Sociology, Anthropology, and Development

An Annotated Bibliography of World Bank Publications 1975 – 1993

Michael M. Cernea
with the assistance of April Adams

Foreword by Ismail Serageldin

Environmentally Sustainable Development Studies and Monographs Series Paper No. 3
The World Bank, Washington, D.C.

© 1994 The International Bank
for Reconstruction and Development/The World Bank
1818 H Street, N.W., Washington, D.C. 20433 U.S.A.

All rights reserved
Manufactured in the United States of America

First printing November 1994

This report has been prepared by the staff of the World Bank. The judgments expressed do not necessarily reflect the views of the Board of Executive Directors or the governments they represent.

ISBN 0-8213-2781-X

Library of Congress Cataloging-in-Publication Data

Cernea, Michael M.
    Sociology, anthropology, and development : an annotated
bibliography of World Bank publications 1975–1993 / Michael
M. Cernea with April L. Adams.
       p.   cm. — (Environmentally sustainable development studies
and monographs series ; no. 3)
    Includes index.
    ISBN 0-8213-2781-X
    1. Sociology—Bibliography.   2. Anthropology—Bibliography.
3. Economic development—Bibliography.   I. Adams, April L., 1960– .
II. Title.   III. Series.
Z7164.S68C47   1994
[HM41]
016.301—dc20   94-1864
                                                                             CIP

Contents

Foreword Ismail Serageldin   v

Abstract   ix

Acknowledgments   xi

How to Obtain the Annotated Publications xiii

Introduction
Enriching Social Science by Applying It:
The Test of Development Practice *Michael M. Cernea 1*

Part One: Social Science and Development   7
1. Use of Social Science in Development   9
2. Project Preparation, Design, and Appraisal 23
3. Project Implementation, Monitoring, and Evaluation   33

Part Two: Social Organization and Social Actors   41
4. Social Organization and Institutional Development 43
5. Participation   *51*
6. Poverty Reduction   *59*
7. Culture, Beliefs, and Values *65*
8. Women, Family Systems, and Gender Analysis   *83*
9. Indigenous and Tribal People *91*

Part Three: Settlement and Resettlement   99
10. Settlement and Involuntary Resettlement   *101*

Part Four: Social Variables in Environmental Management *125*
11. Environment and Development *127*
12. Land and Land Tenure *133*
13. Water and the Sociology of Irrigation *137*
14. Forests and Social Forestry *141*
15. Rangelands and Pastoralism *149*
16. Parks and Biosphere Reserves *153*

Part Five: Social Policy in Sectoral Analysis *157*
17. Housing and Urban Development *159*
18. Rural Development *163*
19. Agricultural Extension *167*
20. Education *171*
21. Health *197*
22. Roads *199*
23. Energy Use *201*

Part Six: Social Research and Methodologies *205*
24. Social Research Methods *207*
25. Social Impact Assessment *213*
26. General Publications in Anthropology and Sociology *217*

Part Seven: Appendixes *221*
1 Informal Papers and Publications *223*
2 Index of Works at a Glance *241*
3 Index of Authors *281*
4 Index of Geographic Locations and Populations *293*
5 Bio-Data *301*

Foreword

The World Bank is widely perceived as an institution dominated by economists and economics. This view is frequently accompanied by a belief that the Bank is not concerned with noneconomic social science. Such a view does not do justice either to the institution or to the distinguished corps of sociologists, anthropologists, and political scientists on the Bank's staff or to those contributing as consultants.

This rich, annotated inventory of publications attests to both the breadth and quality of the noneconomic social science work done at the World Bank. The many works listed here, and the many other unpublished works that lie behind them, are of sound quality, often path breaking, critical, and challenging, creatively conducting the social analysis required for development work. While each paper listed in the compendium looks at only one facet of a particular problem, when taken together they illuminate the special contribution that these social sciences make to the understanding and the practice of development.

Nevertheless, sociologists and anthropologists sometimes point to the fact that the noneconomic social sciences are not full partners in the decision-making concerning the policy and project investment decisions that guide the development business, both in governments and in international financial organizations such as the World Bank. What are the grounds for this contention?

The answer, I believe, lies in part in the dominant paradigm of development and its evolving nature over time, and partly in the nature of financial institutions. On the question of paradigm, I believe that the rise of the economic paradigm in the 1960s and 1970s—displacing the engineers and the technicians from their previously dominant role—came about as the assessment of entire programs of investment, rather than individual projects, became the norm, and as the importance of sectoral and macro policies became widely recognized. The dominance of economic analysis became complete with the combined effects of the debt crisis of the 1980s with its concomitant emphasis on rigorous management of the macroeconomy, and the collapse of the centrally planned economies in the late 1980s and early 1990s. Markets and the private sector not only were recognized as essential parts of the development equation, but also in some quarters they started to be seen as almost sufficient to ensure development.

True development, however, must be people centered and gender conscious. The ruthless efficiency of the market as an allocator of resources must be tempered by a caring and nurturing state. Strong, effective, and efficient governments are essential to development for they alone can create the requisite enabling environment that allows the private sector and the civil society to flourish. And today, more than ever before, we also recognize that sustainability should be an essential dimension of development. Pursuing sustainability requires marrying the concerns of the economists and the financial analysts to those of the sociologists and anthropologists and to those of the ecologists. Thus, the social scientists' role and their contribution is embedded in our current—still evolving—paradigm.

The social analysis on which development investment decisions must be based should have three characteristics. It must be based on a coherent analytical framework; must be predictive and it must be prescriptive as well. Rising to the challenge of meeting these three criteria constitutes the intellectual agenda for the noneconomic social science work at the World Bank in the years ahead. A word about each is pertinent.

First, a coherent analytical framework is essential to show that the approach is more than case-by-case description and is *not* subject to individual researchers' biases. The contribution to the evolving paradigm—as distinct from contributions to the decisions about individual operations where descriptive material and insight may do much good indeed—requires a coherent and clear analytical framework that one associates with systematic analysis and decisionmaking. This framework must become more explicit than it is today.

Second, because we are primarily concerned with development, we are concerned with the future. Because we are concerned with investments, we are concerned with predicting likely outcomes. Thus, it is perhaps interesting to read a very insightful and detailed discussion as to why the Somali state unravelled. But to affect the decisionmaking process, we need a predictive dimension that will try to tell us whether the same—or similar risks—lie in store in another situation, or what the likely outcomes are of efforts to restore the social cohesion of Somalia. For decisionmaking, it is essential to try to predict likely outcomes, no matter how many caveats are tacked onto the predictions.

Third, predictive analysis by itself is not enough, however. For instance, one brilliant analysis of the sociocultural determinants of fertility in Africa led the authors to conclude that the patterns of fertility decline in Africa were likely to be much slower than conventional thinking indicated. Yet the analysis stopped short of proposing what to do about this. Design different development programs? Abandon current efforts at family planning? Continue the efforts currently underway, but accept that the outcomes are likely to be slower in materializing? By not being prescriptive as well as predictive, that analysis cannot easily be incorporated into decisionmaking either by the government officials, who have to approve budgets and adopt policies, or by the international financial institutions, including the World Bank, that must make decisions about supporting policies and funding programs and projects.

The present volume, prepared by Michael M. Cernea, the Bank's Senior Adviser for Social Policy and Sociology, convincingly demonstrates that the foundation is already well laid for the social scientists at the World Bank to rise to these three challenges. Much has already been done, but more remains.

The distinguished men and women whose writings are presented and summarized in these pages have the skills, experience, and dedication to make this necessary additional contribution to the evolving development paradigm.

It is hoped that sociologists and anthropologists elsewhere will join in this creative and applied development effort. By so doing, they will be making a truly great contribution to improving the lot of the billions of impoverished human beings who are the *raison d'être* for all development analysis and practice.

Ismail Serageldin

Abstract

The body of writings described in this volume consists of selected publications authored by sociologists and anthropologists working as regular World Bank staff or as consultants to the Bank. These works were published during less than two decades, essentially from 1975 to 1993.

The bibliography covers the topical areas within which Bank sociologists and anthropologists have done most of their work. They have drawn from, and contributed to, the theories of social change and development; the sociology and anthropology of population settlement and resettlement; the sociology of education; the sociology of agriculture and natural resource management; the anthropological study of indigenous and tribal people, and other important domains. The publications annotated in this volume are grouped under headings such as Social Organization, Settlement and Resettlement, Social Variables in Environmental Management, Social Policy in Sectoral Perspective, and Social Research and Methodology. Special sub-sections are devoted to works about the general theoretical and epistemological issues of translating social science knowledge into policy and programs.

Primarily, the bibliography is intended to help locate publications. However, *the larger purpose* of the annotations is to provide substantive information about the *sets of ideas* put forward in this body of sociological and anthropological writings, and to indicate how social science knowledge is being used to craft development programs and policies.

Acknowledgments

Grateful thanks are extended to Ismail Serageldin, Mohamed T. El-Ashry, Andrew Steer, Pierre Landell-Mills, Ruth Cernea, and Scott Guggenheim, who gave their support and advice to the preparation of this annotated bibliography, and to those colleagues who contributed by preparing the initial summaries of their papers. Gracie M. Ochieng spent long hours in desktopping this volume for printing, and Alicia Hetzner aptly contributed to the editorial preparation of the manuscript for publication.

How to Obtain the Annotated Publications

The titles listed in the main part of the bibliography have been published either by the World Bank or other institutions and should be readily available through major libraries worldwide, commercial distributors, or the World Bank Bookstore (walk-in traffic only), 1818 H Street, N.W., Washington, D.C. 20433, U.S.A., tel 202/473-1155, fax 202/676-0581. Orders from inside the United States should be directed to: World Bank, P.O. Box 7247-7956, Philadelphia, P.A. 19170-8619, U.S.A., tel 202 473-1155, fax 202 676-0581. Orders from outside the United States must be placed with local distributors. For out-of-print World Bank publications, microfiche copies may be obtained from National Technical Information Service, 5285 Port Royal Road, Springfield, V.A. 22161, U.S.A., tel 703 487 4650, fax 703 321 8547.

Many of the listed studies have been reprinted in several countries in journals, anthologies, or other volumes. To facilitate readers' access, references are given to all available versions of each title known to have been republished; these references immediately follow the primary citation.

In addition, individual departments in the Bank issue informal papers and documents for in-house distribution, some of which are of a sociological or anthropological nature. These are listed in Annex I. Because these publications are not available through the World Bank's commercial sales network, interested readers should contact the originating department or author in the Bank. Studies reprinted in the *World Bank Reprint Series* generally are available free from the author on request.

Introduction
Enriching Social Science by Applying It: The Test of Development Practice

Michael M. Cernea

A double perplexity led to the preparation of this *Annotated Bibliography*: that of others and, at times, my own.[1]

Frequently, when I mention to someone that sociologists and anthropologists work at the World Bank, an incredulous or puzzled expression fleetingly passes over the face of my interlocutor, unfailingly followed by the question—"*What does a sociologist do at the World Bank?*"

I have learned to take this confusion in stride, given how little is known about either the World Bank or the professional practice of sociology.

It is, however, my turn to be puzzled when such surprise is shown not by a member of the general public, but by fellow social scientists who teach sociology or anthropology at some prominent academic institution. Why is it that many social scientists don't realize that there is both need and room for their disciplines' intellectual voices in formulating development policy and programs? And why is it not yet realized that propitious room already exists in—at least—some development organizations?

This bibliography may contribute to answering such questions in substance. Primarily, the bibliography is intended to help locate World Bank anthropological and sociological publications on development issues. But beyond showing "*what sociologists do,*" this compendium intends to convey the *sets of thoughts and findings* generated by the authors and to indicate how social science knowledge is used in development programs and policy formulation.

The body of writings described in this volume consists of selected publications authored by sociologists and anthropologists working as regular World Bank staff or as consultants to the Bank. The majority have been published either by the World Bank or directly by university presses such as Oxford University Press and Johns Hopkins University Press. In addition, the bibliography also informs about numerous studies and articles printed in various research

2 Introduction

journals worldwide. These works have been published during less than two decades, from 1975 to 1993.

While this bibliography mainly shows how social science enriches development work, it also strongly suggests the reverse: that development-oriented research and applied work enrich the social sciences. Although this was not the goal pursued in creating this bibliography, any support it provides to documenting this reverse influence will not be disclaimed. For this intellectual enrichment is a two-way avenue. And in this vein, I would hope that this volume might itself become an explicit invitation to further reflection about using this two-way avenue.

We believe that the present volume could prove useful to readers for these purposes: for social research, for applied work in development, or for academic training. We hope that the volume will enhance the capacity to *actually apply* sociology and anthropology, to teach these disciplines persuasively in better connection with ongoing social change, and to expand the disciplinary frontiers.

Potential Users

The three audiences for which this bibliography is intended are: (a) the social science community involved in applied development studies; (b) the broader community of development practitioners; and (c) academics—scholars and students.

Responding to the interests of the first audience, the bibliography aims to be a vehicle for exchanging experience and promoting interdisciplinary links. Economic studies lead the field of development research, but noneconomic development studies, particularly in sociology and anthropology, are generating findings and ideas indispensable to multidisciplinary approaches. More information about, and critical assessment of accumulated experience in noneconomic development studies are essential in order to further carry out social research with competence, moral responsibility, and increased applicability.

For the second audience, the bibliography informs about the social analyses, methods, approaches, and theories that are available to those development practitioners who do not have a formal social science background. Government officials, planners, decisionmakers, and project managers may perceive better what kind of help they can obtain by when working with development-oriented social scientists.

Responding to the third audience, the bibliography aims to facilitate the use of these publications in schools, universities, and other places of learning and training. My colleagues and I feel that the scholars working on theory building or on the epistemology of social research must reflect also on developments applied research, because often the latter is at the cutting edge of social science advances. Currently, however, such reflective work is rarely done, if at all.[2]

In turn, curriculum designers need to know where to find publications that discuss the use of social knowledge and the practice of sociology and anthropology.

The growing and deliberate use of social science in crafting development programs represents a change in the relationship between social research and society. Broader awareness of the significant corpus of social research on development (part of which is described in this volume) may facilitate this relationship.

Social Science in Development Work

Obviously, the intellectual territory covered in this bibliography is young. In many respects, it is new to both sociology and anthropology. Relatively little time has elapsed since the crystallization of a clear trend toward using noneconomic social sciences in international development aid programs. The World Bank is a case in point: the institution is fifty years old and has relied on economic science from its very beginning, yet it has opened up towards noneconomic social science knowledge only slowly during the last two decades. In some development agencies this trend started perhaps somewhat earlier, but in others, sadly, it has not yet started at all. The paradigm governing the practice of development interventions does not account yet for some important social variables.

While valuable work in this domain is now being carried out worldwide, it is insufficiently interconnected.[3] The work of the social scientists at and in connection with the World Bank is just one fraction of this international effort. But it is a significant one, given its far reaching effects through the Bank's programs on the lives of many people around the world. This body of social analytical work needs to be better known and more closely linked to the work of development practitioners elsewhere.

The extent to which social sciences are used within the development activities supported by the World Bank depends on the recognition given to social variables in the Bank's development paradigm(s) and in the staff's thought patterns. Although these sociocultural variables are intrinsic to development, their recognition is not fully commensurate with their true weight in real life. Because these variables are difficult to measure, it is comfortably easy to abstract them from economic models even though it is impossible to bypass them in practice. However, there is clear progress in the World Bank's consideration of their relevance for inducing development, as shown by this volume itself.

During the last eight to ten years, the Bank's corps of noneconomic social scientists—mainly anthropologists, sociologists, and political scientists—has probably become *the largest group of this kind in the world that works together in one location actually practicing development sociology and anthropology*. In this process they often break open new trails, chart untraveled territory, and push the frontiers of these disciplines forward.[4]

Social scientists' capacity sociology to answer the complex riddles of development practice is growing. Beaten paths do not exist and the need to innovate and experiment is paramount. The variety of roles performed and honed by social scientists in development—from field researchers to project designers, to policy formulators, to impact evaluators, or even to managers of development programs—is illustrated and demonstrated in many of these annotated publications.

Particularly significant and consequential is the shift from work on discrete projects to work on formulating *development policies* and *sectoral strategies*. Compared to much of the literature generally available, a distinct novelty reflected in the publications listed in this volume is their clear orientation towards *social action*. These studies and their authors do not shy away from assuming the difficult responsibility of making predictions and prescriptions for change and social improvements, and from discharging these responsibilities with care and prudence.

Key Topical Areas and the Structure of the Bibliography

To facilitate rapid retrieval and use by the reader, the annotations have been grouped into several main sections pertaining to broad categories such as: social organization, institutions, social actors, environment and natural resources management, project cycle stages, research methods, and evaluation.

The key areas in which Bank sociologists and anthropologists have done most of their research and applied work appear quite clearly: the sociology and anthropology of population settlement and resettlement, the sociology of education, the sociology of agriculture and natural resource management, urban development, gender analysis, the social issues of poverty alleviation, participation, social impact assessment, and anthropological studies of indigenous and tribal people, among others. A relevant body of writings has also been produced about the epistemological issues of translating knowledge into policy and programs.

Since many of the annotated publications deal with more than one subject, they could have been listed in several topical sections of the bibliography. However, each publication is listed only once. Therefore the reader searching for one topic is well advised to consult related sections of the bibliography. For instance, the majority of the publications about land or social forestry are listed in those specific subsections, but some may be listed in the subsections on project appraisal or implementation, depending on the main emphasis given in the study itself. Similarly, publications included in the subsection on monitoring and evaluation may be relevant for readers interested in social impact assessment. Therefore, some cross references have been explicitly included.

Criteria for Inclusion

For anthropologists and sociologists who are Bank staff members, this bibliography includes works published during their tenure with the Bank, but not works published before they joined the Bank. For consultants, whose primary institutional affiliation is outside the Bank, only the publications resulting from their Bank assignments are included. Many consultants reside in the countries in which Bank-assisted projects are implemented, and often their social research has been initiated actually as a result of these programs.

In keeping with the subject matter of this bibliography, a few publications by authors with related specialties (political scientists, psychologists, urban planners, archaeologists) on topics such as culture, cultural property, participation, or religion in relation to development are also included.[5] To help the reader retrieve relevant materials, an *index of titles*, one of *authors*, and one of *geographic locations* and populations have been included in this volume.

Grey Literature

The vast majority of publications annotated in this bibliography is commercially available in bookstores and libraries. However, much of the anthropologists' and sociologists' work within at the Bank goes into the preparation of a variety of collective, yet anonymous documents—project appraisal reports, field supervision reports, project completion reports, sector reports, country studies, and similar materials. These are multi-disciplinary products and become official documents, often with no name of author attribution. The serious student of development social science would find many of them enormously interesting, but listing all such documents would be an impossible task. However, a handful of major World Bank *policy* statements with substantial contributions by social scientists (for example, "operational policy notes," "operational manual statements" or "operational directives," which are available publicly as well) have been included.

In addition, a considerable socioanthropological "grey literature" exists within the World Bank, consisting of working papers, notes and studies which do not reach the formal publication stage, despite their valuable content. *Annex 1* of the bibliography includes just some of these informal materials, which are intended primarily for in-house circulation. However, some have been duplicated in a sufficient number of copies and can be obtained by contacting their authors directly.

Not all studies and articles produced during the period covered in this bibliography could be traced and listed, particularly some studies published by consultants. But should this bibliography prove useful and in demand, updated editions will be reissued periodically. Comments from readers are eagerly invited.

Notes

1. The author is the World Bank's Senior Advisor for Sociology and Social Policy.
2. James Coleman called attention to the need for sociology to theorize and reflect upon its own social role in affecting societal change. He wrote: "The content of the theory must be such as to account for the action of engaging in the construction of social theory. If, in a theory of social change, there is no role of sociological knowledge in affecting social change, the theory cannot account for the act of theorizing itself." (James T. Coleman, *Foundations of Social Theory*, Cambridge and London: The Belknap Press of Harvard University Press, 1990), 610.
3. See Allan Hoben, "Anthropology and Development," *Annual Review of Anthropology* no. 1, 1982.
4. For a more detailed description of the work of anthropologists and sociologists at the World Bank, see Michael M. Cernea, *Sociologists in a Development Agency*, World Bank Reprint Series no. 463, 1991; or Michael M. Cernea, *Anthropological and Sociological Research for Policy Development on Population Resettlement*, in **Anthropological Approaches to Involuntary Resettlement: Policy, Practice, and Theory**, ed. M. M. Cernea and S.E. Guggenheim (Boulder, Col.: Westview Press, 1993). See also an interesting study written by an outside researcher who analyzed, among other things, the impact exercised over the course of several years by the World Bank's Sociological Group on the Bank's policies and activities: Nüket Kardam, "Development Approaches and the Role of Policy Advocacy: The Case of the World Bank," *World Development* 21(11) (1993): 1773-86.
5. However, it is not the purpose of this bibliography to cover the Bank's publications in those related disciplines. For interested readers, a general (but not annotated) catalogue of World Bank publications in print, the *World Bank Index of Publications and Guide to Information Products and Services*, can be obtained free by writing to the World Bank Bookstore, 1818 H Street N.W., Washington, D.C. 20433, U.S.A.

Part One

Social Science and Development

Use of Social Science in Development

1.1 Butcher, David. "Human and Institutional Development." In Czech Conroy and Miles Litvinoff, eds. *The Greening of Aid. Sustainable Livelihoods in Practice.* London: Earthscan Publications Ltd. 1988.

As objects of study, institutions have been popular with sociologists, political theorists, and governments. Institutions tend to appear, grow, and atrophy in old age and are sometimes transplanted with varying degrees of success.

The present concern by the development community arises from a realization of the importance of institutions and their development as prerequisites to lasting development. Not only are formal organizations, ministries and parastatals often ill equipped to perform their functions, but there is need to develop lower-level institutions if development assistance is to be useful in its intended purpose.

The five case study projects analyzed in this chapter vary greatly in design, operational level within the recipient country, and objectives. Common factors are the fact that all five projects focus on beneficiary organization and that all claim project replicability or sustainability. In the absence of an established methodology for assessing sustainability, the author analyzes external and internal organizational factors that directly influence a project's success and presents their implications for development donors.

1.2 Cernea, Michael M. "Anthropological and Sociological Research for Policy Development on Population Resettlement." In M.M. Cernea and S.E. Guggenheim, eds. *Anthropological Approaches to Involuntary Resettlement: Policy, Practice, and Theory.* Boulder, Col.: Westview Press. 1993.

A revised version of this study has been published as "Social Science Research and the Crafting of Policy on Population Resettlement." Journal of Knowledge and Policy 6(3-4). 1993.

Social science knowledge must be used not just to evaluate program results but primarily to formulate development policies themselves. Explicit social policies are required to guide, inspire, or mitigate public sector programs that aim to accelerate economic growth and development.

In the first section, the author argues that the most effective strategy for translating major lessons from past assessment studies into future programs is not simply to improve planning procedures, but to modify policies. He takes issue with some alternative views on such strategies. The cognitive dissonance displayed by government planners *vis-a-vis* the negative social effects of development-caused population displacements. Further, the author reconstructs the history and summarizes the content of the World Bank's policy regarding involuntary population resettlement. This is followed by a discussion of methodological lessons about converting social theory and research into policy, given the institutional transactions intrinsic to development bureaucracies. The final section reviews actual effects of the new resettlement policy at two levels: policy replication and project planning and execution, with examples from India, Colombia, Mexico, Brazil, and other countries.

1.3   Cernea, Michael M. "The Sociologist's Approach to Sustainable Development." *Finance & Development* 30(4) (December 1993).

The case for sustainable development is usually made in economic and ecological terms. Many think that if they can only "get the economics right", everything else will fall into place. Soothing as this econo-mythical invocation may be, it is nonetheless one-sided. The social components of sustainability are no less important than the economic and technical ones.

The sociological perspective contributes at least two sets of elements to the arsenal of tools for achieving sustainable development. First, it provides a set of concepts that help explain social action and people's complex forms of social organization. Second, it offers a set of social techniques with which to prompt coordinated social action, inhibit detrimental behavior, craft alternative social arrangements, and help develop social capital.

Program designers searching for increased sustainability often are not aware of the vast repertories of social management "tools" and cultural levers that can be marshalled to mobilize social energy and coordinated action for inducing development. A relevant dimension of sustainability, argues the author, is the presence or absence of forms of social organization structurally suited to manage the environment. The individual actions of multiple users may easily combine to produce adverse system-level outcomes. Atomistic sets of individual users need to be organized into interactive and culturally cohesive groups in order to foster the capacity to manage and enforce adequate rules, rights, and obligations.

If a high degree of social organization is itself a strategic resource for development, creating organizations is equal to creating new social capital. The author defines the concepts of "organizational intensity," "organizational density," and "social capital."

He argues that investments must be made to foster organizations that accumulate human experience and knowledge, which are social capital. New and growing social capital is indispensable for the social sustainability of development.

1.4 Cernea, Michael M., ed. *Putting People First: Sociological Variables in Development*. 2nd ed., revised and enlarged. New York and London: Oxford University Press. 1991.

The basic tenet of this book is that people are, and should be, the starting point, the center, and the end goal of every development intervention. In sociological terms, "putting people first" in projects means making social organization the explicit concern of development policies and programs, and constructing development projects around the modes of production, cultural patterns, needs, and potential of the populations in the project area.

Rather than a simple reprint of the 1st 1985 ed., this 2nd ed. is a new volume. It seeks to capture the newly emerging trends in development thinking and practice that are likely to characterize the 1990s. Some authors went back to the field to update cases investigated earlier and report new findings. One chapter has been dropped, two new chapters have been included, and most other chapters have been rewritten and expanded.

The contributors provide sociological and anthropological analyses of issues that are central to induced rural development. This book distills lessons gained from development experience, brings to light both recognized and unrecognized sociological variables of development programs, and proposes new models and methodologies for addressing these variables.

This edition highlights more explicitly the issues of natural resources management (water, forests, land, and fisheries); the environmental implications of development programs; and the development of social capital through investments in forming grassroots organizations and promoting participation.

After a decade of structural adjustment programs, this volume draws attention to adverse consequences of development such as the impoverishment of some social groups, the forced displacement and resettlement of populations, and the deterioration of common property assets. The authors are concerned with understanding the conditions for long-term sustainability of development investments.

Detailed annotations for each chapter of this 2nd ed. are included in this bibliography under the author's name. These chapters are:

- "Knowledge from Social Science for Development Policies and Projects" by Michael M. Cernea
- "Planning Technical and Social Change in Irrigated Areas" by E. Walter Coward, Jr.
- "Developing Irrigators' Organizations: A Learning Process Approach" by Benjamin U. Bagadion and Francis F. Korten
- "Middle-Level Farmer Organizations as Links between Farms and Central Irrigation Systems" by David M. Freeman and Max K. Lowdermilk
- "A Sociological Framework for the Analysis of New Land Settlements" by Thayer Scudder
- "Involuntary Resettlement: Social Research, Policy, and Planning" by Michael M. Cernea
- "Pastoral Production Systems and Livestock Development Projects: An East African Perspective" by Neville Dyson-Hudson
- "Social and Cultural Characteristics in Small-Scale Fishery Development" by Richard B. Pollnac
- "Sociological and Environmental Dimensions of Social Forestry Projects" by Scott Guggenheim and John Spears
- "The Social Actors of Participatory Afforestation Strategies" by Michael M. Cernea
- "Social Analysis in Rural Road Projects" by Cynthia Cook
- "When People Don't Come First: Some Sociological Lessons from Completed Projects" by Conrad Phillip Kottak
- "Fitting Projects to People" by Norman Uphoff
- "Shortcut and Participatory Methods for Gaining Social Information for Projects" by Robert Chambers.

1.5 Cernea, Michael M., ed. *Putting People First: Sociological Variables in Development Projects*. (1st ed.). New York: Oxford University Press. 1985.

For content of this volume see entry 1.3 on the 2nd ed.

1.6 Cernea, Michael M. *Mengutamakan Manusia Di Dalam Pembangunan: Variabel-variabel Sosiologi di dalam Pembangunan Pedesaan*. Jakarta: Penerbit Universitas Indonesia. 1988.

*This is a complete translation into Bahasa Indonesia of **Putting People First: Sociological Variables in Development Projects**. (1st ed.). For content of this volume see entry 1.3.*

1.7 Cernea, Michael M. "Knowledge from Social Science for Development Policies and Projects." In M.M. Cernea, ed. *Putting People First: Sociological Variables in Rural Development*. 2nd ed. New York, London: Oxford University Press. 1991.

Also published in Hari Mohan Mathur, ed. The Human Dimension of Development: Perspectives from Anthropology. New Delhi: Concept Publishing Company. 1990.

In this introductory chapter to the 2nd ed. of *Putting People First*, the author stresses that the call to "put people first" in development programs is not simply a slogan but reflects a realistic recognition of the centrality of social actors in any development, spontaneous or induced. This call entails a formidable work program for the social sciences in order to identify the pertinent social variables in every "technical," "financial," or "administrative" development intervention.

The author argues that sociologists must deal hands on with the nuts and bolts of development activities and not shy away from the mundane, pragmatic questions of translating plans into reality in a sociologically sound manner. To increase their relevance, they must not only analyze and explain, but also assist in transforming society and improving people's lives.

The planning models for inducing development are far from perfect. Although sociologists should learn to work within existing frameworks, they must at the same time challenge, criticize, and change them with their input. Financially induced development programs need sociological knowledge and must explicitly recognize sociocultural variables. The range of entrance points for sociological knowledge and skills should be expanded to all segments of development planning. Sociologists have an obligation to contribute their skills and knowledge, and design purposively for social action.

The range of practically usable products generated by social scientists is narrow and insufficient. Action methodologies should be formulated to enrich this domain. The support for people's participation will be effective if advocacy is accompanied by methodology.

The teaching of sociology and anthropology in universities must radically change, so that universities can avoid producing new cohorts of sociologically incompetent technical experts and economically illiterate sociologists. More work should be directed to formulating sociological techniques and methodologies for eliciting coordinated social action.

1.8 Cernea, Michael M. "Sociologists in a Development Agency: Experiences from the World Bank." In Michael Schönhuth, ed. *The Socio-Cultural Dimension in*

Development: The Contribution of Sociologists and Social Anthropologists to the Work of Development Agencies. Eschborn, Germany: GTZ. 1991.

Also published as World Bank Reprint Series no. 463. Washington, D.C.

The author describes the work of sociologists and anthropologists in the World Bank, in several operational and policy domains. He starts from two fundamental premises: first, that anthropologists and sociologists possess distinct professional knowledge about social organization, social structure, and cultural change that is sorely needed for inducing sustainable development; and second, that development agencies must firmly institutionalize social science expertise within their organizational structures and everyday work patterns.

The author criticizes the imbalanced skills mix of development agencies, heavily skewed towards economists. The work pattern of development agencies results from the very nature of financially and exogenously induced development, pursued through planning and projects, whereas most of the history of human development has been spontaneous and endogenously generated.

Financially induced development runs the risk of creating social imbalances, particularly when planned interventions are informed by inadequate models and knowledge. To avoid this, the design of development programs that marshall vast financial and technical resources must be organized around the social actors, the people themselves.

Based on his experience at the World Bank, the author urges a diversification of the entry points for sociological and anthropological knowledge in the work processes and products of development agencies. Social scientists must locate the key junctures within the work of these agencies and insert their contributions into what are often products of team work. It is crucial to incorporate social analysis in the agencies' overall policies, not only piecemeal in individual projects.

1.9 Cernea, Michael M. *Using Knowledge from Social Science in Development Projects.* World Bank Discussion Paper no. 114. Washington, D.C. 1991.

Financially induced development aims to accelerate the pace of economic growth and social change. However, accelerating development through investment projects often risks creating social imbalances.

The author contends that such risks are aggravated when planning is guided by technocentric or econocratic models, which typically overlook social and cultural variables. Using social science knowledge and methods in designing project strategies can minimize such risks. It can also help fit the project better to the existing local sociocultural fabric or help create new patterns of social organization.

This paper emphasizes the complementarity rather than the opposition between the two approaches through which social sciences attempt to influence society—the "enlightenment approach" and the "engineering approach". State-of-the-art knowledge and methods from social sciences need to be converted into operationally usable know-how and models for action and learning.

The author argues that the conventional "entrance points" for sociological and anthropological knowledge in the planning for development are few and of little consequence. New entrance points must be opened up. For carrying out action-oriented applied research work, sociologists and anthropologists must go outside the academic cocoon of their disciplines. They must undertake policy-oriented inquiry and restructure their research work to fit operational frameworks and practical demands.

The institutionalization of development oriented, applied social science requires harmonizing the cognitive identity and the professional identity of those who practice in this area. This would entail at least: (a) formalizing the position of the social analyst within the organizational structure of technical and development agencies; (b) substantially changing the university curriculum for training future social scientists and social workers oriented towards development work; and (c) introducing and exposing economists and technical specialists to social science knowledge.

1.10 Cernea, Michael M. *Social Science Knowledge for Development Interventions.* HIID Development Discussion Paper no. 334. Cambridge, Mass.: Harvard University. 1990.

Repeated failures have plagued many development programs that were—and failed because they were—sociologically ill-informed or ill-conceived. Financially induced development interventions aim to accelerate the pace of economic growth and social change, but often avoid addressing head on the social imbalances they engender.

Development projects should depart from the long used technocentric and econocratic models of planned interventions and explicitly make space in their design for social organization variables. Since the core of any development process is its actors, defining the role of people in project strategies is a design and resource allocation matter. Models adopted in projects that do not put people first inevitably clash with the model intrinsic to the real social process of development. A substantially modified paradigm for planning development interventions is therefore necessary.

The author argues that in undertaking action-oriented applied development work, sociologists and anthropologists must go outside the academic cocoon of their disciplines, must carry out policy-concerned social inquiry and must restructure the content of their project-related research to fit operational frameworks and practical demands. The range of their contributions must expand to all segments of induced development, from policy formulation to project implementation.

New "products" of anthropological and sociological work must be generated by development oriented social scientists. State-of-the-art social science knowledge needs to be methodically converted into usable "packages" of know-how and models for action.

The institutionalization of development social science requires intensified interplay between the cognitive identity and the professional identity of those who practice in this area. This entails formalizing the position of the social analyst within the organizational structure of technical and development agencies, changing the university curriculum for social scientists oriented to development work, and exposing economists and technical specialists to systematic social science education.

1.11 Kardam, Nüket "Development Approaches and the Role of Policy Advocacy: The Case of the World Bank." *World Development* 21(11):1773-86. 1993.

This paper explores how policy innovation occurs in international organizations and explains it in terms of four factors: independence of the international organization within the international regime of which it is a member; external pressure; the consistency of new issues with organizational goals and procedures; and internal policy advocacy. Internal policy advocacy, not often considered in the development literature, is seen as an intervening variable between the first three factors and the response to innovation.

The first section of the paper addresses the conditions under which international organizations respond to new issues, considering different combinations of these four factors with examples.

The second section focuses on a case study on internal advocacy efforts in the World Bank by a group of staff members, informally organized as the Bank's Sociological Group. The group advocated the recognition of the importance of sociocultural variables in projects and was successful in having them incorporated in various Bank projects and guidelines, for example, project appraisal guidelines, involuntary resettlement policy, and the assessment of impacts on tribal populations incorporated. in World Bank operations.

While external pressure played a role, these insiders were the ones who introduced the issues in ways that fit the goals and procedures of the World Bank despite a sometimes reluctant environment. This contributed to the enactment of new policy guidelines, to the hiring of more staff with social science training, and, in general, to the increased legitimacy of these issues in the activities of the World Bank.

1.12 Kottak, Conrad Phillip. "When People Don't Come First: Some Sociological Lessons from Completed Projects." In M.M. Cernea, ed. *Putting People First: Sociological Variables in Rural Development*. 2nd ed. New York, London: Oxford University Press. 1991.

Also published as "Dimensions of Culture in Development." In G.C. Uhlenbeck ed. Proceedings of the International Symposium on the Cultural Dimension of Development, September 1985. The Hague: Colophon. 1987.

Based on a secondary analysis of sixty-eight primary evaluations of completed projects, this chapter constructs an empirical demonstration of the importance of bringing sociological and anthropological concepts into project design from the very beginning. The author discusses projects which failed, as well as projects which succeeded.

Through his analysis of ex post findings on both kinds of projects, compared with the results of a "blind" analysis of the quality of the respective project inception reports (Bank appraisal documents) for the same projects, the author is able to show that sociocultural analysis makes a significant difference in the chances for project success. The payoff from analysis is often measurable in concrete economic terms: the author found that the average economic rate of return for rural development projects which have incorporated sociocultural analysis was more than double that for projects which had been poorly appraised from a sociological viewpoint.

The author argues that a "people orientation" involves considerably more than encouraging direct participation in project design or implementation. Many of the underlying principles of social structure, which are explicit in sociological models, are buried in cultural practice and are not necessarily articulated conceptually by members of a cultural group and vary tremendously from one geographic area to another. Yet these principles have to be understood and taken into account by development interventions.

The retrospective analysis of project results confirms how essential it is for the technical experts to recognize and address this cultural variability with the help of professional sociologists. The paper specifies which social variables and approaches have proved crucial to a project's success or failure and should undoubtedly be built into future projects.

1.13 Lethem, Francis J., and Heli Perrett. *Human Factors in Project Work.* World Bank Staff Working Paper no. 397. Washington, D.C. 1980.

This paper proposes a framework to make the consideration of social and behavioral factors a useful and efficient part of project work. In particular, project managers should consider the following questions:

- Is the expected demand for the project's goods and services likely to materialize in the face of existing traditional alternatives, general lack of interest, or other obstacles?

- Is the proposed design, that is, the choice of technology, architectural plans, and institutional arrangements (including the degree of involvement of local people in project planning, construction, maintenance ,or management) likely to work and be beneficial to users and appropriate to their social environment?

- Are the project populations likely to gain access to the intended project benefits as expected, or are there risks from unintended consequences to the people in the project's area of influence?

- Most importantly, what possible "social" measures or activities may be built into the project's design or implementation arrangements to improve their efficiency or outcome?

The authors discuss and recommend a set of special social techniques, and show how they may fit into the project cycle. The annex to this paper contains models of terms of reference, checklists, and guidelines for use by practicing social analysts.

1.14 Lipset, Seymour Martin. "The Social Requisites of Democracy Revisited. 1993 Presidential Address." *American Sociological Review* 59(1):1-22. February 1994.

This paper discusses the factors and processes affecting the prospects for the institutionalization of democracy throughout the world. An earlier version was prepared by the author as an invitational lecture at a World Bank senior management seminar on governance and was subsequently considerable expanded. The resulting and published version is the text of the Presidential Address delivered by the author at the 1993 annual meeting of the American Sociological Association.

The author surveys cultural and economic variables, religious traditions, various electoral systems, the importance of a participatory civil society, and the methods through which political parties should be structured to maintain stability. He concludes that there is need for considerable caution about the long-term prospects for stable democracy in many of the newer systems given their low level of legitimacy. During the 1980s, the processes of political democratization occurred at the same time as a profound economic crisis in many countries. Such conditions have already caused breakdowns of democratization in a number of countries.

What new democracies need above all to attain legitimacy is efficacy, argues the author, particularly in the economic arena, but also in the polity. If they can take the high road to economic development, they can keep their political houses in order. The opposite is true as well: governments that defy the elementary laws of supply and demand will fail to develop and to institutionalize genuinely democratic functions.

1.15 Rogers, Everett M., Nat J. Colletta, and Joseph Mbindyo. "Social and Cultural Influences on Human Development Policies and Programs." In P.T. Knight, ed. *Implementing Programs of Human Development*. World Bank Staff Working Paper no. 403. Washington, D.C. 1980.

The authors emphasize that noneconomic variables are gaining increasing attention from development specialists and that the strategy of anti-poverty policies and programs has often been predicated on expected behavioral change. To be effective, however, planning for behavioral change must consider the influences of macrosocial and cultural factors.

The authors identify the major sociocultural factors involved in economic development in terms of their influence on human development programs, and derive recommendations for future policy. Success, the authors suggest, rests on using a holistic approach emphasizing the interaction of values, institutions, and processes of behavioral change, and recognizing the variations encountered at the microlevels of village and urban communities.

1.16 Serageldin, Ismail. "Public Administration in the 1990s: Rising to the Challenge." In *Public Administration in the Nineties: Trends and Innovations*. Proceedings of the Twelfth International Congress of Administrative Sciences. Brussels: International Institute of Administrative Sciences. 1992.

Administration science as a social discipline is presented in the 1990s with an extraordinary opportunity to redesign the structures of governance and administration—internationally, nationally, and locally. The author outlines the current challenges facing the practitioners of this discipline and the various levels at which its use must help the development process. At the international level there is a need to reinforce or devise new supranational entities to keep pace with the growing challenges facing humanity.

At the national level the challenges for countries in transition are all the greater because they demand major transformations of the functions and structures of public administration at a time of economic crisis and financial duress.

Reform of public administration ranks among the most intractable yet absolutely necessary tasks facing most governments in the world outside of the OECD today. The author discusses problems commonly encountered in the course of efforts to achieve public accountability, to restaff public administrations, to introduce quality control, and build administrative capacity.

Three important guidelines recommended by the author for developing the institutions of the future are: assigning greater importance to the strategy-making function; adopting a participatory approach; and using pragmatism in the search for solutions.

1.17   Serageldin, Ismail. "The Human Dimension of Structural Adjustment Programmes: World Bank's Perspective." In A. Adedeji, S. Rasheed, and M. Morrison, eds. *The Human Dimension of Africa's Persistent Economic Crisis*. Kent, England: Hans Zell Publishers. 1990.

The severity and depth of the African crisis have challenged the international development community as have few other problems. In recognition of this, the World Bank has made assisting African governments in redressing the decline in African economic performance an institutional priority.

Despite twenty five years of development programs supported by multilateral and bilateral institutions, two thirds of the rural population and one third of the urban population of Sub-Saharan African remain below the absolute poverty level. The author highlights the multi-faceted nature of the problem of poverty in Africa. Basic needs, women's issues, the environment, external debt, and institutional deficiencies each represent a dimension of the larger problem, for the alleviation of which the sine-qua-non is economic growth. The engine of economic growth in Africa, the author contends, can only be improvement of agricultural performance.

The author discusses the World Bank's current initiatives throughout Africa to increase agricultural productivity, promote economic policy changes, and to address the individual dimensions of the larger poverty problem. Poverty alleviation efforts will only bear fruit if consistent progress is made on many, if not all, fronts simultaneously, an ambitious agenda which the Bank is trying to pursue.

1.18 Serageldin, Ismail, and Pierre Landell-Mills. "Governance and the External Factor." In *Proceedings of the World Bank Annual Conference on Development Economics 1991*. Washington, D.C.: World Bank. 1992.

The design and functioning of governmental systems is currently much debated. Aid agencies are increasingly preoccupied by how governance influences the effectiveness of aid and promotes economic growth. Nondemocratic governments are coming under increasing pressure to reform. A corollary to this view is the widespread conviction that centrally controlled economies are inefficient and that liberal market policies offer better prospects for rapid growth.

This paper offers a conceptual framework for analyzing these issues. It defines the core characteristics of good governance that enjoy wide acceptance internationally and examines how such characteristics may be legitimately and effectively fostered in developing countries through support from external development agencies.

1.19 Serageldin, Ismail, and Michel Noël. "Tackling the Social Dimensions of Adjustment in Africa." *Finance & Development* (September 1990): 18-20.

Programs of adjustment and development in Africa cannot be sustainable in the longer term unless the poor fully participate in the emerging economic environment. Adjustment programs provide the opportunity to focus attention on, and marshall efforts for tackling the problems of the poor.

To support African governments in their quest to integrate poverty reduction policies and programs into their adjustment and development efforts, The United Nations Development Programme, the African Development Bank, and the World Bank launched the Social Dimensions of Adjustment (SDA) program in 1987. Based on a comprehensive conceptual framework, the SDA program aims at improving macro and sectoral policy management, designing social action programs, strengthening national informational systems, and stepping up training and institutional development in thirty participating countries.

The author explains the basic strategies of the SDA program and describes its four areas of focus: the SDA program helps governments include social dimensions in the macroeconomic policymaking process from the earliest stage; it is helping African governments implement social action programs in conjunction with their policy reform programs; it is providing assistance with data collection and surveys to improve the quality and increase the quantity of data on social indicators; and it is helping participating countries develop their own capacity to design and implement social strategies.

1.20 Uphoff, Norman. "Political Considerations in Human Development." In P.T. Knight, ed. *Implementing Programs of Human Development*. World Bank Staff Working Paper no. 403. Washington, D.C. 1980.

Drawing on concepts and terminology familiar to economists, this study addresses poverty-reducing human development in terms of political analysis and strategy. It begins by examining general considerations for policy analysis, such as the imperative of political "solvency," the reality of power stratification, the criterion of policy feasibility, and the shape of cost and benefit time paths.

Themes specific to poverty-oriented human development are considered next, ranging from the political weakness of poorer sectors to advantages of distributive, rather than redistributive, strategies. An analysis follows of political differences among and within the main program areas (education, health, nutrition, and, to a lesser extent, population) involving legitimacy, visibility, targetability, and corruptibility.

The implications of differences among national political systems are also highlighted. The author moves from a "macro" to a "micro" framework by addressing the politics of actors, decisions and interests associated with different stages of program design and implementation.

Project Preparation, Design, and Appraisal

2.1 Bamberger, Michael, and Abdul Aziz, eds. *The Design and Management of Sustainable Poverty Alleviation Projects in South Asia.* World Bank Economic Development Institute Seminar Report Series. Washington, D.C. 1993.

This publication is based on the papers prepared for a sociological and economic seminar on the design and management of poverty alleviation in South Asia, organized jointly by the World Bank and the Institute for Social and Economic Change in Bangalore. The findings and recommendations arising from this seminar are presented in this volume, which seeks to integrate sociological and anthropological approaches to understanding poverty and poverty alleviation with conventional economic approaches.

The volume is divided into five parts. Part 1 reviews the poverty situation in South Asia and describes and assesses the main approaches to poverty alleviation. A comparison is also drawn between approaches to poverty alleviation in South Asia, Africa, and Latin America. Part 2 reviews sector experience in poverty alleviation in Asia and includes papers on population; health and nutrition; rural development; housing and urban development; the role of credit in poverty alleviation; and gender issues in anti-poverty programs. Part 3 discusses decentralization, targeted poverty projects, and survival strategies of poor households. Part 4 proposes guidelines for the selection, design, implementation, and sustainability of poverty alleviation programs. The chapters in this section place particular emphasis on participatory approaches to the formulation, implementation, and sustainability of projects. Part 5 presents the summary and conclusions.

There are a number of areas in which sociological and anthropological theory and methods contributed to this publication. First, there is an emphasis throughout on the importance of participatory approaches to the identification, implementation, and sustainability of poverty programs and policies. The chapters on guidelines by Neil O'Sullivan explain in detail how to apply the ZOPP Participatory Logical Framework approach and other participatory methods such as Rapid Assessment. The sector reviews also emphasize the participatory approach, particularly the reviews of housing and urban development and population, health and nutrition.

Second, the participatory approach was further emphasized by including field visits and on-site project evaluations. The main findings are presented in Chapter 8.

Third, the role of nongovernmental organizations (NGOs) in poverty alleviation is emphasized. All of the sector reviews stress the importance of NGOs in reaching the poor and in cost-effective delivery of services to the poor. Chapter 6 discusses the role of credit in poverty alleviation and argues that most of the successful experiences in the use of credit as an instrument of poverty alleviation in Asia have been managed by NGOs.

Fourth, the need to understand the gender dimensions of poverty and poverty alleviation are emphasized throughout. Chapter 7 presents an in-depth review of the Asian experience in gender issues related to poverty alleviation, and a chapter of the guidelines is devoted to the design of gender sensitive poverty reduction projects.

Fifth, the theme of decentralization is examined and a case study is presented on lessons from Karnataka (at the time, one of the Indian states which had progressed furthest in the implementation of decentralized policies) on the linkages between decentralization and the accessibility of public resources to the poor.

Sixth, the issue of sustainable approaches to poverty alleviation is stressed throughout, with a chapter of the guidelines devoted to the design and management of sustainable approaches to poverty alleviation.

Finally, the concept of survival strategies of poor households is introduced. Chapter 10 reviews the Latin American and African literature on interhousehold networks and survival strategies of the poor. Short case studies are presented to illustrate some of the survival strategies adopted in urban areas of South India. These are taken from the first phase of a study on survival strategies in South India which was commissioned for the seminar but which will continue for another year. One outcome of the sociological and economic seminar is a research project on survival strategies.

2.2 Bennett, Lynn, and Mike Goldberg. *Providing Enterprise Development and Financial Services to Women: A Decade of Bank Experience in Asia.* World Bank Technical Paper no. 236. Washington, D.C. 1993.

In both South and East Asia, credit has been the most popular financial service offered in World Bank enterprise development and financial services projects to low income clients, particularly women (EDFS/W). Savings mobilization is less frequently included in project designs, and deposit rates are rarely specified. This indicates a lack of appreciation for the benefits that could accrue to both the clients and the implementing institution by providing savings facilities.

To assist in understanding the targeting and project design choices made by Asia Region EDFS/W projects, enterprises are classified into four stages of development: (a) subsistence enterprises; (b) new microenterprises; (c) growth-oriented microenterprises; and (d) mature microenterprises and small scale industries. These operations differ in terms of the size of investment, the scale of operations, and marketing complexity, with women clients most active at the subsistence level of operations.

The paper analyzes the tradeoffs involved in the choice of a minimalist or an integrated services model of service delivery, and discusses the role of social intermediation in the development of sustainable systems. The rapid growth of EDFS/W projects has been tempered recently by the lack of practical guidelines. There is a need for guidance on what works to enable financial institutions to reach groups that are not adequately serviced (such as women and small farmers) and still maintain strict financial discipline. Also, it is critical that subsidies, which may initially be required to build these mechanisms and "extend the frontier" of EDFS services to women and the poor, are transparent and do not undermine the financial viability and business orientation of the financial institution.

Given the Bank's emphasis on poverty alleviation, the paper concludes that it would be useful to broaden Bank experience over time by encouraging the development of EDFS/W projects as one element in a coordinated country-specific strategy for poverty alleviation. Such an approach would require reconsideration of the structure and sequence of financial, enterprise development and social intermediation services in Asian projects.

2.3 **Cernea, Michael M. "Entrance Points for Sociological Knowledge in Planned Rural Development." In H. Schwartzweller, ed.** *Research in Rural Sociology and Development*. **Greenwich, Conn.: JAI Press. 1987.**

The question addressed in this study is *how* and *when* sociological knowledge can be infused into the planning process, along with economic and technical expertise. The author rejects general yet vague and diffuse social advocacy. He argues that to successfully introduce the application of sociological knowledge into the planning processes and other activities of large-scale organizations (development agencies, governments), practicing sociologists must identify the "entry points" of those organizations or processes.

Each "entry point" is likely to require a different kind of sociological input, functionally tailored to fit the needs existing at that juncture. This requires a flexible "packaging" of the knowledge offered by the social scientist which may consist of: research data; project designs; proposals for institutional arrangements;

communication strategies; evaluation techniques; or other recommendations. For example, the entry points in a development project cycle are: project preparation; project appraisal; implementation and supervision, among others. At each of these entry points, a different kind of work and intellectual input must be generated by the social scientist, adjusted in content and "packaging" to meet the needs of that activity.

Inability to find specific entry points or lack of concern or ability to integrate knowledge appropriately with the activity in question accounts for many failures in the practice of sociology and missed opportunities to put sociological and anthropological knowledge to work.

2.4 Cernea, Michael M. "The Sukuma: A Socio-Cultural Profile." Working Paper c-1, vol. I, Annex to the Tanzania Mwanza-Shinyanga Rural Development Project Staff Appraisal Report. World Bank. Washington, D.C. 1978.

The paper is a description and discussion of the cultural, demographic, and economic characteristics and settlement patterns of the population living in the project area—the *Sukumaland* in Tanzania. Drawing their cultural profile, the author selectively highlights those features of *Sukuma* social organization which (a) may be conducive to support for and participation in the Mwanza-Shinyanga project; (b) may be a cultural source of resistance to proposed project innovations; or (c) may be most affected by the planned changes.

Responding to the need to sociologically inform project appraisal, design, and implementation, the sociocultural profile covers the historic origins of the population; its political structure; economic system; community organization patterns; tenure arrangements for land, water, and grazing areas; the family *Kaya* as a productive unit with its specific farming system and division of labor; the inheritance system; and the population's migratory movements and villagization process.

2.5 Cernea, Michael M., and Scott McLeod. "The Village Self-Help Program in Mwanza-Shinyanga: Socio-Cultural Feasibility Assessment." Working Paper c-9, vol. II, Annex to the Tanzania Mwanza-Shinyanga Rural Development Project Staff Appraisal Report. World Bank. Washington, D.C. 1978.

The paper presents the full design—social, technical, organizational, and financial—of the Village Self-Help Program (VSHP) initiated in two regions of Tanzania (Mwanza and Shinyanga) under a new rural development project in 1978. The VSHP, proposed during preparation of the larger project, was considerably redesigned during the appraisal stage as a "mechanism enabling villages to identify their priority projects, to mobilize villages' own resources for these projects, and to facilitate the provision of government services to support these projects."

In this multidisciplinary working paper (part of the project's appraisal documents), the sociologist analyzed the sociocultural feasibility of the VSHP by examining local social organization patterns, the traditions of group action and mutual help, and the mobilization capacity of the local leadership. The paper describes basic sociocultural patterns of the *Sukuma* culture, such as *Banamhala* (the leading body of village elders), *Basumba Batale* (communal organization by age group), and the *Mwonga* system (a system of labor contribution by one person per household for one work day).

In the case of *Malika ga Mbina* (dance societies), the sociological analysis demonstrates that what at first sight may appear to be merely a loose group created to perform dancing at community celebrations is, in fact, a complex form of social organization that facilitates labor exchanges between farmers at times of peak demand, has a structured authority system and a ramified network of communicators who convey messages between members and leaders.

The paper concludes that the new project can benefit from building upon and capturing the development potential of *Sukuma* culture traditions. While the values exist for activating such organizational modalities, the government has rarely been able to identify and capitalize on such traditions to promote new self help initiatives.

2.6 Hecht, Robert M. "Land and Water Rights and the Design of Small Scale Irrigation Projects: The Case of Baluchistan." *Irrigation and Drainage Systems*. 4:59-76. 1990.

In countries around the world where small-scale irrigation systems are being improved, the design and functioning of these upgraded systems will be greatly enhanced if pre-existing patterns of land and water rights and established procedures for system operation are taken into account. An appreciation of these rights and procedures can greatly influence the layout of the water distribution network, water management practices, anticipated cropping patterns, and the related incidence of project benefits.

Failure to do so will almost certainly have an adverse effect upon the functioning of the irrigation system, and can often result in serious conflicts. This is illustrated by the case of small-scale irrigation development in Baluchistan Province, Pakistan, where limited analysis of property rights and management practices, and lack of consultation with intended beneficiaries caused major delays during the initial stages of project implementation.

However, by introducing a "methodology for social action" that included an assessment of property rights and extensive consultation with affected households during the design and construction phases, the physical features and operating procedures for the upgraded irrigation system were crafted in a manner which maximized economic returns within the range of options acceptable to the local community.

2.7 Hecht, Robert M. "Salvage Anthropology: The Redesign of a Rural Development Project in Guinea." In M. Horowitz and T. Painter, eds. *Anthropology and Rural Development in West Africa.* Boulder, Col.: Westview Press. 1986.

Why work with peasant smallholders as a means of increasing agricultural production in Africa when larger-scale, more "rational" production is needed? It was a particularly arrogant variation of this vision of agrarian change that informed the Agricultural Production Capacity and Development Project in Guinea described by the author.

The original project, which he was asked to help redesign, required large transfers of American techniques and equipment to Guinea, even though they were poorly adapted to the capital mix of most peasant producers affected by the project. Through a re-analysis of the rural economy and social fabric of project areas, the author was able to recommend improvements in production techniques for a follow-on project that would not overload small-holders with debt-inducing equipment.

Projects are based on considerations of internal rates of return, profit, and rates at which "modern" but often technically inappropriate techniques will presumably be adopted by rural producers. Typically these economic considerations are divorced from the social reality which they address. Under these conditions, it is no surprise that many projects fail. When these difficulties become serious enough, the anthropologist may be called in to salvage a foundering project through an examination of "interstitial" (that is, social) factors neglected by planners.

2.8 Horowitz, Michael M. "Social Analysis Working Paper for the Zimbabwe Rural Afforestation Project." Working Paper no. 20. Binghamton, N.Y.: Institute for Development Anthropology. 1982.

Zimbabwe's Rural Afforestation Project was predicated on the validity of two assumptions: (a) smallholders on communal lands *perceive* the deficit between production and consumption of wood for fuel and construction as a problem requiring a solution; and (b) smallholders *possess* the appropriate resources of land, labor, and capital, and *are willing and able* to invest them in ways recommended by the Forestry Commission. If either of these assumptions were unsound, the project would have difficulty in achieving its objectives of enhanced well-being of smallholders and the retardation and ultimate reversal of environmental degradation associated with overcutting the indigenous woodlands.

The paper is the outcome of the author's field work as a member of the World Bank appraisal mission for Zimbabwe's Rural Afforestation Project. The author confronts the project's basic assumptions with sociological data and analysis, identifies the socioeconomic issues most salient to successful project implementation, and recommends appropriate directions for training of project staff, research, monitoring, and evaluation.

2.9 Molnar, Augusta. "Rapid Rural Appraisal Methodology Applied to Project Planning and Implementation in Natural Resource Management." In Timothy Finan and John van Willigen, eds. *Soundings: Rapid and Reliable research Methods for Practicing Anthropologists*. NAPA Bulletin 10. 1991.

As part of a review of rapid appraisal methodologies being used in the fields of natural resource management and forestry, a series of interviews were carried out with various practitioners, mostly social scientists, to assess the state-of-the art in the application of rapid appraisal technologies. The paper examines the tradeoffs in the use of different mixes of methods and degrees of reliability.

2.10 Molnar, Augusta. Community Forestry: Rapid Appraisal. Community Forestry Note 3. United Nations Food and Agriculture Organization. Rome. 1989.

The use of Rapid Appraisal methodologies as an alternative to traditional survey methodologies is increasing in forestry and natural resource management planning. This manual summarizes the range of methodologies in use in 1988 and guides practitioners in the uses of RRA techniques for planning, monitoring, evaluation, and promotion of participatory processes in community forestry development.

2.11 Noronha, Raymond J., and Francis J. Lethem. *Traditional Land Tenures and Land Use Systems in the Design of Agricultural Projects*. World Bank Staff Working Paper no. 561. Washington, D.C. 1983.

Also available in French.

This paper provides agricultural project designers with an analytical basis and rationale for examining traditional land tenure and land use systems, and suggests how to make operational use of such information for key project decisions.

The feasibility of agricultural project implementation and its intended impact depends on farmer behavior, which is often determined by traditional tenurial and land use patterns, whether or not they are reflected in formal legislation. Understanding such patterns helps project designers to answer such questions as whether land would be available for the project; what impact the proposed inputs are likely to have and whether they would be accepted; how these inputs should be introduced and who is likely to adopt them and receive benefits; whether labor for project works would be forthcoming; and whether traditional forms of organization would be viable as support for project organizations.

2.12 Noronha, Raymond, and John Spears. "The Sociological Dimensions of Forestry Project Design." In M.M. Cernea, ed. *Putting People First: 1st ed.* New York: Oxford University Press. 1985.

A translation of this study into Bahasa Indonesia is published in the volume Mengutamakan Manusia Di Dalam Pembangunan: Variabel-variabel Sosiologi di dalam Pembangunan Pedesaan. Jakarta: Penerbit Universitas Indonesia. 1988.

Social forestry projects differ from conventional forestry in that they serve local needs through the active involvement of the beneficiaries in the design and implementation of the reforestation efforts and the sharing of forest produce. Social forestry involves the production and use of forest products in a sector of the economy which is mainly nonmonetized and implies different attitudes and skills on the part of foresters whose role is changed from protecting forests *against* the people to working *with* people to grow trees.

The design of projects with and for people implies an understanding of group processes and socioeconomic and cultural patterns. A sociologist is therefore an essential member of a team to design a social forestry project. Proposed solutions must be acceptable to the beneficiary population living in and around the forest.

The authors, a sociologist and a forester, discuss the four main areas requiring sociological inquiry which is almost invariably necessary for preparing forestry projects: (a) population, (b) land, (c) labor, and (d) social organization. They identify aspects of project design which require additional refinement once the sociocultural data are available, and offer advice for their incorporation into community forestry programs.

2.13 Salmen, Lawrence F. "Beneficiary Assessment: Improving the Design and Implementation of Development Projects." In *Evaluation Review* 13(3):273-91. 1989.

Beneficiary assessment is a tool that can provide project personnel with information about community-based factors that may foster or limit project success. This method involves participant observation and intensive qualitative interviewing in the project communities by nationals trained to develop information attuned to the needs of local project management.

This review presents the evidence accumulated from use of beneficiary assessment in World Bank projects since its introduction in 1982, examining how it has been utilized and to what effect, together with observations on how it may, in the future, be operationalized more extensively. These experiences illustrate a number of insights to be gained from use of this method: adequate communication between project staff and beneficiaries is often lacking; ignorance of the various social strata within the community can lead to inequitable/inefficient implementation; the role of community participation in project success is not always sufficiently understood; and there is a demonstrated need for project management to understand the living conditions, economic realities, and felt needs of beneficiaries.

The following are several World Bank internal documents specifying policy and procedural guidelines, primarily related to social and environmental issues. Bank social scientists have participated in the preparation and writing of these institutional guidelines, which are among the most important and consequential in-house codifications of goals and norms for designing and implementing Bank-assisted development programs.

2.14 World Bank. Operational Directive 4.01: *Environmental Assessment.* October 3, 1991 (a revision of the former OD 4.00, Annex A. October 1989).

2.15 World Bank. Operational Directive 4.02: *Environmental Action Plans.* July 21, 1992.

2.16 World Bank. Operational Directive 4.30: *Involuntary Re-settlement.* June 29, 1990.

2.17 World Bank. Operational Directive 4.20: *Indigenous Peoples.* September 17, 1991.

2.18 World Bank. Operational Directive 4.00: Annex B. *Environmental Policy for Dam and Reservoir Projects.* April 28, 1989.

2.19 World Bank. Operational Directive 14.70: *Involving Nongovernmental Organizations in Bank-Supported Activities.* August 28, 1989.

2.20 World Bank. Operational Policy Note 11.02: *Wildlands—Their Protection and Management in Economic Development.* June 2, 1986.

2.21   World Bank. Operational Policy Note 11.03: *Management of Cultural Property in Bank-Financed Projects*. September 1986.

2.22   World Bank. Operational Policy Note 10.08: *Operations Issues in the Treatment of Involuntary Resettlement in Bank-Financed Projects*. October 8, 1986.

2.23   World Bank. Operational Manual Statement 2.33: *Social Issues Associated with Involuntary Resettlement in Bank-Financed Projects*. February 1980.

2.24   World Bank. Operational Manual Statement 2.20: *Project Appraisal*. February 6, 1984.

Additional publications relevant to this topic can be found in Section 24.

Project Implementation, Monitoring, and Evaluation

3.1 **Bamberger, Michael. "The Politics of Evaluation in Developing Countries."** *Evaluation and Program Planning* 14:325-39. 1991.

After reviewing approaches to program evaluation in the United States, the author identifies the major stakeholders involved in evaluations in developing countries and discusses the concerns of each one and the areas of potential conflict between stakeholder priorities. A major theme is the role of donor agencies in defining the kinds of evaluations which are conducted and the issues on which they focus.

The author argues that donors are mainly concerned with ensuring the effective implementation of the projects they are financing and that this has made it often difficult for developing countries to focus on broader issues of program evaluation, impact assessment or sustainability evaluation.

3.2 **Bamberger, Michael, and Shabbir Cheema.** *Case Studies of Project Sustainability: Implications for Policy and Operations from Asian Experience.* Economic Development Institute Seminar Series. World Bank. Washington, D.C. 1990.

There is a growing awareness that both donors and governments have tended to focus on project implementation and that much less attention has been paid to issues of operation, maintenance and sustainability. While many countries have developed quite elaborate systems for monitoring project implementation, very few countries produce even the most rudimentary information on project operation and maintenance or the extent to which projects do actually produce their intended benefits.

This paper discusses the causes and consequences of this lack of attention to project sustainability in Asia and assessed sustainability experience in Bangladesh by focusing on commissioned case studies of three major projects.

Chapter 1 discusses the concept of sustainability, its importance to developing countries, and the factors affecting the sustainability of projects. Chapter 2 reviews project sustainability experience in agriculture, and in rural and urban development in Asia.

Chapters 3 through 5 summarize the Bangladesh case studies prepared on the First Integrated Rural Development Project, the Agricultural University Project, and the Universal Primary Education project.

Chapter 6 considers some of the policy issues which arise in trying to ensure more sustainable projects, while Chapter 7 discusses the implications for project design and implementation. The annex presents a sustainability checklist which can be used to develop an index of the degree of sustainability of projects.

3.3 Bamberger, Michael. "The Monitoring and Evaluation of Public Sector Programs in Asia: Why Are Development Programs Monitored but Not Evaluated?" *Evaluation Review* 13(1):223-42. 1989.

The author discusses why most countries have reasonably adequate systems for monitoring the implementation of development projects but almost none have even rudimentary systems for monitoring and evaluation of projects once they become operational.

3.4 Bamberger, Michael, and Viqar Ahmed. *Monitoring and Evaluating Development Projects: The South Asian Experience.* Economic Development Institute Seminar Series. World Bank. Washington D.C. 1989.

The authors describe the organizational arrangements for monitoring and evaluating development projects in South Asia, and report on the opinions of monitoring and evaluation practitioners, development planners, and project managers on the strengths and weaknesses of these arrangements and on the management systems and research methodologies used for monitoring and evaluation in the region.

The information is derived from a South Asian Seminar organized by the Economic Development Institute and held in Lahore in 1987. The report describes the current status of monitoring and evaluation in each country and assesses the strengths and weaknesses of current systems and methodologies. Recommendations are included with respect to organizational arrangements for monitoring and evaluation at the national, sectoral and project levels; management issues; methodological issues; and the organization of monitoring and evaluation training programs.

3.5 Bamberger, Michael, and Eleanor Hewitt. *Monitoring and Evaluating Urban Development Programs: A Handbook for Program Managers and Researchers.* World Bank Technical Paper no. 53. Washington, D.C. 1987.

Also published in French.

This volume is a comprehensive handbook for urban policymakers, managers and evaluation practitioners in developing countries which draws on recent developments in urban sociology, economics, and urban planning. It provides guidance on all stages of the design and implementation of a monitoring and evaluation system tailored to the specific context of urban sector projects.

The handbook recommends various alternative options with respect to scope, key research issues, and organization of monitoring and evaluation systems. The systems described can be applied either to self-contained individual projects or to comprehensive multi-component urban development programs.

3.6   Bamberger, Michael, and Eleanor Hewitt. *A Manager's Guide to Monitoring and Evaluating Urban Development Programs: A Handbook for Program Managers and Researchers*. World Bank Technical Paper no. 54. Washington, D.C. 1987.

Also published in Chinese, French, and Spanish.

This summary of the above handbook (see entry 3.5) was prepared to assist managers and policymakers in using the handbook and understanding the overall principles and key issues on which impact evaluation choices must be based.

3.7   Bamberger, Michael, and others. *Evaluation of Sites and Services Projects: The Experience from Lusaka, Zambia*. World Bank Staff Working Paper no. 548. Washington, D.C. 1982.

The findings of a comprehensive evaluation of the First Lusaka Upgrading and Sites and Services Housing Project are presented and discussed by the author. The evaluation included both short-term, operationally oriented studies and more comprehensive, socioeconomic impact studies. The report contains four main parts. The first discusses the project and the political and economic context within which it evolved, while the remaining parts present the main evaluation findings with respect to design and organization, and efficiency of project implementation and project impact.

3.8   Bamberger, Michael, and others. *Evaluation of Sites and Services Projects: The Experience from El Salvador*. World Bank Staff Working Paper no. 549. Washington, D.C. 1982.

Also published in Spanish.

The author reports on the five year evaluation of the first Sites and Services Housing Project in El Salvador, which was part of a four country research project sponsored by the World Bank and the International Development Research Centre of Canada. Three main types of study were conducted: short term studies on topics such as project demand and reasons for participant turnover; medium-range studies to evaluate the efficiency and impact of individual project components; and long-range policy studies to estimate project impact on participants and on housing policies. The report also contains a methodological appendix.

3.9 Cernea, Michael M. *Measuring Project Impact: Monitoring and Evaluation in the PIDER Rural Development Project—Mexico*. World Bank Staff Working Paper no. 332. Washington, D.C. 1979.

The Mexico's nationwide program for rural development (PIDER), one of the largest of its kind in the world, developed an original and extensive system for monitoring its implementation and for the ongoing evaluation of its impact. The strengths and weaknesses of this system are analyzed in this case study.

The paper synthesizes the lessons to be derived from PIDER's experience across the following range of methodological issues: types of information to be collected; definition of the investigation unit; data generation tools; disaggregation of the data collection process; aggregation of monitoring data and evaluation findings; feedback of information to management; and the organizational structures required for monitoring and evaluation.

PIDER management's sensitivity to the sociology of rural development resulted, inter alia, in significant efforts to elicit grassroots community participation in development planning. Systematic guidelines for promoting this participation, as proposed by the Research Center for Rural Development (CIDER) program are presented in the study.

3.10 Cernea, Michael M., and Benjamin J. Tepping. *A System for Monitoring and Evaluating Agricultural Extension Projects*. World Bank Staff Working Paper no. 272. Washington, D.C. 1977.

Based on fieldwork in India, the authors have designed and recommended a system of monitoring and evaluation for agricultural extension and research projects. Grounded in sociology and statistics, the proposed system is conceived as a management tool to ensure that the extension organization is operating efficiently, with close contacts with the beneficiary farmers. The system also enables management to take corrective action when necessary and provides policymakers with appropriate information on performance.

The paper describes the components of the recommended system: a conceptual framework; a set of indicators for monitoring project implementation; a set of indicators for estimating impact on farmers; and a design for a data generation system consisting of a combination of sample surveys and ad hoc studies to produce information on the chosen indicators.

Recommendations for the establishment, composition, and staffing of a monitoring and evaluation unit are included, and an implementation timetable for periodic studies is suggested. Detailed statistical specifications were prepared describing sample allocations, recommended sampling procedures, draft questionnaires and appropriate data collection and processing techniques.

3.11 Murphy, Josette. "Good Enough, Soon Enough: A User-Oriented Approach to Monitoring and Evaluation in Extension Agencies." *Rural Extension Bulletin 1:4-8*. Agricultural Extension and Rural Development Center, University of Reading, England. February 1993.

Information required for management is not necessarily the same as information needed for research purposes. In order to perform their central function of making choices, managers need information available in a form which makes it easy to understand and use, and that reaches them before they have to take the relevant decisions. This article outlines recent attempts by United Nations agencies, the International Fund for Agricultural Development, the Food and Agriculture Organization, and the World Bank to identify the types of information needed by the two separate activities of "monitoring" and "evaluation". It identifies the specific information needs of managers of extension agencies and puts forward seven key principles for the design of management information systems. Application of these principles should result in systems which will provide information "good enough, soon enough" to meet the needs of decisionmakers.

3.12 Murphy, Josette, and Timothy Marchant. *Monitoring and Evaluation in Extension Agencies*. World Bank Technical Paper no. 79. Washington, D.C. 1988.

Managers in charge of development programs will be more effective if they have access to systematic, decision-oriented information on implementing progress as well as on the immediate effects of the program. This is particularly true for managers in extension agencies which provide services to a large, dispersed population, as measuring the provision and effect of such services raises conceptual and technical problems.

Evaluating the efficiency and long-term impact of any development program remains a complex task which requires an innovative approach. Recent efforts to strengthen agricultural extension agencies emphasize the importance of internal monitoring activities that ascertain whether the extension services are being made available to the intended beneficiaries, whether the farmers are taking advantage of them, whether the farmers are adopting the extension recommendations on a sustained basis, if not why not, and with what immediate consequences.

The author provides guidelines for managers and technical staff in extension agencies who plan, organize, implement, and utilize monitoring activities and, when necessary, subsequent evaluations. It defines the information needs of extension managers, discusses administrative and logistic requirements, and reviews techniques for data collection, analysis, presentation, and dissemination which experience has shown to be realistic and timely for extension agencies.

3.13 Murphy, Josette. *Using Evaluations for Planning and Management: An Introduction*. Working Paper no. 2. International Service for National Agricultural Research (ISNAR). The Hague. 1985.

3.14 Narayan, Deepa. *Participatory Evaluation: Tools for Managing Change in Water and Sanitation*. World Bank Technical Paper no. 217. Washington, D.C. 1993.

A mounting body of evidence from around the world is demonstrating the validity of involving communities and service users at all levels in the development process—including data collection, planning, management, and monitoring and evaluation.

The author presents a framework of indicators and processes for conducting participatory evaluation in order to make possible ongoing adjustments and adaptation in projects, to promote effective learning, and to support local decisionmaking, both at the community level and the projects level.

3.15 Narayan, Deepa. *Workshop on Goals and Indicators for Monitoring and Evaluation for Water Supply and Sanitation in Geneva, Switzerland*. UNDP-World Bank Water and Sanitation Program. Washington, D.C. 1991.

The author presents workshop findings reflecting discussion of a framework of indicators of sustainability, effective use, and replicability developed by her.

3.16 Perrett, Heli E. *Using Communication Support in Projects: World Bank's Experience*. World Bank Staff Working Paper no. 551. Washington, D.C. 1982.

This paper outlines how support for communication and information dissemination to project area populations enters into Bank project work in various sectors of lending. It recommends how communication support activities should be designed and carried out during the project cycle, and addresses some commonly experienced difficulties and alternatives which should be kept in mind when designing and implementing activities to support better communication.

3.17 Salmen, Lawrence. "Participant-Observer Evaluation of Upgrading Projects in Two Latin American Cities: La Paz and Guayaquil." In Reinhard J. Skinner, and others., eds. *Shelter Upgrading for the Urban Poor: Evaluation of Third World Experience*. Manila: Publishing House Inc. 1987.

The participant-observer evaluation research discussed in this chapter was undertaken as an effort to heighten the awareness of World Bank and executing agency personnel of project beneficiaries' point of view. This evaluation looks at World-Bank assisted urban projects in two Latin American cities. The primary focus of the evaluation is on urban upgrading of low-income neighborhoods and low-cost housing. Secondary attention was given to credit extended for home improvement and for small business programs.

The evaluation was conducted by the author over a period of 16 months, with an initial residence of four months at project sites in each of the two cities, followed by a later stay of three months at each site. The primary methodology employed consisted of participant observation and qualitative interviewing. This chapter discusses this concept of monitoring and evaluation and demonstrates its practicality based on the author's urban upgrading project experiences in 1982 and 1983.

3.18 Salmen, Lawrence. *Listen to the People*. New York: Oxford University Press. 1987.

This account of the author's experience living among the poor beneficiaries of World Bank urban development projects in La Paz, Bolivia and Guayaquil, Ecuador testifies to the effectiveness with which anthropological techniques of participant observation can be applied in the context of economic development projects. It demonstrates how the evaluations made by participant observers have enabled project managers to identify and address some of the problems they encountered and to adapt projects to the values and needs of the poor.

The book also describes the application of the methodology elsewhere—housing projects in Thailand, fishing and artisanal cooperatives in Brazil, and agricultural projects in Bolivia—using observers from the developing countries themselves. It also reports on the advantages and pitfalls of the participant-observer evaluation method, and its uses in the design and management of development projects.

Additional publications relevant to this topic can be found in Section 25.

Part Two

Social Organization and Social Actors

Social Organization and Institutional Development

4.1 Bamberger, Michael, and others. "Resource Mobilization and the Household Economy of Kenya." *Canadian Journal of African Studies* 19(2):409-21. 1985.

In light of a review of empirical studies on rural-urban income transfers in Kenya, the authors report on their study of the role of social welfare organizations as a mechanism for promoting transfers of money and goods between workers who have migrated to the city and the rural areas from which they come in western Kenya. It was found that these transfers represent a major source of investment in infrastructure projects and, to a lesser extent, a source of credit for small-business development in rural areas.

4.2 Bouman, F.J.A. "Indigenous Savings and Credit Societies in the Developing World." In J.D. Von Pischke, D.W. Adams, and G. Donald, eds. *Rural Financial Markets in Developing Countries*. Baltimore and London: The Johns Hopkins University Press. 1983.

Informally organized groups of farmers or townspeople who each periodically contribute money in small sums and receive one large amount at one time in rotation constitute an informal mechanism that mobilizes savings and in some cases supports productive investments. Rotating savings and credit associations (ROSCAs) are characterized by simple procedures, informality, accessibility, flexibility, and adaptability to many purposes. ROSCAs in Cameroon and Liberia existed before the introduction of Western currency and monetization of the economy, operating on brass bracelets, food, and other commodities.

Contractual saving has traditionally been the prime motivator of these societies, but the credit element seems to become more important with the promise of economic opportunities. Members now use them to start a business, replace trading stock and machinery, or invest in their children's education. The author opposes suggestions for integrating formal and informal capital markets, pointing out that the survival of ROSCAs even in sophisticated city economies suggests that there is still a need for this type of traditional institution based on local knowledge, collective support, and social control.

4.3 Cernea, Michael M. *Nongovernmental Organizations and Local Development.* World Bank Discussion Paper no. 40. Washington, D.C. 1988.

Recent years have witnessed the explosive emergence of nongovernmental organizations (NGOs) as major actors in development activities. Although NGOs are not a novel social phenomenon, the scale and pace at which NGOs have been expanding, the new functions and roles they are taking up, and their increased sophistication and mobilization capabilities represent new and significant trends.

The author discusses NGOs' roles and strategies for future NGO development and identifies three current trends in NGO expansion: growth in numbers and constituencies, broadening functions, and more complex internal institutional structures. He argues that despite the growing flow of financial resources channeled through NGOs, the central contribution of NGOs is not to financially induce development, but to organize people into structures for group action.

The author discusses the nature, functions and types of NGOs vis-a-vis local government and the state. A category of "economic NGOs" is identified within the typology of grassroots associations as being most closely related to the economic and productive activities of their membership and their needs for various kinds of production-related services. Patterns of NGO strengths and weaknesses are analyzed and NGOs' capacity for outreach to the poor is emphasized. The constraints on NGOs' roles and impact include limited replicability of NGO activities, limited self-sustainability, and limited capacity for technical analysis.

International and bilateral development agencies, including the World Bank, can work with NGOs and strengthen their role. Two strategic directions for further NGO development are organizational buildup and the creation of favorable domestic policy environments.

4.4 Cernea, Michael M. "Farmer Organizations and Institution Building for Sustainable Development." *Regional Development Dialogue* 8(2):1-24. 1987.

Also available as World Bank Reprint Series no. 414. Washington, D.C. 1987.

The author discusses the necessity of building institutional and organizational structures for ensuring the long-term sustainability of investments in agricultural development programs. Recognizing the importance of establishing adequate patterns of social organization, and of building durable organizational structures at the grass roots, is crucial for the manner in which development projects and strategies are conceptualized, designed, and implemented.

Much too often, organizational variables have received insufficient recognition in both theory and practice. Consequently, less knowledge and funding and fewer skills than necessary have been allocated to address these variables through social science research and in actual development interventions.

The paper reports the findings of an analysis of the factors that contribute to long-term sustainability of induced development processes, including institutional and organizational factors. The analysis covers 25 development projects financed by the World Bank, of which 13 proved to be nonsustainable only a few years after their completion. The analysis sheds light on the premises of sustainability and, conversely, on the causes of nonsustainable interventions. The empirical findings are followed by a discussion of their implications and of the social engineering approaches required in development programs.

4.5 Cernea, Michael M. "Modernization and Development Potential of Traditional Grassroots Peasant Organizations." In M. Attir, B. Holzner, Z. Suda, eds. *Directions of Change: Modernization Process in Theory and Reality*. Boulder, Col.: Westview Press. 1981.

This chapter focuses on the importance of structure building for development-oriented activities, in particular the social organization of agricultural production activities in traditional peasant societies. The author examines organizational underdevelopment in peasant societies, which are characterized by a low degree of division of labor, undifferentiated skills among the producers, and a low or uneven development of specialized and distinct organizations created solely for supporting productive activities.

Recognizing, however, the development potential of traditional peasant economic organizations, the author argues that, instead of routinely regarding traditional organizations as a constraint, they should be utilized wherever possible as a resource for development.

As an overview of the "state of the art" regarding the use of traditional organizations in rural development projects, the author reports on a review of 164 World Bank-supported rural development projects started between 1973 and 1977, which indicated that elaborating the social methodology and technologies for organization building should be regarded as a high priority for social scientists involved in the study and support of rural development.

The final section of the paper contains a discussion of the major issues related to informal peasant organizations and defines issues for further debate.

4.6 Cernea, Michael M. "The Organization and the Individual: The Economic Rationale of Cooperative Farm Members." *Journal of Rural Cooperation* 3(1). Jerusalem Academy Press. 1975.

This paper analyzes the relationship between farmers' behavior as productive agents and their ideas concerning economic incentives, benefits, income generation, and prices. Farmers' economic beliefs, ideas, and perceptions vary enormously; this set of mental representations can be collectively termed their economic psychology or economic culture.

Farmers' understanding of the economic contexts within which they conduct their productive and market-exchange activities and manage their household economy, may or may not be accurate. Regardless, contends the author, their economic psychology commands or mediates their day-to-day economic behavior and choices, their way of reasoning about market opportunities, their individual relationship *vis-a-vis* various economic organizations and activities, their decisions about family labor allocation, savings, and investments.

The economic rationality which commands a farmer's activity as owner-manager of a private plot is different, and often in conflict with, the type of economic rationality that underlies the activities of cooperative farms in which the same farmer may be a member. Such conflicting rationalities explain behavior patterns that are in contradictory. Without sensitivity towards farmers' economic culture and value systems, policymakers and planners cannot properly understand how elements within this economic culture foster or impede economic behavior and can hardly anticipate farmers' responses to the use of economic levers.

4.7 Hecht, Robert M. "The Transformation of Lineage Production in Southern Ivory Coast." *Ethnology* 23(4):261-77. 1984.

The author attempts to demonstrate the value of a theory of transformation of production systems in explaining rapid social and economic change. He argues that the model of lineage production is useful in understanding the social behavior of incipient cocoa and coffee farmers in southern Ivory coast during 1920-1945.

This model appears to be fruitful in studying a wide range of precapitalist agrarian societies, in Africa and elsewhere, especially in land surplus economies, where control over labor rather than land is crucial for production, and where a low level of technology limits the nature and scope of control over persons and their material output.

More specifically, the author argues that the evolution of rural society in southern Ivory Coast during 1920-1980 can best be explained as a shift from lineage to small-scale capitalist farm production, from an extended kin system to a peasant system. This transition was shaped by factors internal to the dynamics of the lineage configuration, including farm expansion and the intensification of labor, which imposed demands that could not be met by extended kin workers; and by external factors including government policies on public investment, cocoa and coffee marketing, land tenure, and education.

4.8 Hussi, Pekka, Josette Murphy, and others. *The Development of Cooperatives and Other Rural Organizations: The Role of the World Bank.* World Bank Technical Paper no. 199. Washington, D.C. 1993.

Recent initiatives by governments and donors to restructure African economies include efforts to redefine the policy framework for, and the role of, cooperatives and other farmer organizations. These organizations, if they are genuine, member-controlled, and efficient, can provide their members with opportunities to contribute to and benefit from the development of the private sector.

This report reviews the lessons from experience in Bank-funded projects and provides operational guidelines at three levels: (a) the need for an enabling environment; (b) internal functions and structures of rural organizations, and (c) donor assistance coordination.

4.9 Ibrahim, Saad E. and Nicholas Hopkins, eds. *Arab Society: Social Science Perspectives.* Cairo: The American University in Cairo. 1978.

This book is designed as an introduction to the major social and cultural contours and problems of Arab society and an investigation of the social basis for Arab unity. The authors move from consideration of social processes to the ways in which people understand how these processes affect them.

Part one raises general questions of Arab unity and Arab identity. Part two presents a series of reflections on the study of Arab society, and introduces the various methodological approaches that are illustrated throughout the book. Part three discusses the demographic transformations of the Arab world, both population growth and urban migration. Part four considers the transformation of the roles of men, women, and the family in a changing society. Part five examines problems of social change in rural areas with particular attention to the role of the state. Part six addresses problems of political transformation, nation building, ethnicity, and the case of Palestine. Finally, part seven examines the transformation of value systems through the analysis of changes in religion.

4.10 Partridge, William L. "The Human Ecology of Tropical Land Settlement in Latin America: An Overview." In D. Schumann and W.L. Partridge, eds. *The Human Ecology of Tropical Land Settlement in Latin America*. Boulder, Col.: Westview Press. 1989.

The author presents a cultural analysis which reviews the literature from Latin America over several decades on smallholder settlement and its interdependence with plantation agribusiness and cattle ranching in the Latin American tropics. This overview provides the analytical framework for the larger volume as a whole (see entry no. 4.14 below).

The author argues that this interaction dates from the earliest days of European settlement of the tropics, and represents the persistence of a cultural tradition rather than being the product of recent conditions. Furthermore, he believes, smallholders cannot be accurately understood nor can adequate policies affecting them be formulated, unless their interdependence on the other two types of communities is analyzed.

4.11 Pollnac, Richard B. "Social and Cultural Characteristics in Small-scale Fishery Development." In M.M. Cernea, ed. *Putting People First: Sociological Variables in Rural Development*. 2nd ed. New York, London: Oxford University Press. 1991.

Because sociological knowledge has more frequently been applied to farming activities, planners tend to mechanically extrapolate farming community models to fishing communities, without consideration of the social and cultural differences between the two. In contrast, the author inventories the characteristics analytically that distinguish fishing communities from other types of communities and explains why changes induced by fishery development projects tend to unfold differently than changes in other sectors.

Harvest fisheries are distinguished from aquaculture, and both types are further defined by scale and aquatic niche. The amount of cooperation among producers, their shifting residence and irregular work hours, the unpredictability of resources and the high perishability of the product all entail unusual consequences for development interventions.

Income structures in small-scale fishing communities strongly affect investment opportunities. Frequently, only wealthy fishermen or other investors can afford the costly new technology to increase productivity. This new technology gives them a further advantage over poorer fishermen, increasing social and economic stratification and polarization. In some instances, labor-intensive fishing systems are preferable to technologically more efficient systems which may displace local labor and create social problems outweighing the anticipated gains in economic efficiency.

The author describes specific organizational arrangements which can help keep the ownership of new means of production in the hands of smaller fishermen, and addresses the role of cooperatives in fishery development programs. Changes in social organization are perhaps the most difficult to initiate, and the fishermen's cooperative is a problem-prone organization, yet the governments of many developing countries consider cooperatives to be the most adequate institutional vehicle for fishery development projects.

The paper offers recommendations to fishery project planners and managers on the use of sociological information in project design and implementation. Examples of how the data can be obtained and converted into operational recommendations are provided.

4.12 Schumann, D. and William L. Partridge, eds. *The Human Ecology of Tropical Land Settlement in Latin America*. Boulder, Col.: Westview Press. 1989.

This volume is a collection of papers that examine smallholder settlement in the Central and South American tropics and subtropics and their interdependence upon other patterns of human settlement on the frontier. The introductory chapter compares experiences in Latin America with findings from Asia and Africa. Subsequent chapters explore the interactions between plantations, ranches, and small farms, including economic, social, political, and environmental spheres of activity. An epilogue highlights the ecological consequences of this pattern of agricultural expansion of frontier areas.

Contributors include Leopoldo Bartolome, Jane Collins, Robert Goodland, Luz Graciela Joly, Jim Jones, George Ledec, Maxine Margolis, Emilio Moran, Michael Painter, William Partridge, Jorge Uquillas, Connie Weil, Jim Weil, and John Wilson.

Additional publications relevant to this topic can be found in Sections 8 through 15.

Participation

5.1 Bamberger, Michael, and Khalid Shams. *Community Participation in Project Management: The Asian Experience*. Kuala Lumpur: Asian and Pacific Development Centre. 1989.

The authors report on the discussions and conclusions of a seminar organized by the World Bank and the Asian and Pacific Development Centre to analyze experiences with community participation and to assess its potential benefits for increasing the efficiency of project management and sustainability. Six review papers were commissioned to examine experiences of NGOs and governments in the use of participatory approaches in urban and rural development projects in Asia. Chapters on the policy and operational implications of participatory approaches are also included.

5.2 Bamberger, Michael. *Community Participation, Development Planning and Project Management*. Economic Development Institute Policy Seminar Report no. 13. World Bank. Washington, D.C. 1988.

This paper summarizes the conclusions of a broad discussion organized to help the World Bank define how it should strengthen the focus on participatory approaches to development in the Bank's training programs. Participants in the discussion included NGOs and experts in community participation. A number of sector review papers were prepared to assess community participation experiences in rural development, urban development, family planning, and health programs.

5.3 Bhatnagar, Bhuvan and Aubrey Williams, eds. *Participatory Development and the World Bank: Potential Directions for Change*. World Bank Discussion Paper no. 183. Washington, D.C. 1992.

The Bank's operational experience over many years shows that projects tend to be more sustainable and yield higher returns when they involve those they are intended to help. However, Bank staff have been challenged to ask themselves whether they are approaching the idea of participation in the right way. How and to what extent can external agencies such as the Bank encourage participatory government?

This report reflects the outcome of an international workshop exploring these issues. The workshop, supported by the Swedish International Development Authority, as

52 Participation

well as this volume, were organized around the twenty-one priority questions of the Bank-wide learning group on participation relating to important aspects of participation and development, and issues relevant to strengthening Bank support for participatory approaches.

5.4   Bhatnagar, Bhuvan. "Participatory Development and the World Bank: Opportunities and Concerns." In B. Bhatnagar and A. Williams, eds. *Participatory Development and the World Bank: Potential Directions for Change*. World Bank Discussion Paper no. 183. Washington, D.C. 1992.

Based on information provided by World Bank project managers, members of the core team of the Bank-wide participatory development learning group, academics, and development practitioners, this chapter addresses eleven priority questions on participatory development identified by members of the learning group's core team.

Rather than describing participatory development as viewed from within the Bank, the chapter focuses instead on the utility of the questions themselves as a basis for investigation. It takes a broad look at three areas of concerns and issues that could eventually lead to policy recommendations for the Bank: concerns related to the definition of participation; issues related to borrowing governments that are members of the World Bank Group; and issues related to the Bank's commitment and capacity to support participation in Bank-financed activities.

5.5   Cernea, Michael M. *The Building Blocks of Participation: Testing Bottom-up Planning*. World Bank Discussion Paper no. 166. Washington, D.C. 1992.

A summary version is published in B. Bhatnagar and A. Williams, eds. *Participatory Development and the World Bank: Potential Directions for Change*. World Bank Discussion Paper no. 183. Washington, D.C. 1992.

How can a planner build the capacity for mobilizing community participation into a project? This paper answers that question by analyzing, step by step, one case rich in experience: Mexico's Decentralization Project and its predecessor, the PIDER program. The period encompassed stretches from the early 1970s to the 1990s.

The public's participation in government-initiated development programs is essentially a matter of social organization. It requires identification of social actors, goal definition, linkages between planners and the local community, establishment of information channels, procedures for consultative decisionmaking and resource allocation, and mobilization mechanisms. These institutional and social arrangements, argues the author, are the "software" of development programs, but creating it requires a systematic methodology, to be formulated through applied social research.

Mexico's PIDER program developed a bottom-up planning methodology to give local communities a role as *social actors in bottom-up planning.* A "capacity-building" team was set up inside PIDER to construct the new framework for participatory planning. Six components of this capacity-building process are discussed: (a) creation of a multidisciplinary capacity-building group; (b) formulation of a conceptual framework; (c) sociological analysis of the social actors; (d) action research and social experiments with the new planning methods; (e) staff training; and (f) formal institutionalization of the new methodology. The paper describes the action-research process, with its field experiments which produced a planning methodology for initiating and executing local projects by combining financial and equity resources from the public sector and the beneficiaries themselves.

The new Decentralization and Regional Development Program for the disadvantaged states, started in 1990 after Mexico's economic crisis, has reintroduced the earlier participatory approaches. The paper defines the key lessons about sound social engineering learned from the two projects.

5.6 Dichter, Thomas. "Demystifying Popular Participation: Institutional Mechanisms for Popular Participation." In B. Bhatnagar and A. Williams, eds. *Participatory Development and the World Bank: Potential Directions for Change.* World Bank Discussion Paper no. 183. Washington, D.C. 1992.

The growing literature on popular participation provides detailed answers to the institution-related questions posed by the World Bank's participatory development learning group. According to the author, however, the literature does not address the problem of quality. What might be of most help on the institutional front is not a set of "how to's," but rather a guide to some of the cultural mismatches inside institutions (including the Bank) that result in poor-quality promotion of participation.

The author presents several examples of cultural mismatches and suggests six steps that the Bank could take to foster greater respect for participatory development.

5.7 Elmendorf, Mary. "Public Participation and Acceptance." In C.G. Gunnerson and J.M. Kalbermatten, eds. *Environmental Impacts of International Civil Engineering Projects and Practices.* New York: American Society of Civil Engineers. 1978.

Engineers can perform the technical planning to supply irrigation or drinking water, but people at the grassroots level must be included for effective utilization and management of the water supply system. Systems which have been essentially user-built and -planned, and for which the technology dictating their design has been within the maintenance capabilities of the users, are the most likely to be effective.

54 *Participation*

The author presents three case studies to illustrate her argument. The two cases in Mexico, both successful potable water supply projects, involved several levels of participation. In the third case, an irrigation project in Kenya, participation was seriously limited by linguistic and cultural factors.

Based on the conclusions drawn from these cases, the author recommends that: (a) members of a community be involved in the *early* stages of project planning; (b) simplified methodologies for data collection be adapted to village needs and perceptions; (c) surveys be structured on a community zone basis in order to elicit early evidence of inequities or special needs; (d) information about various alternatives for water supply and waste disposal be shared at public meetings with families present in order to broaden the basis of understanding and support; and that (e) recognition be given to the importance of membership in formal and informal networks, so that group decisions related to cooperative efforts can reinforce individual decisions for improving the quality of life of all households.

5.8   Falloux, François, and Lee Talbott. "Political Involvement and Popular Participation." In F. Falloux and L. Talbott, eds. *Crisis and Opportunity: Environment and Development in Africa.* London: Earthscan, Ltd. 1992.

The central theme of this chapter is that in the process of creating a National Environmental Action Plan (NEAP), synergistic interaction between the state and its people is the key to success. The author examines the actual degree of interaction in the creation of the NEAPs of Madagascar, Rwanda, Ghana, Uganda, and Guinea. Participation varied considerably according to the commitment of the head of government, the involvement of democratically elected members of parliament, decentralization of analysis and input to regional and local levels, and diversity of support by organizations other than a single political party.

The authors warn, however, that there is a danger of excess participation if various segments of society are not properly integrated in the NEAP process. Knowledge of a country's society is an essential starting point. The authors summarize lessons learned from international experience with participation of local organizations and make recommendations for a more integrated, and decentralized environment in which to promote effective popular participation.

5.9   Narayan, Deepa. *Participatory Materials Toolkit: Training of Trainers and for Community Empowerment.* Washington, D.C.: World Bank. 1994.

Based on fifteen years' experience, this toolkit is a compilation of visual materials to support twenty-five activities to facilitate participatory decisionmaking, both at the community level and the project level.

5.10 Narayan, Deepa. "Participatory Gender Analysis Tools for the Community and Agency Level." In W. Wakeman, ed. *Gender Issues Sourcebook for the Water and Sanitation Sector*. Washington, D.C.: Water and Sanitation Collaborative Council. 1994.

Gender analysis is a powerful tool for planning, implementation, and evaluation, and for raising awareness about gender issues. However, there is a relative lack of experience with participatory application of tools for gender analysis at the community and project level. In this chapter, the author highlights some principles of participatory gender analysis with brief descriptions of ten related activities.

5.11 Paul, Samuel. *Community Participation in Development Projects: the World Bank Experience*. World Bank Discussion Paper no. 6. Washington, D.C. 1987.

This paper reviews the experience of Bank-assisted projects with community participation (CP) in the urban housing, health, and irrigation sectors. A sample of forty projects with potential for CP and ten successful projects without CP were selected from these sectors for analysis within a conceptual framework that draws attention to the objectives, intensity, and instruments of CP and their interrelationships. The author argues that the mix of objectives, intensity, and instruments of CP tends to vary depending on the nature of projects and their context. The multiplicity of approaches to an interpretation of Cp in the literature and in the world of practice can be better understood within this analytical framework.

For the purposes of this study, the author identifies five objectives of CP: (a) empowerment; (b) building beneficiary capacity; (c) increasing project effectiveness (d) improving project efficiency; and (e) project cost sharing. He summarizes project experience in relation to success in achieving the five objectives; the intensity of CP in a given project, ranging from information sharing to decisionmaking in operational aspects of projects; the presence or absence of critical project inputs such as technology and supervision; and initiative for incorporating CP into project strategies. The author draws lessons from the project outcomes and analyzes their implications for Bank policies.

5.12 Racelis, Mary. "The United Nations Children's Fund: Experience with People's Participation." In B. Bhatnagar and A. Williams, eds. *Participatory Development and the World Bank: Potential Directions for Change*. World Bank Discussion Paper no. 183. Washington, D.C. 1992.

UNICEF has capitalized on its mandate to enhance the well-being of children, which by its nature generates interest in local participation and commonality of concern.

UNICEF's policies, programs, structure, and procedures emphasize participatory approaches.

The author presents an overview of UNICEF's experience with popular participation, focusing on four areas: UNICEF's policies and programs encouraging participation, participation in the country programming process, social mobilization techniques, and other participation-inducing procedures.

5.13 Rudquist, Anders. "The Swedish International Development Authority: Experience with Popular Participation." In B. Bhatnagar and A. Williams, eds. *Participatory Development and the World Bank: Potential Directions for Change*. World Bank Discussion Paper no. 183. Washington, D.C. 1992.

The author recounts the experience of the Swedish International Development Authority (SIDA) with popular participation against the background of the main objectives of Swedish development cooperation. First, he relates SIDA's policies and program planning procedure. Subsequently, he discusses participatory experiences in SIDA-financed programs and reports on responses offered by a selection of SIDA officials to the World Bank learning group's priority questions on participation.

5.14 Uphoff, Norman. "Monitoring and Evaluating Popular Participation in World Bank-Assisted Projects." In B. Bhatnagar and A. Williams, eds. *Participatory Development and the World Bank: Potential Directions for Change*. World Bank Discussion Paper no. 183. Washington, D.C. 1992.

Monitoring and evaluating participatory components in World Bank-supported projects should be done in ways that strengthen intended beneficiaries' capacities to help manage project activities and sustain project benefits. The cost of such monitoring and evaluation is more easily justified if the expenditure helps to build up management capabilities among local communities, rather than just producing information for monitoring and evaluation of project activities.

Accordingly, this paper considers methodologies that can contribute to longer-term participatory operation and maintenance. The methods discussed fall into two categories representing two basic perspectives: the "outsider's" view expressed in "objectified" terms, and the "insider's" view, representing reality as understood by persons within their own culture. Monitoring and evaluating participation must be undertaken from both perspectives in order to effectively support the processes and potential that participation can evoke.

5.15 Uphoff, Norman. "Fitting Projects to People." In M.M. Cernea, ed. *Putting People First: Sociological Variables in Rural Development.* 2nd ed. New York, London: Oxford University Press. 1991.

If "people's participation" in financially induced development programs is to be more than a trendy slogan, planners and managers must face the task of organizing participation—they must identify and mobilize the specific social actors whose participation is sought, and open practical ways in which they can participate in project design, execution, and monitoring.

To chart such ways, the author discusses problems confronted in projects lacking adequate popular participation. He analyzes several areas in project planning where planners need to seriously rethink project design in order to bring more people into the decisionmaking process.

The author reviews three rural development projects in Ghana, Mexico, and Nepal. Despite their relatively innovative designs, all three projects were hindered by an excessive dependence on centralized, nonparticipatory planning. Even where planners started to allow for consultation, as in the Mexican case, further analysis showed that lasting patterns of social organization for participation were not established. The author uses the experience gained from these three cases to define five ways of ensuring beneficiaries' participation in project design and implementation.

This chapter examines participation not only in project decisionmaking, but also in gathering the knowledge used to design a project. The author notes areas in which local expertise can make a substantive contribution to project design: obtaining socioeconomic data, monitoring and evaluating the project, checking the validity of sociocultural information gathered by outsiders, providing technical knowledge, and contributing historical information about earlier projects and the reasons for their success or failure.

Finally, he addresses the issue of working with local organizations, noting that some institutions are more suitable than others for carrying out development programs, and discusses some of the potential pitfalls in promoting genuine participation.

Poverty Reduction

6.1 Cernea, Michael M. **Poverty Risks from Population Displacement in Water Resources Development**. HIID Development Discussion Paper no. 355. Cambridge, Mass.: Harvard University. 1990.

The counter-development risks and effects of many development programs are often overlooked by planners. Failure to recognize these risks from the outset and to adopt measures for avoiding or mitigating them explains why certain adverse effects often snowball.

A class of programs that provides great benefits are the water resource development programs. Benefits—irrigation, energy, flood control, drinking water, and better navigation—usually greatly exceed the negative effects. Yet such programs also entail high economic, health, and social risks and casualties for the upstream population dislocated by reservoir submergence. Impoverishment and social disarticulation, the essential adverse impacts of displacement, are documented based on empirical evidence from India, Brazil, Kenya, Nepal, and other countries. The deleterious effects of compensation in cash, as opposed to land for land, are demonstrated in light of experiences from the Saguling and Civata reservoirs in Indonesia, the Narayanpur dam in Karnataka, India, and the Kulekhani reservoir in Nepal.

Generalizing from a vast body of empirical material, the author derives a seven-dimensional model of the impoverishment processes typically unleashed by forced displacement. The dimensions are: (a) landlessness, (b) unemployment, (c) homelessness, (d) marginalization, (e) food insecurity, (f) increased morbidity and mortality, and (g) social disarticulation. This predictive model is intended to serve as a "self destroying prophecy" by informing planners and decisionmakers about processes that must be prevented through careful planning and commensurate resource allocation.

The author recommends that four frameworks which facilitate preventive and mitigating measures be incorporated into projects: policy frameworks, legal frameworks, planning frameworks, and organizational frameworks. Production-based approaches are recommended for reestablishing self-sufficiency and improving living standards of relocated populations.

6.2 Esman, Milton J. and John D. Montgomery. "The Administration of Human Development." In P.T. Knight, ed. *Implementing Programs of Human Development*. World Bank Staff Working Paper no. 403. Washington, D.C. 1980.

The authors identify and analyze the administrative dimensions of programs designed to reduce poverty in developing countries. They focus on human development activities, primarily in health, nutrition, family planning, and elementary and nonformal education, but the findings have application to a broad range of programs oriented to the poor in urban as well as rural areas.

The administrative stance that will evoke appropriate responses from intended users differs radically from that of the "command style" of conventional bureaucracies. The authors accordingly indicate the analytical and operational means available to governments and donor agencies for improving administrative performance, propose a short agenda for applied research, and identify a number of policy issues that remain to be resolved. Their special focus is on the needs of program and project planners and administrators, and of the international agencies working with them in the search for better ways to reduce global poverty.

6.3 Grootaert, Christian, and Timothy Marchant. *The Social Dimensions of Adjustment Priority Survey: An Instrument for the Rapid Identification and Monitoring of Policy Target Groups*. World Bank Social Dimensions of Adjustment Working Paper no. 12. Washington, D.C. 1991.

This paper describes approaches developed or proposed by a special unit created in the World Bank to study the social effects of structural adjustment programs. The authors describe the planning and implementing of the Priority Survey, designed to profile households vulnerable to adjustment programs and to provide a mechanism to monitor social and economic variables for different population groups. They discuss survey sampling, questionnaire design, field logistics, data processing and systems design, and the analysis and presentation of the initial results. The paper includes technical annexes covering survey data processing system design requirements and specifications of analytical tables.

6.4 Grootaert, Christian, Timothy Marchant, and others. *The Social Dimensions of Adjustment Integrated Survey: A Survey to Measure Poverty and Understand the Effects of Policy Change on Households*. World Bank Social Dimensions of Adjustment Working Paper no. 14. Washington, D.C. 1991.

The authors describe the steps used for the Integrated Survey, designed to study household behavior in greater depth than the Priority Survey, and to examine household responses to different socioeconomic settings. The paper covers issues of sampling, questionnaire design, field logistics, data processing and systems design, and analysis and presentation of initial results.

6.5 **Safilios-Rothschild, Constantina. "The Role of the Family: a Neglected Aspect of Poverty." In P.T. Knight, ed.** *Implementing Programs of Human Development.* World Bank Staff Working Paper no. 403. Washington, D.C. 1980.

The author analyzes the role of the family under circumstances of absolute poverty, deriving implications for anti-poverty policies. To delineate the relevant dimensions of the family's role in development, the author emphasizes the fluid and dynamic nature of family, household and kin networks, and the inapplicability of Western models to family systems in other cultures. She reviews the evidence concerning variables such as family power and decisionmaking; patterns of inequality in the intrafamilial division of labor and such resources as food, health care, and education; and the mediating role of kinship.

After examining the strategies used by families to cope with poverty, the author analyzes the impact of development policies and programs on family structure and dynamics, emphasizing the spread of female-headed households and changes in the prevailing division of labor and role interdependencies.

6.6 **Salmen, Lawrence.** *Reducing Poverty: an Institutional Perspective.* World Bank Poverty and Social Policy Series Paper no. 1. Washington, D.C. 1992.

The World Bank's central operating paradigm, this paper maintains, is the "miracle of the market"—those who need goods and services offer prices that stimulate others to supply them. This principle of demand organizes service delivery to the rich and powerful, whose purchasing power or connections stimulate those services that interest them.

People-oriented service organizations are usually supply-driven providers that try to induce clients to consume what is judged to be good for them. Experience suggests that poverty-reduction efforts would be more successful if they were energized more by demand than supply. To this end, the Bank would do well to begin viewing the poor less as passive beneficiaries and more as customers whom it can help enable to pay the costs for what the beneficiaries see will better their lives.

Successful use of qualitative techniques for understanding the needs of the poor, such as focus group interviews, social marketing, beneficiary assessment interviews, and participant observation are described in this paper. It also recommends development assistance to nurture a "thickening social web" of non-governmental organizations and increased use of local independent consultants to understand the grassroots realities that Bank staff have difficulty mastering in several two- or three-week missions a year. The combination of attention to both informal and formal institutions leads to a sustainable approach to poverty reduction.

6.7 Salmen, Lawrence. "Reducing Poverty." In *Public Administration and Development* 11(3):295-302. 1991.

Since the early 1970s, the World Bank has recognized that economic growth alone will not reduce poverty. Yet it has not fully accepted the fact that effective poverty reduction requires a "learning process approach," rather than the "blueprint approach" commonly used by development agencies.

To facilitate the learning process approach, the Bank should consider using qualified intermediary, grassroots and non-governmental organizations; stimulating pluralism and competition; and encouraging cooperation between central and local institutions. However, helping the poor will require more administrative resources than heretofore provided, making funds available for careful and flexible project design, staff exposure to poverty conditions and programs, training in and use of appropriate interdisciplinary fields, monitoring and evaluation, and continual project revision.

6.8 World Bank. *Poverty Reduction Handbook*. Washington, D.C. 1993.

This handbook, based on lessons learned from operations and research, is intended to help operationalize the two-pronged strategy for poverty reduction articulated in the *World Development Report (WDR) 1990*. This strategy is based on broad economic growth to generate income-earning opportunities and improved health care, education, and other social services to help the poor take advantage of these opportunities. The handbook is a collective product to which many Bank staff and consultants (including economists, education specialists, anthropologists, sociologists, health experts, and political scientists) have contributed.

The Handbook provides an operational context for poverty analysis and the design of country assistance strategies by discussing poverty profiles and poverty assessments and reviewing the treatment of poverty reduction in country strategy papers, adjustment operations, and investment projects. It highlights the continuum of sectoral and macroeconomic issues that preoccupy Bank operational managers.

The Handbook has three parts: Part I covers the preparation of country poverty assessments, including the country poverty profile and the analysis of policies and public expenditures; Part II deals with the design of Bank country assistance strategies, including lending operations; and Part III discusses investments aimed at improving country poverty data and monitoring Bank programs.

Lessons from experience are an important part of the Handbook. The annex to Chapter 3 contains summaries of social sector public expenditure reviews for Bolivia, Brazil, Costa Rica, Guatemala, and Honduras. The annex to Chapter 4 contains eight sample summary poverty assessments for Bolivia, Egypt, India, Indonesia, Malawi, Malaysia, Mexico, and Venezuela. The annex to Chapter 7 compiles thirty project summaries illustrating poverty reduction projects and components in different sectoral and country contexts.

Culture, Beliefs, and Values

7.1   Ardouin, Claude. "What Models for African Museums? West African Prospects." In I. Serageldin and J. Taboroff, eds. *Culture and Development in Africa: Proceedings of an International Conference*. Washington, D.C.: World Bank. 1993.

After several decades of economic development in Africa it is now clear that cultural parameters and processes are at least as important as the economic aspects of the evolution of African societies. Cultural identities represent a reference point for the self identities of both individuals and communities and constitute an important factor in individual and social equilibrium. In African societies today, which are undergoing rapid change and subjected to powerful external influences, this equilibrium is frequently damaged or destroyed.

Integrating culture and cultural heritage into the global vision of development introduces a new dimension into the activities of institutions concerned with culture. This context is increasingly shaping development options for Africa's museums. As institutions inherited from the colonial period or based on Western models, African museums are commonly in an equivocal situation. Although they are generally considered obligatory, museums are rarely perceived as dynamic development tools.

However, over the past few years new movements and approaches have been developing that redefine the museum's role. In addition to their role of safeguarding the traditional cultural heritage, museum professionals increasingly believe that the narrow ethnographic and folkloric vision must be replaced by a more complex and dynamic view of material heritage as a range of historical products created by the activity of different human groups in the past and the present. The author presents an overview of different potential perspectives for museums and describes how they can diversify their fields of activity in order to be involved in their communities' lives and communicate with their different publics.

7.2   Bryant, Coralie. "Culture, Management, and Institutional Assessment." In I. Serageldin and J. Taboroff, eds. *Culture and Development in Africa: Proceedings of an International Conference*. Washington, D.C.: World Bank. 1993.

Culturally congruent management approaches are adapted to local norms and practices, with attention to how motivation, incentives, communication, coordination, and organization take place within a culture. When people participate in decision making, they bring their own knowledge of how their culture and social system can adapt to and advance change.

The World Bank is undertaking a regional study of indigenous management with the objective of deepening understanding through empirical data of how culture impacts upon management and how African development managers might become more effective in that context. The three major components of the study are governance and culture, participation, and local organizational life. These three topics point to a need for institutional assessment that can inform country operations at various levels. The paper concludes with a discussion of the data required and the appropriate methodology to understand what processes work in a given culture while others don't, and why decision making occurs as it does.

7.3 **Cernea, Michael M. "Culture and Organization: The Social Sustainability of Induced Development." In** *Sustainable Development* **1(2):18-29. Australia. 1993.**

Also published in reduced form in M.A. Faris and M.H. Khan, eds. **Sustainable Agriculture in Egypt.** *Boulder, Col. and London: Lynne Rienner. 1993.*

When economic development is accelerated through government programs, such interventions must lead to durable, self-sustaining development, rather than only cause what the author calls passing "growth blips" or "development spurts." This requires strengthening local capacities, supporting indigenous entrepreneurship and unlocking the propensity for self-organization within the local culture.

Building up a "culture of sustainable development" is essential in this respect, as culture is humanity's basic mechanism for *adaptation* to nature as well as for *transforming* our natural environment. This includes agricultural production, within which people must use, manage, and transform natural resources in a sustainable manner.

The author proposes the concepts of *organizational intensity* and *organizational density* as tools for defining and measuring sociocultural components of sustainable development. Successful strategies invest in programs that are not only technology-intensive, but also organization-intensive. Such strategies lead to constructed social environments with higher degrees of organizational density: thus they create social capital. The higher the organizational density of a given society and the better the fit between organization, technology and the management of natural resources, the higher the likelihood for sustainable development.

Failure to strengthen local organizations increases the risks of overall failure, particularly in programs of *induced* development. Economic failures can often be prevented by a strategy of investing more in "organization-ness," that is, by fostering adequate association among resource users.

7.4 Colletta, Nat J., and Umar Khayam. **Culture for Development: Toward an Indonesian Applied Anthropology.** Jakarta: OBOR Press. 1987.

7.5 Colletta, Nat J. "**Cultural Revitalization, Nonformal Education, and Village Development in Sri Lanka.**" *Comparative Education Review* 26(2):271-86. 1982.

The author reports the results of a study of the Sarvodaya Shramadana movement and draws conclusions for other community development projects. Sarvodaya is a nonprofit, nongovernmental community education and development movement working in nearly 3000 villages in Sri Lanka. "Sarvodaya" means universal awakening and "Shramadana" means sharing of one's time, energy, and thought for the good of all.

7.6 Colletta, Nat J. "**The Fusing of Cultures in Micronesia: Community Learning System Model.**" *Journal of Asian-Pacific and World Perspectives* 5(2). Winter 1981-82.

7.7 Davis, Shelton H. "**The Globalization of Traditional Cultures.**" *Northeast Indian Quarterly* 8(1):42-3. 1991.

This essay describes the role which the cultures of the world's indigenous peoples can play in the resolution of contemporary social issues. Specific attention focuses on indigenous ecological knowledge, indigenous credit institutions, and the care of the elderly in traditional societies.

7.8 de Maret, Pierre. "**Archaeological Research, Site Protection, and Employment Generation: Central African Perspectives.**" In I. Serageldin and J. Taboroff, eds. *Culture and Development in Africa: Proceedings of an International Conference.* Washington, D.C.: World Bank. 1993.

The present crisis in Africa is at least as much a moral and identity crisis as an economic and political one. For several years the necessity of taking into account the cultural dimension has been acknowledged by a growing number of development policy makers although, to date, most of the development projects integrate this problem only in a very limited way.

As recognition of the necessity to take into account the sociocultural dimension of development gains ground, social and cultural anthropology will have a more significant role to play, and with them archaeology. In addition, from a political point of view archaeology offers a unique opportunity to counteract the growth of tribalism by revealing the cultural diversity in precolonial times and the fact that, historically, most cultures in the region trace their origins to a common stock.

Archaeologically, Central Africa is the least known part of the continent and probably the largest of the last unknown regions of the world. In most of the region finances and trained staff are usually lacking. The little research being done is carried out by expatriates during brief missions. The author lists a number of archaeological research topics directly relevant to present-day inhabitants, such as the origins of food production and metallurgy and the emergence of societies in connection with state formation and trade. Strategies to promote conservation and valorization of cultural property include institution building, education, support through development projects, education, and the development of tourism and handicraft production to increase employment and income.

7.9 Etounga-Manguellé, Daniel. "Culture and Development: African Responses." In I. Serageldin and J. Taboroff, eds. *Culture and Development in Africa: Proceedings of an International Conference*. Washington, D.C.: World Bank. 1993.

Since the early 1970s, awareness has grown of the importance of culture in the social, economic, and political evolution of contemporary societies. In Africa, this awareness seems to focus on reasserting cultural identity, which Africans perceived as threatened by the emphasis placed during the first decades of independence on purely economic development.

The author contends, that African executives and managers must reflect on changes needed for African society as a whole and search for the means to speed the evolution of African enterprises to adapt to an environment dominated by international competition. He describes the experience of his own consulting firm which conducts seminars on cultural adjustment for African executives. The methodology of the seminars addresses the belief that African cultures can negatively influence their societies' economic performance. Participants in the seminars reflect and discover for themselves what needs to be done to change cultural patterns.

7.10 Goodland, Robert, and Maryla Webb. *The Management of Cultural Property in World Bank-Assisted Projects: Archaeological, Historical, Religious, and Natural Unique Sites*. World Bank Technical Paper no. 62. Washington, D.C. 1989.

"Cultural property" (a United Nations term) denotes sites or artifacts of archaeological, paleontological, historic, religious, and unique natural value. The term encompasses remains left by previous human inhabitants as well as unique natural environmental features. Worldwide, cultural property is rapidly, irreversibly, and unnecessarily being depleted because of rapid population growth and poorly planned economic development. This loss represents a permanent diminution of the international and national patrimony.

During the past decade, many development projects financed by the World Bank have included cultural property concerns. (Thirty-five of these are described in detail in part II of the volume.) Therefore, the Bank has adopted a general policy to help preserve cultural property and prevent its elimination or deterioration.

When potential projects are being identified, pertinent authorities and experts are consulted and/or reconnaissance surveys are made to assess the cultural property elements of the proposed project site. If cultural property is present, relevant government authorities and other experts are called upon to help design mitigatory measures. Nations are best served if economic progress and the preservation of cultural property are carefully planned so as to be mutually enhancing.

7.11 Klitgaard, Robert. "Taking Culture into Account: From 'Let's' to 'How." In I. Serageldin and J. Taboroff, eds. *Culture and Development in Africa: Proceedings of an International Conference.* Washington, D.C.: World Bank. 1993.

Forty years ago, some of the foremost social scientists of the day met in Paris to discuss taking culture into account in economic development. They were unanimous on the need to enhance understanding of economic development, cultural change, and their interrelationships. The author calls this convergence of views the "let's" point, but notes that the conferees were less impressive in saying "how."

There is agreement that culture should be taken into consideration, and people have studied culture scientifically for over a century, yet there are as yet no well developed theories, no practical guidelines, nor any close professional links between those who study culture and those who make development policy. The author offers the following explanation: "cultural differences" between anthropologists (humanists) and economists (scientists); the fear that taking culture into account will lead to oversimplification and discrimination; the scientific difficulty of specifying the ways that cultures and policy choices interact; and a limited and misguided understanding of policy analysis.

The author makes recommendations for overcoming these difficulties. Beyond this, he argues, part of "taking culture into account" should mean understanding how "cultural dimensions" enter into utility functions and production functions of various kinds. Anthropological literature has been of little help so far in this sort of "taking culture into account," although anthropology has contributed in critiquing ideas about development; long-term, in-depth ethnographic description; championing the voiceless and advocating popular participation in development; and avoiding oversimplification.

The author stresses the need to take the scientific side of cultural studies more seriously. The current concepts of policy analysis and the role of social sciences must be enriched and experimented with and new processes of policy analysis and participatory management must be devised.

7.12 Kottak, Conrad Phillip. "Culture and Economic Development." *American Anthropologist* 92(3):723-31. 1990.

This essay informs anthropologists about the results of the World Bank-supported study comparing primary evaluations of 68 completed projects. Through his analysis of ex post findings on both successful and failed projects, compared with the results of a "blind" analysis of the quality of the respective Bank project appraisal documents for the same projects, the author is able to show that incorporating sociocultural analysis in project design from the very beginning makes a significant difference in the chances for project success. In reporting the results of this study, the author focuses on the relevance of Romer's rule to development theory.

7.13 Marc, Alexandre O. "Community Participation in the Conservation of Cultural Heritage." In I. Serageldin and J. Taboroff, eds. *Culture and Development in Africa: Proceedings of an International Conference.* Washington, D.C.: World Bank. 1993.

In Africa, conserving cultural heritages is made particularly difficult by weak institutional capabilities, lack of resources, isolation of many culturally essential sites, and a general lack of awareness of the value of cultural heritage preservation. However, involving people in cultural heritage preservation raises awareness of the importance of the past for people facing rapid changes.

The author reviews the concepts of community participation in cultural heritage preservation. Participation can be seen as an end in itself or as a means to improve the effectiveness of a project. In the authors opinion, the two views are not contradictory; it is possible to view participation as both a means and an end. In either case, if people are to provide their time and resources, the activity has to have a value for them. The design of participatory approaches in cultural heritage conservation is discussed with particular attention to institutional capabilities, and sharing benefits, implementation, and management.

7.14 McIntosh, Susan Keech. "Archaeological Heritage Management and Site Inventory Systems in Africa: The Role of Development." In I. Serageldin and J. Taboroff, eds. *Culture and Development in Africa: Proceedings of an International Conference.* Washington, D.C.: World Bank. 1993.

For Africans, who experienced to varying degrees the loss of their past under colonialism, the archaeological heritage is closely connected to important national agendas. It also represents a part of the global patrimony, a contribution to the collective memory of mankind. However, the disappearance of large chunks of the archaeological record is a direct consequence of development activities, although many African countries have created legislation to protect archaeological sites. Given limited national resources to enforce this legislation fully, the author argues that development agencies should ensure that the investigation and mitigation steps needed for their own compliance with local laws are taken prior to project implementation.

The author examines fundamental aspects of archaeological heritage management (AHM), particularly two topics widely identified as the most troublesome aspects of AHM in Africa today: basic site inventories and the training of Africans to undertake AHM. She argues that inventory work must be radically restructured to ensure data of sufficient quality, and that African archaeologists need specialized training in computerized information systems, air photo interpretation, management theory, and conservation practices.

7.15 Nyang, Sulayman S. "The Cultural Consequences of Development in Africa." In I. Serageldin and J. Taboroff, eds. *Culture and Development in Africa: Proceedings of an International Conference.* Washington, D.C.: World Bank. 1993.

The role and place of culture in the development of countries in Africa, Asia, and Latin America has not received serious attention among economists and other specialists engaged in development programs. Conventional wisdom argued for a universal, unilinear history in which societies move from agrarian to industrialized societies.

At the time of decolonization, African nationalist leaders believed that the African peoples would not exercise much influence in the world until they were in full control of their political systems. This attitude toward power had serious consequences for African development because it instructed Africans to accept the primacy of politics and to subordinate the cultural to the political. By linking the primacy of politics to the notion that things foreign are the highest status symbols, many of this generation of African leaders led to cultural alienation in their societies.

Religious traditions and their cultural consequences in Africa have political implications. However, so long as donors and scholars involved in development studies deny or ignore the relevance of these cultural factors, chances are that

Africans will continue to be the victims of xenophilia and any homegrown development that is rooted in the history, culture, and psychology of African peoples will be stymied. Policy makers must develop a better understanding of their cultural landscapes.

7.16 Putnam, Robert D. "Democracy, Development, and the Civic Community: Evidence from an Italian Experiment." In I. Serageldin and J. Taboroff, eds. *Culture and Development in Africa: Proceedings of an International Conference*. Washington, D.C.: World Bank. 1993.

In 1970, the Italian parliament approved a portentous reform, replacing centralized administration with a nationwide set of twenty regional governments. This reform was one of few recent attempts to create new representative institutions in the nation-states of the West. Because of the dramatic social, cultural, economic, and political differences among the various regions, this experiment was ideal for a comparative study of the dynamics and ecology of institutional development, offering the opportunity to examine the evolution of the new organizations, formally identical, in their diverse social, economic, cultural and political settings.

For the past twenty-two years a study by the author and two collaborators has closely followed the evolution of a number of nascent regional institutions representing the full range of different environments along the Italian peninsula. The central question posed is: what are the conditions for creating strong, responsive, effective, representative institutions? The author presents an overview of the methodologies used in the survey, the indicators used to measure institutional performance, and observations made.

The author concludes that in northern Italy norms of reciprocity and networks of civic engagement have undergirded levels of economic and institutional performance which are much higher than in the South, where norms and networks of civic engagement have been historically lacking and mutual suspicion and corruption were regarded as normal. The Italian experiment suggests that building social capital is a key to both effective government and economic growth.

7.17 Ravenhill, Philip. "Public Education, National Collections, and Museum Scholarship in Africa." In I. Serageldin and J. Taboroff, eds. *Culture and Development in Africa: Proceedings of an International Conference*. Washington, D.C.: World Bank. 1993.

No phrase has been so much used with so little definition as "cultural heritage." In practice, the use of these words tends to obfuscate real issues that must be confronted if the past is to be useful for the present and preserved for the future. The author defines "cultural heritage" as socially constructed and remembered systems of knowledge, represented by *things* that have come into being through, and bear witness to, this knowledge.

According to the author, Western prejudice *for* explicit, written systems of knowledge and *against* implicit, oral or verbally unarticulated systems of knowledge has quite clearly led to misunderstanding of African ways of being and doing. However, unless the concept of cultural heritage is properly defined, African museums will not be able to rise to the challenge of public education that confronts them.

The author cites positive examples of African museums which have moved to a more expansive and realistic definition of cultural heritage as a result of applying critical thinking and informed scholarship to their missions, rather than continuing a custodial preoccupation with folkloric collections. There is a great need for African museums to shift their orientation to public scholarship that communicates through objects, a collections-based scholarship that uses things to support very serious messages.

7.18 Serageldin, Ismail, and June Taboroff, eds. *Culture and Development in Africa: Proceedings of an International Conference*. Washington, D.C.: World Bank. 1993.

The studies and essays commissioned for this multidisciplinary conference organized by the World Bank in 1992 are published in two volumes. They are grouped under the following headings: (a) Cultural Theory and Development Practice; (b) Culture and Civic Society; (c) Cultural Institutions; (d) Conservation of the Built Historic Environment; (e) Development, Archaeology, and the Environment; and (f) Economic Development—Culture as Cause or Consequence.

The full list of the presentations included in the two volumes is given below. Individual annotations for about half the volume's papers, written by sociologists, anthropologists, political scientists, architects and archaeologists, are included in this bibliography. Two papers written by economists on taking culture, particularly indigenous culture, into account have also been included. These papers are summarized individually in this section of the bibliography under the author's name.

- *"The Challenge of a Holistic Vision: Culture, Empowerment, and the Development Paradigm"* by Ismail Serageldin
- *"Democracy, Development, and the Civic Community: Evidence from an Italian Experiment"* by Robert D. Putnam
- *"Taking Culture into Account: From 'Let's' to 'How'"* by Robert Klitgaard
- *"Development in a Multi-Cultural Context"* by Ali Mazrui
- *"What Cultural Theory Can Contribute to Understanding and Promoting Democracy, Science, and Development"* by Aaron Wildavsky

74 *Culture, Beliefs, and Values*

- *"Indigenous Management Practice: Lessons for Africa's Management in the 1990s"* by Mamadou Dia
- *"Culture, Memory, and Development"* by Wole Soyinka
- *"Culture and Development: African Responses"* by Daniel Etounga-Manguellé
- *"What Models for African Museums? West African Prospects"* by Claude Ardouin
- *"Towards and Integrated Approach: Southern African Museums Map Out Strategies"* by Dawson Munjeri
- *"Community Participation in the Conservation of Cultural Heritage"* by Alexandre O. Marc
- *"Public Education, National Collections, and Museum Scholarship in Africa"* by Phillip Ravenhill
- *"Architectural and Urban Heritage: The Example of the City of Ouidah, Benin"* by Alain Sinou
- *"Earth—The Once and Future Building Material: The Potential in Developing Africa"* by Neville Agnew
- *"Bringing Cultural Heritage into the Development Agenda: Summary Findings of a Report on Cultural Heritage in Environmental Assessments in Sub-Saharan Africa"* by June Taboroff
- *"Revitalizing Historic Cities: Towards a Public-Private Partnership"* by Ismail Serageldin
- *"Archaeological Research, Site Protection, and Employment Generation: Central African Perspectives"* by Pierre de Maret
- *"Archaeological Heritage Management and Site Inventory Systems in Africa: The Role of Development"* by Susan Keech McIntosh
- *"Valuing the Past, Envisioning the Future: Local Perspectives on Environmental and Cultural Heritage in Ghana"* by Ann B. Stahl
- *"The Cultural Consequences of Development in Africa"* by Sulayman S. Nyang
- *"Culture, Management, and Institutional Assessment"* by Coralie Bryant
- *"Cultural Dimensions of Conflict Management and Development: Some Lessons from the Sudan"* by Francis Deng.

7.19   Serageldin, Ismail. "The Challenge of a Holistic Vision: Culture, Empowerment, and the Development Paradigm." In I. Serageldin and J. Taboroff, eds. *Culture and Development in Africa: Proceedings of an International Conference*. Washington, D.C.: World Bank. 1993.

Since the early years of its operation, the World Bank has regularly added new sectors to its activities and has been evolving its concepts for understanding and dealing with development issues. In the early 1970s a major debate within the Bank on the issue of poverty resulted in a milestone research study on "redistribution with growth" and a call for dealing with the problems of the global poor. The 1980s saw the introduction of structural adjustment lending and sectoral adjustment lending.

Today, some staff members of the Bank are grappling with the issues of cultural identity and empowerment of the people in relation to development, conscious of the fact that they are at the threshold of a complex and different vision of development.

The author calls for a new focus of the development paradigm on the two intertwined issues of promotion of cultural identity and empowerment of the people. The first is unlikely to happen without the second, nor can empowerment be developed in isolation from the cultural realities of a society. Such a cultural framework is indispensable for relevant, effective institutions rooted in authenticity and tradition yet open to modernity and change. The lessons of failure in Africa frequently can be traced to the absence of such institutions.

Good governance, which emphasizes transparency, accountability, participation, the rule of law, and, implicitly, the guarantees of the civil and human rights needed for effective participation, enables people to pursue fulfillment subject to the limits of the law and the discipline of the market. Calls for empowerment and good governance do not necessarily prescribe a particular form of government and do not in and of themselves constitute interference in the domestic affairs of an individual state.

The author concludes by enumerating six areas in which the World Bank can, and to a significant extent already does, work to promote good governance: transparency; accountability; institutional pluralism; participation; the rule of law; and pilot and experimental approaches toward implementing good governance.

7.20 Serageldin, Ismail. "Cultural Continuity and Cultural Authenticity: The Architectural Sculptures of Aboudramane and Kingelez." In *Home and the World: Architectural Sculpture by Two Contemporary African Artists*. 1992-1995. Exhibition Catalogue. New York: Museum for African Art. 1993.

Few issues affect contemporary African societies as deeply as a sense of lost identity and a corollary search for cultural "authenticity." Many Africans seek to return to the roots of the precolonial African heritage, however, the author argues that this approach is narrow and romantic. The past must be decoded through the contemporary perspective, sifting the relevant from the timebound. This approach seeks to explore and revitalize African myths and images and ground them in a critical investigation of the meaning of being African now.

The author interprets the work of two African sculptors. One reasserts the essential and timeless in the African heritage, while the other carries the imported forms of modern African architecture to extremes, challenging the premises that underlie the creation of the modern African urban environment. Both artists address a rapidly

76 *Culture, Beliefs, and Values*

evolving reality and seek to assert a unique African identity that is organically joined to an evolving world.

7.21 Serageldin, Ismail. "Contemporary Expressions of Islam in Buildings: the Religious and the Secular." In *Expressions of Islam in Buildings*. Geneva: The Aga Khan Trust for Culture. 1991.

Understanding the position of intellectuals of the Muslim world in the context of the unprecedented sociocultural turmoil which is currently shaking Muslim societies is the key to understanding the issues of the spiritual and the temporal in the built environment of contemporary Muslim societies. The evolving idea of cultural identity has been badly shaken over the last thirty years. The secularization and modernity embraced by the elites of most newly independent Muslim societies has given way to a powerful, new call for a return to traditional values.

Societal issues, such as maintenance of the sense of self and community, the social functions of the mosque in contemporary communities, and the degree to which social culture is capable of integrating new external elements, are the basis for understanding the architecture of the mosque in contemporary Muslim societies. Against this background, the author presents an overview of the changing function of mosques, the symbolism of mosque architecture, notable contemporary mosque projects, and current architectural trends and patterns.

7.22 Serageldin, Ismail. "Faith and the Environment," "Islamic Culture and Non-Muslim Contributions," and "Architecture and Society." In I. Serageldin, ed. *Space for Freedom: The Search for Architectural Excellence in Muslim Societies*. Geneva: Aga Khan Award for Architecture and London: Butterworth Architecture. 1989.

The basic approach of the first of three chapters by the author contained in this volume is to return to the original sources of Islamic doctrine in order to relate them to the historic context and present realities of the built environment of Muslim societies. The author guides us through a discussion of basic Islamic principles and their particular applications to the built environment. He calls for continuous painstaking analysis of past achievements and present reality in order to transcend the simplistic, physical reading of the Muslim heritage and promote a deeper understanding of self and society within the context of an Islamic world vision.

In his second chapter, the author examines the meaning of historical heritage for the contemporary architect and points out that, in the case of Cairo, the city's culture through history has incorporated the contributions of several religions other than Islam, welded together in a cosmopolitan, urban society.

The role of the architect in defining the image of progress that a society, and particularly its elite, holds of itself is the subject of the author's third chapter in this volume. Architects must acquire the sophistication to decode the symbolic content of the Muslim heritage, read the signs and trends of the present, understand the relationship of their individual buildings with the wider community, and pull all of this together in the design of structures which can take their place in the historical continuity of world architecture. The author calls for an improvement in the relationship between Muslim societies and their architects, and a nurturing of real talent in order to meet the challenge of building in the Muslim world today.

7.23 Serageldin, Ismail. "Financing the Adaptive Reuse of Culturally Significant Areas." In Y. Raj Isar, ed. *The Challenge to Our Cultural Heritage: Why Preserve the Past?* Washington, D.C.: Smithsonian Institution Press and Paris: UNESCO. 1986.

Many ancient city centers in developing countries are being engulfed by the rising tide of urbanization. These old city centers are jewels of architecture and urban design and are frequently listed as part not only of the national heritage, but of the world heritage as well. Such cities as Fez, Kairawan, and Cairo have enormous treasures of buildings and urban complexes that deserve to be safeguarded. However, in the LDCs where most of these cities are located, the massive scale of the challenge is matched by a paucity of resources. The World Bank has had experience dealing with these problems, notably by financing projects in Lahore, and Tunis.

Two key problems face conservation planners: the uses to which the land and buildings are put, which are inappropriate and need change; and the fear that restoration and conservation will be enormously expensive and that adequate financing cannot be obtained. The author argues that these two issues must be addressed by describing the nature of the problems, by defining "adaptive reuse" as a suitable approach to the problem, and by exploring approaches to financing that should enable municipalities to undertake such problems with minimal drain on their resources. He concludes with the presentation of a case study, the award-winning Hafsia revitalization project in Tunis, which has been partially financed by the World Bank.

7.24 Serageldin, Ismail, and others. "International Labor Migration in the Middle East and North Africa: Current and Prospective Dimensions, 1975-85." In L.O. Michalak and J.W. Solacuse, eds. *Social Legislation in the Contemporary Middle East*. Berkeley, Cal.: University of California. 1986.

International labor migration in the Middle East and North Africa (MENA) has become a factor of major economic and social significance for virtually every country in the region. The oil price increases of 1973-74 triggered a profound change in the

78 *Culture, Beliefs, and Values*

scale of international labor migration. At the same time that employment demand slackened in the West European economies, the economic boom in the Gulf States and Libya pushed the limits of their capacity to absorb their burgeoning incomes. Purchasing the services of armies of expatriate workers helped to reduce their petrodollar surpluses.

The authors summarize their assessment of international labor migration in the MENA region, which is based primarily on a 1981 World Bank research project. This project differs from most other studies of labor migration in the region in that it includes computer modeling of manpower requirements and supply by sector, occupation, and nationality for nineteen countries in the region, as well as an assessment of the implications of the projections for 1975-1985.

The authors discuss the factors contributing to the oil-endowed states' current and projected reliance on imported workers, the changing occupational requirements for migrant workers, their numbers and nationality composition, and the costs and benefits of migration. They point out a number of issues for further consideration and conclude by urging the labor importing and exporting countries of the region to cooperate more closely and develop a system of information sharing, joint planning, and regulation of labor migration in order to mitigate the adverse consequences and enhance the beneficial consequences of labor migration.

7.25 Serageldin, Ismail. "A Unified Approach to the Character and Islamic Heritage of the Arab City." In I. Serageldin and S. Al-Sadek, eds. *The Arab City: Its Character and Islamic Cultural Heritage*. Washington, D.C. and Riyadh, Saudi Arabia: The Arab Urban Development Institute. 1982.

A unified approach to the character and Islamic heritage of the Arab city must proceed from the recognition that the Arab city is an interwoven tapestry of elements, some of them physical, some of them non-physical. The Arab city is an organic entity, and its physical expression is only one expression of its being.

The non-physical dimension is comprised of the threads of thought, whether religious, scientific, or in art; socioeconomic and sociocultural institutions; and the law and institutions of power which shape the basic organization of the social structure.

The physical dimension consist of the threads of city structure as a whole, reflecting the organic nature of Islam; the scale and distribution of urban complexes within the urban fiber; architecture of individual buildings, including the relations between them; and fine arts and decoration.

The author stresses the importance of the inter-relatedness of the non-physical and physical dimensions of the Arab city and argues that the threads of the tapestry must not be ruptured as the past is linked to the future and that both physical and non-physical elements must continue to interact in the cities of today and the plans for the cities of tomorrow.

7.26 Stahl, Ann B. "Valuing the Past, Envisioning the Future: Local Perspectives on Environmental and Cultural Heritage in Ghana." In I. Serageldin and J. Taboroff, eds. *Culture and Development in Africa: Proceedings of an International Conference.* Washington, D.C.: World Bank. 1993.

Studies focused on technological and environmental change during the last five centuries should be of special interest for development studies. Two insights generated by these studies have significant implications for development initiatives in rural areas today. First is the decline of traditional technologies that resulted from increased availability of manufactured, often imported, goods and the importance of these technologies during contemporary crises. Second is the diversity of subsistence adaptations subsumed under the gloss "agriculture" and the planning problems that stem from resultant misunderstanding of how rural peoples exploit their environment.

In addition, there is a pressing need to counteract the dichotomous European way of thinking which draws sharp boundaries between such concepts as traditional and modern, primitive and civilized, and inefficient and efficient. One means of accomplishing this is to foster a renewed pride of place and past at the local level. Foreign researchers and international agencies must assist African nations in developing cultural heritage plans. Furthermore, there is great potential to involve rural people in cultural heritage programs. Foreign specialists should conduct local training programs in conservation, curation, and field excavation and should be encouraged to enter into dialogue with local officials regarding their needs.

7.27 Taboroff, June. "Bringing Cultural Heritage into the Development Agenda: Summary Findings of a Report on Cultural Heritage in Environmental Assessments in Sub-Saharan Africa." In I. Serageldin and J. Taboroff, eds. *Culture and Development in Africa: Proceedings of an International Conference.* Washington, D.C.: World Bank. 1993.

Archaeological remains constitute for many African countries the only objective source material for the study of their precolonial history. Traditional art forms are a reservoir of potent symbols to be put to new purposes. They are used by contemporary African artists who find original ways of incorporating them with new elements in the ongoing process of renewal. Archaeology may, in some cases, contribute to practical solutions on an everyday level where high technology has failed, for example in agriculture and mining.

The author summarizes the broad conclusions she reached in her region-wide survey of cultural heritage issues and sketches the broad outlines of the current institutional and legal framework for cultural property conservation in Sub-Saharan Africa. Most national institutions do not have the adequate financial and human resources to protect cultural property, and the effectiveness of heritage protection legislation is generally low.

Several mechanisms exist for overcoming the obstacle of national policy that disregards cultural heritage: country environmental action plans, environmental assessment, environmental projects or project components, and training. The author concludes with recommendations for using these mechanisms for strengthening the protection of cultural property.

7.28 Wildavsky, Aaron. "What Cultural Theory Can Contribute to Understanding and Promoting Democracy, Science, and Development." In I. Serageldin and J. Taboroff, eds. *Culture and Development in Africa: Proceedings of an International Conference*. Washington, D.C.: World Bank. 1993.

By far the biggest blind spot in political theory in general, and economic development and political democracy in particular, is the failure to treat fatalism and egalitarianism as cultures (viable ways of life whose adherents share values justifying preferred patterns of social relations) on a par with hierarchies and individualism. Yet the importance of fatalism and egalitarianism for democracy and development can hardly be doubted.

Cultural theory leads to the expectation that markets work not because they are made up of autonomous individuals free of social sanctions but because they are made up of distinctive social beings who, in acting in a particular way, and generating a particular set of beliefs, are able to secure a way of life that emphasizes accumulation. The energetic, skillful, and lucky are able to operate through the personal networks to which this mode of social organization gives rise, while the less energetic, less skillful, and less lucky find themselves always at the peripheries of other peoples' networks and never at the centers of their own. This division is the normal state of affairs when group relations are absent or little developed.

Cultural theory goes on to show that a quite different bifurcation is found in the reaches of social life in which group relationships predominate and individualism is muted. Here it is the dynamics of group formation—boundary creation, internal differentiation, incorporation, and exclusion—that continually separate the hierarchists and the egalitarians.

If hierarchy is under attack, which is the nature of current economic transitions in many regions, there are two quite separate directions in which it is being dismantled: one away from collectivized patterns and toward individualized ones; and the other away from differentiated statuses towards equalized ones. With measures of culture in place it will be possible to understand these dynamics of sociocultural change and make empirically based policy recommendations to further economic development.

Even now there is general agreement that fatalism should be decreased and that individualism and hierarchy must work together for economic growth. This understanding of institutionally generated motivations that work for and against economic growth will help create cultural instruments for doing better.

Women, Family Systems, and Gender Analysis

8.1 Bamberger, Michael. "Gender Issues in Poverty Alleviation in Socialist Economies." In Rita Raj-Hashim and Noeleen Heyzer, eds. *Gender, Economic Growth and Poverty*. Kuala Lumpur: Asian and Pacific Development Centre. 1991.

One characteristic of the transition process in former socialist countries in Europe and Asia is that relatively effective social safety nets and policies of seeking gender equality in the labor market have tended to be weakened during the transition to a market economy. In many other ways, the situation of women with respect to poverty alleviation, access to educational and health services and labor force participation in socialist economies has many similarities with the situation in countries such as India and Bangladesh. This paper also examines how gender is taken into account in the strategies which the World Bank is seeking to develop for countries such as Bangladesh, India, China and Viet Nam.

8.2 Bennett, Lynn. "Expanding Women's Access to Credit in the World Bank Context." *Hunger Notes* 17(3):16-20. 1992.

In the past, there have been two strong currents in World Bank projects each of which pursued goals that were considered mutually exclusive: (1) to expand access to resources for marginal groups, and (2) to promote self-sustaining financial institutions. The author explains why old Bank-funded targeted credit projects, which tended to be formal and large-scale, failed and how, over the last decade, new types of NGO-managed, informal targeted credit programs have emerged.

The success rates of these new targeted credit projects on the one hand, and the expanding number of Bank projects with NGO involvement and an enterprise support or finance service (ESFS) component for women on the other, lead the author to conclude that the above mentioned goals need not be mutually exclusive. She argues for more emphasis on institution building because projects which do not build financially viable institutions do a disservice to women in the long run.

8.3 Bennett, Lynn. *Women, Poverty, and Productivity in India*. Economic Development Institute Seminar Paper no. 43. World Bank. Washington, D.C. 1992.

This publication is based on a more detailed study, *Gender and Poverty in India* (see below), of women's involvement in key sectors of the Indian economy, the returns they are getting, and the constraints they face in increasing their access to, and productivity in, these sectors. This shorter version is intended for use as a training material by the Economic Development Institute and is aimed at World Bank borrower country policy makers and civil servants.

8.4   Bennett, Lynn, and others. *Gender and Poverty in India.* World Bank Country Study. Washington, D.C. 1991.

Despite their statistical "invisibility" in prevailing measures of labor force participation, women are vital and productive workers in the Indian economy. Their economic productivity is particularly critical for India's estimated 60 million households below the poverty line: studies show that the poorer the family, the more it depends for its survival on the earnings of a woman. Yet India invests far less in its women workers than in its working men and women receive a smaller share of health care, education, and productive assets that could increase their returns to labor.

Within an integrative framework that recognizes the cultural as well as the economic dimensions of Indian women's situation, this report analyzes the current role of women in Indian agriculture, dairying, forestry, and the urban informal sector. In each case sector-specific policy and program recommendations are offered. Special attention is also given to women's health and education—particularly as they relate to women's productivity.

Both government and NGO initiatives as they have evolved over the past several decades are reviewed and assessed. In addition to broad recommendations about overall approaches to integrating gender issues in India's development planning, the report suggests specific means by which women can gain wider access to the help, skills, and tools they lack.

8.5   Bennett, Lynn, and Meena Acharya. *Women and the Subsistence Sector: Economic Participation and Household Decisionmaking in Nepal.* World Bank Staff Working Paper no. 526. Washington, D.C. 1982.

This paper analyzes how several sociocultural, economic and demographic factors affect the extent and structure of female economic participation in the largely subsistence economy of rural Nepal. It investigates the relationship between these variables and the extent of women's input into the household decision making process.

Among the specific hypotheses examined is the assumption that the strength of female decision making in the household is positively affected by women's participation in the market economy and negatively affected by their confinement to subsistence agricultural production and domestic work. The paper also investigates the hypothesis that women's decision making input is inversely related to the income status of the household.

An extensive methodological annex describes the complimentary quantitative and qualitative approaches to data collection which were combined in the study. The survey instruments used to collect time allocation, decision making and other quantitative data are presented, along with a condensed version of the field guide to the collection of in-depth anthropological material on women and households.

8.6 Cernea, Michael M. "Anthropology and Family Production Systems in Africa." Foreword to Michael M. Horowitz and T. Painter, eds. *Anthropology and Rural Development in West Africa*. Boulder, Col.: Westview Press. 1986.

8.7 Cernea, Michael M. "Macrosocial Change, Feminization of Agriculture and Peasant Women's Threefold Economic Role." *Sociologia Ruralis* 18(2-3):107-24. 1978.

Within the framework of structural changes in Rumanian agriculture during the 1960s and 1970s, including the collectivization of agriculture, the role of women was a window revealing trends in the broader development process. The assumption at the time was that the collectivization of traditional rural societies was beneficial to women's development, that it improved their economic situation and reduced their heavy workload.

The author contends that the real process was different, more complex and contradictory. Changes in land tenure and production patterns multiplied women's roles, often putting additional burdens on women rather than improving their condition and advancing their status.

The three key roles of women which evolved were: production agents in the collective farm (often substituting for men who took urban-based jobs for cash); key laborers on the small family plots allocated by the collective to each member family; and family caregivers and housekeepers. The extraordinary increase in demands placed on women's labor resulted in an unanticipated feminization of key sectors of agriculture.

8.8 Cernea, Michael M. "L'Exploitation Familiale des Coopérateurs—Project Social ou Rémanence Economique?" In Placide Rambaud, ed. *Sociologie Rurale*. Paris: Editions Mouton. 1976.

Family-based enterprises have often been considered one of the reasons for the inferior efficiency of agricultural production compared to industry. However, no social system has entirely eliminated family enterprises. The peculiar labor mobilization powers of the family make family farms an important factor in agricultural production everywhere.

In collectivized agriculture, one of the structural characteristics of the agricultural cooperative is its considerable dependence on the socioeconomic micro-units represented by family farms. The author examines these relationships, both institutionalized and informal, which shed light on the nature of agricultural cooperatives in planned economies and explain the surviving roles of families within cooperatives. Even asset dispossession and many other restrictions, imposed by the political systems in planned socialist economies on the peasant family farm, have not succeeded in completely annihilating the productive functions of the peasant family as a unit of social organization.

The economic data presented in the paper demonstrate that small, family-managed plots in Rumania achieved a much higher productivity, both in crops and in animal husbandry, than the collective farms. They succeeded in producing a much larger proportion of the country's food than the proportion of land they control.

The author reveals the intrinsically contradictory relationship between families and cooperatives by examining family activities, illustrating how family units resist dependence and maintain productive functions of their own.

8.9 Cernea, Michael M. "The Large Scale Formal Organization and the Family Primary Group." *Journal of Marriage and the Family* 37:927-36. 1975.

This paper examines the relationship between the family as a primary group and the cooperative farm as a type of large formal organization, emphasizing the influence of the family on the formal organization in which it participates. Data from Rumania show how the family has survived as a work unit inside the inhospitable structure of the collective farm, despite the efforts of the political system to deprive the peasant family of its productive assets and functions.

On the contrary, empirical evidence shows the ability of the family to mobilize labor effectively, and to partly "control" the functioning of the collective farm organization. Data showing preference for working in family teams as well as a new type of contractual relationship between families and cooperatives are reported and interpreted.

8.10 Dyson, Mary. "Mentor's Mandate: First, Listen! Women's Roles Examined at Global Assembly." *World Bank Environmental Bulletin* 4(1):7. Washington, D.C. 1992.

The Global Assembly of Women and the Environment (Miami, November 1991) was dedicated to demonstrating to the world community women's capacity as environmental managers, the elements of leadership necessary for such activities, and the policies which can advance or hinder such efforts.

The eight Bank mentors who attended the assembly listened to 218 "success stories" involving water, waste, energy, or environmentally friendly systems. Criteria for success stories were replicability, affordability, sustainability, and visibility, combined with demonstrated women's leadership and social organization. Key factors were: (a) building on locally generated initiatives; (b) building on the efforts of local leaders and local communities; (c) using site-specific designs; (d) adopting an integrated approach; and (e) promoting technology based on local resources and materials.

8.11 Kudat, Ayse. *Women and Human Settlements Development*. Nairobi: United Nations Center for Human Settlements. 1989.

The backlog of unmet demand for housing is increasing in developing countries, but governmental capacity to satisfy it is limited. There is a growing awareness of the need to enhance the capacity of people to help themselves to meet this demand. The necessity of using the contributions of women to shelter development in an effective manner is increasingly being felt.

Before they volunteer their time, labor, and other resources to development, however, their contributions and needs must be recognized, the conditions under which their contributions are made must be improved, and their participation as thinkers, managers, and professionals in policy and decision making has to be enhanced.

The author gives an overview of settlement trends and how they affect women, the impact of housing policies on women, and other related issues, such as women's access to land and housing finance. The global housing situation, she argues, represents an immense challenge, requiring adoption of bold and innovative human settlement policies.

The author recommends policies and stresses that these policies must be adopted with explicit recognition of the role of women in development, accompanied by programs and projects to enhance women's participation in development, both as beneficiaries and as contributors.

8.12 Molnar, Augusta. "Women and Forestry in the Developing World." *Journal of Society and Natural Resources* 2(4). 1991.

This article summarizes various experiences accumulated in developing countries concerning the involvement of women in reforestation, particularly in social forestry. Approaches in use are described and some of the successful strategies being implemented by government and/or voluntary agencies from different regions of the world are analyzed.

8.13 Moser, Caroline. O. *Gender Planning and Development: Theory, Practice and Training.* London: Routledge. 1993.

This book focuses on the interrelationship between gender and development, the formulation of gender policy, and the implementation of gender planning practice. It attempts to improve current development policy, which, because of incorrect assumptions, often discriminates against or misses women. The author provides the conceptual rationale for key principles of gender planning. These relate to gender roles and needs, control over resources and decision making within the household, and developing country policy approaches to women in development. From extensive research and teaching experience in gender planning, the author shows how such principles are translated into methodological procedures, tools, and techniques that are integrated into a gender planning process.

The author considers whether constraints in the implementation of gender planning are technical or political in nature, and analyses both institutional structures and operational procedures to integrate gender particularly into the project planning cycle. The role that training plays in creating gender awareness and providing appropriate tools and techniques is emphasized with practical exercises for trainers provided.

8.14 Moser, Caroline. O. "Adjustment from Below: Low-Income Women, Time and the Triple Role in Guayaquil, Ecuador." In H. Afshar and C. Dennis, eds. *Women, Recession and Adjustment in the Third World.* London: Macmillan. 1992.

Widespread concern now exists about deteriorating standards of living and the severe erosion of the "human resource base" in many developing countries after a decade of crisis from debt and recession and the resulting economic structural adjustment policies (SAPs). The fact that the social costs of SAPs have been most heavily carried by the low-income population in both rural and urban areas has resulted in proposals to modify the adjustment process to include a "human face" and strengthen the human resource base.

To assist the formulation of policy, the World Bank, in collaboration with the UNDP and the African Development Bank, has embarked on an extensive research program to monitor the effects of SAPs in sub-Saharan Africa, setting up the Social Dimensions of Adjustment unit and undertaking the Permanent Household Survey (PHS), a large-scale structured household interview survey to be undertaken over a five to seven year period. At the same time, a considerable number of detailed micro-level surveys of the effects of SAPs on women have been commissioned.

This study contributes to the ongoing debate concerning the extent to which SAPs have negatively affected members of low income households, particularly gender-related impacts, through the analysis of recent research in Urban Latin America. The objective is also to show policy makers the importance of ensuring that current research methodology, such as the SDA survey, shifts from the household as the unit of analysis, towards a disaggregating approach capable of identifying intra-household differentiation. In addition, the limitations of research which isolates low-income women outside the context of their households are identified.

8.15 Moser, Caroline. O. "**Gender Planning in the Third World: Meeting Practical and Strategic Gender Needs.**" *World Development* 17(11):1799-825. 1989.

Also in T. Wallace and C. Marsh, eds. Changing Perceptions: Writings on Gender and Development. London: Oxfam Publications. 1991.

Spanish translation: "La Planificacion de Genero en el Tercer Mundo: Enfrentando las Necesidades Practicas y Estrategicas de Genero." In V. Guzman, P. Portocarrero, and V. Vargas, eds. Una Nueva Lectura: Genero en el Desarollo. Lima, Peru: Entre Mujeres, Flora Tristan Ediciones.

Recognition of the important role that women play in developing country development has not necessarily been translated into planning practice. This paper describes the development of gender-sensitive planning. By recognizing the different roles and needs of women and men in these societies, gender-conscious development planning uses both better conceptual frameworks and methodological tools.

These tools relate to the categorization of the triple role of women and the distinction between immediate and strategic gender needs. The paper evaluates the capacities of different interventions to meet gender needs, and provides a critique of different policy approaches to "women in development" from a gender planning perspective.

8.16 Murphy, Josette, ed. *Women and Agricultural Technology: Relevance for Research.* Proceedings of an Inter-Center Seminar, March 25-29, Bellagio, Italy. The Rockefeller Foundation and ISNAR. The Hague. 1985.

8.17 Safilios-Rothschild, Constantina. "Women's Groups: An Underutilized Grassroots Institution." In *The Long-Term Perspective Study of Sub-Saharan Africa: vol. 3. Institutional and Sociopolitical Issues.* Washington, D.C. 1990.

The paper emphasizes the great potential of women's groups for development, but argues that creating the conditions necessary to realize their potential would require a careful balance between formalization and maintenance of the advantages of informal contacts, and mutual responsibilities. Usually, for a variety of reasons, not all women belong to organized groups. The more such groups are used as vehicles of development for rural women, the more the participation issue becomes crucial.

The author also discusses several important alternatives for institution building of women's groups: strengthening and linking them with NGOs willing to mediate on their behalf with formal institutions; linking them into federations of rural women that are represented nationally and can create formal employment and not just "income generating opportunities"; and establishing forward and backward linkages among different types of women's groups (for example, producer, transport, and marketing women's groups) that help increase all groups' incomes.

Indigenous and Tribal People

9.1 Brandon, Katrina. "Integrating Conservation and Development." Research Note in *National Geographic* 7(3):371-72. 1991.

This note is a reply to a description of a project involving the Miskito Indians in Nicaragua. It addresses some of the difficulties in linking conservation and development at the local level in areas inhabited by indigenous people.

9.2 Cernea, Michael M. "Indigenous Anthropologists and Development-Oriented Research." In H. Fahim, ed. *Indigenous Anthropology in Non-Western Countries*. Durham, N.C.: Carolina Academic Press 1982.

*Also available as World Bank Reprint Series no. 208. Washington, D.C. 1982, or as a chapter in Hari Mohan Mathur, ed. **The Human Dimension of Development: Perspectives from Anthropology**. New Delhi: Concept Publishing Company. 1990.*

Theoretical and epistemological aspects of the work of indigenous anthropologists in non-western countries are examined. The author argues that applied anthropological research in developing countries by anthropologists from both western and non-western countries contributes to development. In particular, he focuses on how research carried out by anthropologists from developing countries can influence social and cultural change in their own countries.

There is a long history of neglect or disregard for the research of indigenous anthropologists—distrust of their work, underestimation of their contribution, and, often, political hostility. Challenging conventional definitions of anthropology as the study of "other cultures," the author examines the trade-offs—the advantages and disadvantages—which indigenous anthropologists have in performing anthropology within their own culture. He argues, however, that a distinction should be made between the concept of "indigenous anthropologists" and the pseudo-concept of an "indigenous anthropology." The latter undermines the universality of anthropology as a social science.

Indigenous anthropologists and sociologists have an important role to play in the progress of their societies. The author examines the constraints and difficulties of indigenous anthropologists, and calls for increased support for the development of indigenous anthropological research, for expanded cooperation between indigenous and non-indigenous anthropologists, and for more assistance from official development agencies.

9.3 **Davis, Shelton H.** *Indigenous Views of Land and the Environment.* World Bank Discussion Paper no. 188. Washington, D.C. 1993.

In preparation for the *World Development Report 1992*, the author asked a number of individuals affiliated with non-governmental organizations who work with indigenous people to provide reports on indigenous peoples' views of land and the environment. Articles include discussions of the views of the Quichua Indians of eastern Ecuador, the Masai and Samburu pastoralists of Kenya, and the traditional upland swidden farmers of the Philippines.

Each report responds to three questions: (a) What are the traditional views held by indigenous peoples about land and the environment? (b) How have national laws and government policies either corresponded to or conflicted with these views? (c) What types of policies, programs, or projects could more adequately take indigenous views of land and the environment into account?

The reports show, first, that close attachment to the land and the environment, which are fundamental to a people's existence and identity, is the defining characteristic of indigenous peoples throughout the world. Second, there is a practical dimension to this indigenous outlook that is reflected in traditional knowledge and strategies which permit them to make a living in harsh or fragile environments. Third, indigenous peoples throughout the world face serious problems in gaining official recognition of their land and territorial rights. Even when their rights are legally recognized, they are seldom defended in practice. Fourth, all of the indigenous peoples surveyed face severe demographic, and sociocultural stresses in trying to maintain their traditional land and natural resource use strategies. Lastly, the reports highlight that indigenous people are striving to participate in the development and environmental programs planned for their lands. They want to be active designers of their own destinies.

9.4 **Davis, Shelton H., and Jorge Uquillas.** "La Cuestion Territorial y Ecologia entre Pueblos Indigenas de la Selva Baja del Ecuador." In Fundacion Gaia and Cerec. *Derechos Territoriales Indigenas y Ecologia en las Selvas Tropicales de America.* Bogota, Colombia. 1992.

The result of a conference on indigenous land demarcation programs in lowland South America, this article examines the history and current status of indigenous land titling in eastern Ecuador. It discusses macroeconomic factors, such as expanding road building, colonization, and petroleum development, and their effects on indigenous lands and natural resources. Statistical data is provided on the scope and progress in indigenous land titling in Ecuador.

9.5 **Davis, Shelton H. "The Rainforest Guests."** *The Bank's World* 10(6):13-5. 1991.

In April 1991, fifty World Bank staffers met with eight members of the "Alliance of Forest People of Brazil," the Bank's "rainforest guests," at the Bank's headquarters in Washington. The eight representatives had made the journey from Brazil to inform conservation groups and development agencies about their views and experiences concerning tropical forest management and development.

According to the eight representatives, current models for the occupation of the Amazon are destructive to both the forest and its inhabitants. Alternative production models can only succeed to the degree that they are based on the production experience of the local forest dwellers and take their views into account.

9.6 **Davis, Shelton H.** *Land Rights and Indigenous Peoples: The Role of the OAS Inter-American Commission on Human Rights.* Cambridge, Mass.: Cultural Survival, Inc. 1989.

Based upon an investigation at the OAS Inter-American Commission on Human Rights, this study reviews several cases where international remedies were sought for protecting the human rights of indigenous forest-dwelling populations in South America. The cases considered are the Guahibo Indians of Colombia, The Ache Indians of Paraguay, and the Yanomami Indians of Brazil. The study argues that the recognition and protection of indigenous land rights, especially in a context of rapid frontier expansion, is central to the wider question of the protection of the human rights of indigenous populations.

9.7 **Davis, Shelton H.** *Indigenous Peoples, Environmental Protection, and Sustainable Development.* Sustainable Development Occasional Paper Series. Geneva: IUCN. 1988.

This paper describes the role of indigenous peoples and their traditional cultural knowledge in environmental assessment and natural resource management in specific local settings. Case materials are drawn from the Central Selva Natural Resources Management Project in Peru, the Kuna Yala Nature Reserve in Panama, energy development on Indian reservations in the western United States, and the Mackenzie Valley Pipeline Inquiry in Canada. Introductory and concluding comments highlight general issues of project design in areas occupied by tribal and indigenous peoples.

94 *Indigenous and Tribal People*

9.8 Davis, Shelton H. "Sowing the Seeds of Violence." In Robert M. Carmack, ed. *Harvest of Violence: The Maya Indians and the Guatemala Crisis*. Norman, Ok.: Oklahoma University Press. 1988.

This essay is the introduction to a collection of papers by a group of anthropologists on the social and cultural effects of political violence on the Mayan-speaking Indian population of Guatemala. The essay traces the roots of the Guatemalan violence in the country's unequal land distribution system and indicates what international human rights agencies have done to counter the violence. Special attention is focused on the implications of the political democratization process on the country's large indigenous population.

9.9 Davis, Shelton H. "Agrarian Structure and Ethnic Resistance: The Indian in Guatemalan and Salvadoran National Politics." In Remo Guidieri, Francesco Pellizzi, and Stanley J. Tambiah, eds. *Ethnicities and Nations: Processes of Inter-Ethnic Relations in Latin America, Southeast Asia, and the Pacific*. Houston: The Rothko Chapel and University of Texas Press. 1988.

Part of a contribution to a symposium on the comparative study of ethnicity in national politics, this essay considers the historic role of Indians in the national politics of Guatemala and El Salvador. Specific attention is focused on the rise of coffee production in the late 19th century in the incorporation of Central American Indians into the national and international political economies.

The author also discusses the emergence of indigenous political mobilization during the early 1930s in El Salvador and in the 1970s and 1980s in Guatemala. The politics of ethnicity, it is argued, is a critical element in the understanding of the current Central American crisis.

9.10 Dyson, Mary. "Concern for Africa's Forest Peoples: A Touchstone of a Sustainable Development Policy." In *Conservation of West and Central African Rainforests*. World Bank Technical Paper, Environment Series no. 1. Washington, D.C. 1992.

This paper compares past and present definitions of forest peoples in World Bank policy statements, before briefly describing characteristics of the Pygmy groups of West and Central Africa. Examples of completed and current project components in Cameroon, the Congo, and the Central African Republic are given as context to the Bank's new Indigenous Peoples Operational Directive.

9.11 Goodland, Robert. *Tribal Peoples and Economic Development: Human Ecologic Considerations*. World Bank. Washington, D.C. 1982.

This paper provides an overall perspective, interpretation, and rationale of the policy principles that should inform projects that affect indigenous and tribal peoples. Its purpose was to assist the Bank's borrowers and their consultants in the task of designing projects, regulations, or institutions taking into account the special problems that arise when economic development impinges on a tribal society.

The first chapter identifies the tribal people concerned, focussing particularly on relatively isolated, unacculturated tribal groups, and describes the problems associated with the development process as it affects tribal people. The second chapter shows why special attention on the part of the World Bank is needed and the third chapter outlines the particular needs of tribal people to be addressed in implementing policy. Detailed annexes recommend operational measures for the project cycle, designed to mitigate negative impacts of development projects as they affect tribal lands, and information on international documents and national agencies dealing with indigenous tribes.

9.12 Ibrahim, Saad E., and Donald P. Cole. *Saudi Arabian Bedouin: An Assessment of Their Needs*. Cairo Papers in Social Science. Monograph Five. Cairo: The American University in Cairo. 1978.

Little social science research has been conducted on the Bedouin as an important population segment of Saudi Arabia. Currently this group contributes little to the developing Saudi economy and, at the same time, is becoming relatively more deprived in comparison with the urban and farming segments of society.

This study, carried out initially in connection with the need to inform development projects in Saudi Arabia, combines sociological and anthropological methods to identify and assess the needs of this segment of society and to gain an understanding of how they themselves perceive their needs. The goal of the research was not only to present an overview of contemporary Bedouin social and cultural structures, but to furnish precise data required for investments for improving the living standards of the Bedouin and their incorporation as equals in the modern society and economy of Saudi Arabia.

9.13 Partridge, William L. "The Fate of Indigenous Peoples: Consultation and Coordination Can Avoid Conflict." *The Environmental Forum* 7(5):29-30. 1990.

The author outlines a conceptual framework for understanding the multiple objectives of indigenous groups today. He explores the apparently contradictory pressures for conservation of rich cultural heritages with the need for economic development in order to reduce poverty, improve health, and increase human resources. These objectives are not inherently in conflict, but can be reconciled through proactive negotiation and collaboration between indigenous peoples and development professionals.

The World Bank's policy on indigenous people recognizes that many groups actively seek to participate in their countries' development process and to gain access to their share of their countries' development investments. Other indigenous groups, however, avoid interaction with government institutions or lack adequate information about the development process. It is Bank policy to foster the active participation of indigenous groups themselves in the decision making process regarding their future and it is only through their participation that the Bank can pursue its objective to make development investments meet the needs of indigenous people and be compatible with their culture.

9.14 Price, David. *Before the Bulldozer: The Nambiquara Indians and the World Bank.* Cabin John, Md.: Seven Locks Press. 1989.

This volume focuses on the impact of recent development projects financed by the World Bank on a region of Brazil inhabited by the Nambiquara Indians. As late as the 1960s, the Nambiquara were one of the most primitive tribes in South America. Some villages had come in contact with Brazilian society but many Nambiquara continued to live as their ancestors had, wearing no clothes, and using few tools.

Based on the author's experiences as an anthropological consultant to the World Bank on the Polonoroeste project in Brazil, this book is a narrative and a critical analysis of this program to build a highway through the remote western part of Brazil, establish new settlements, and develop the area served by the highway. The author's assignment was to evaluate the program of the National Indian Foundation (FUNAI), the Brazilian governmental agency responsible for Indian affairs, for protecting the Nambiquara Indians, whose traditional territory lay in the path of the planned highway. The protection of the Indians and creation of a reservation providing the Nambiquara with an adequate land base to be guaranteed in perpetuity were conditions on which the Bank's Polonoroeste loan was officially made contingent.

The author is highly critical of the preparation and appraisal of the Polonoroeste project by both the World Bank and the borrowing government. He describes widespread corruption and anti-Indian racial bias within FUNAI and at the highest levels of the Brazilian government. He also chastises World Bank officials for ignoring his warnings concerning FUNAI's incompetence and his other recommendations, and for disavowing responsibility for what has become widely recognized as a major human and environmental failure.

9.15 Warren, D. Michael. *Using Indigenous Knowledge in Agricultural Development.* World Bank Discussion Paper no. 127. Washington, D.C. 1991.

The belief that indigenous knowledge systems are simple and static is changing fast. Certain societies with simple technologies have sophisticated knowledge about their natural resources. Based on a growing body of evidence, the paper argues that by understanding and working with indigenous knowledge and decision making systems, participation, capacity building, and sustainability all can be enhanced in cost-effective ways.

The author reviews three types of development project scenarios: those where local knowledge provided an improved approach to managing natural resources than that of proposed project technologies; those that inadvertently ignored indigenous structures; and those whose success at meeting their objectives can be linked to the deliberate incorporation of indigenous knowledge components. Experience shows that technical solutions to unperceived problems are not readily adopted by local groups. New technologies that duplicate indigenous ones are superfluous, and ignoring tested local approaches to local problems is wasteful.

Part Three

Settlement and Resettlement

Settlement and Involuntary Resettlement

10.1 Ayeni, Julius S.O., and others. "The Kainji Lake Experience in Nigeria." In C. Cook, ed. *Involuntary Resettlement in Africa*. World Bank Technical Paper no. 227 Washington, D.C. Forthcoming.

This resettlement program is believed to have been a success, largely because it was responsive to social and cultural concerns of the affected people. A national park was created in conjunction with the lake, providing unexpected additional income for local residents. Irrigated farming in the drawdown zone has proved to be successful.

However, the creation of the lake has had a negative impact on Fulani pastoralists who were seasonal users of the grazing land. Although attempts were made to address this problem, increasing pressure on grazing land and growing conflicts between farmers and herders continue to pose problems for local communities.

Fisheries have been successfully developed on the lake and have provided short-term benefits to local people. However, the downstream irrigation plans which were originally part of the water resource development project have not materialized.

10.2 Bartolomé, Leopoldo J. "The Yacyretá Experience with Urban Resettlement: Some Lessons and Insights." In M.M. Cernea and S.E. Guggenheim, eds. *Anthropological Approaches to Involuntary Resettlement: Policy, Practice, and Theory*. Boulder, Col.: Westview Press. 1993.

The key to understanding the social consequences of resettlement and, consequently, the design of sound social policies capable of helping people use the new opportunities generated by large-scale projects, lies in the study of adaptive behavior under these peculiar circumstances. In order to progress towards a theory of resettlement, there is a pressing need to widen the empirical basis for theorizing by including as many different groups of people and social, cultural, and national contexts as possible.

The paper discusses the findings and insights the author gained through his nine years' experience as the head of the Urban Resettlement Program on the Argentine side of the Bank-assisted Yacyretá Dam Project. The paper describes the affected population in Argentina, most of which are urban poor living in the city of Posadas, and the relocation policy formulated by the Urban Resettlement and Social Action Program (PRUAS) in the late 1970s.

10.3 Cernea, Michael M., and S.E. Guggenheim, eds. "Resettlement and Development: The Bankwide Review of Projects Involving Involuntary Resettlement 1986-1993." Environment Department. World Bank. Washington, D.C. 1994.

For content, see annotation for this paper in entry number 10.41.

10.4 Cernea, Michael M., and S.E. Guggenheim, eds. *Anthropological Approaches to Involuntary Resettlement: Policy, Practice, and Theory*. Boulder, Col.: Westview Press. 1993.

This volume takes stock of recent social science research, applied action research, and policy work on involuntary resettlement, since the last overview of this field, done in 1981. The articles collected here describe how resettlement has occurred in diverse contexts and are written by social scientists from around the world who are themselves deeply engaged with the practical dimensions of resettlement, as field researchers, advocates, critics, planners, and analysts. This volume thus forms part of an international discussion not just about the theories of resettlement, but about what social scientists can do to improve it.

The contributions to this volume belong to three broad groups depending on their primary focus: policy, practice and theory. The chapters in the first group are concerned with the development and use of policies designed specifically for resettlement; the second group of studies demonstrates that changes in policy must be reflected in a series of institutional reforms, legal procedures, and changes in planning models if they are to have a coherent impact at the field level; the chapters in the third category reflect on more general issues associated with resettlement, such as household decisionmaking, economic alternatives, adaptive potential, and impact analysis.

The following is a full list of the studies contained in this volume; those prepared by World Bank staff are summarized individually in this section of the bibliography under the author's name:

- *"Anthropological Approaches to Involuntary Resettlement: Policy, Practice, and Theory"* by Scott E. Guggenheim and Michael M. Cernea
- *"Anthropological and Sociological Research for Policy Development on Population Resettlement"* by Michael M. Cernea
- *"Legal Aspects of Involuntary Population Resettlement"* by Ibrahim F.I. Shihata

- *"Involuntary Resettlement, Human Capital, and Economic Development"* by G. Edward Schuh
- *"Resettlement Planning in the Brazilian Power Sector: Recent Changes in Approach"* by Maria Teresa Fernandez Serra
- *"Resettlement after Involuntary Displacement: The Karelians in Finland"* by Ulla-Marjatta Mustanoja and Kari J. Mustanoja
- *"The Yacyreta Experience with Urban Resettlement: Some Lessons and Insights"* by Leopoldo J. Bartolome
- *"Resettlement in Ghana: From Akosombo to Kpong"* by V. Q. Adu-Aryee
- *"The Navajo-Hopi Land Dispute and Navajo Relocation"* by David F. Aberle
- *"Peasants, Planners, and Participation: Resettlement in Mexico"* by Scott E. Guggenheim
- *"Resettlement at Manantali, Mali: Short-Term Success, Long-Term Problems"* by Michael M. Horowitz, Dolores Koenig, Curt Grimm, and Yacouba Konate
- *"The Dynamics of Social and Economic Adaptation during Resettlement: The Case of Beles Valley in Ethiopia"* by Francesca Agneta, Stefano Berterame, Mariarita Capirci, Loredana Magni, and Massimo Tommasoli
- *"Involuntary Displacement and the Changing Frontiers of Kinship: A Study of Resettlement in Orissa"* by N.K. Behura and P.K. Nayak
- *"Involuntary Resettlement: A Plea for the Host Population"* by Muneera Salem-Murdock
- *"A Spatial Analysis of Involuntary Community Relocation: A South African Case Study"* by Chris de Wet
- *"Successful Involuntary Resettlement: Lessons from the Costa Rican Arenal Hydroelectric Project"* by William L. Partridge
- *"Disaster-Related Refugee Flows and Development-Caused Population Displacement"* by Michael M. Cernea.

10.5 Cernea, Michael M. "Disaster-Related Refugee Flows and Development-Caused Population Displacement." In M.M. Cernea and S.E. Guggenheim, eds. *Anthropological Approaches to Involuntary Resettlement: Policy, Practice, and Theory*. Boulder, Col.: Westview Press. 1993.

A hardly justified dichotomy in the social science literature dealing with displaced populations separates the study of refugees from the study of populations uprooted by development projects. The author argues that this dichotomy must be overcome by exploring the similarities and differences between these categories of displaced populations. Both literatures, which currently do not "speak to each other," stand to gain theoretically from overcoming their relative isolation and could also compare their respective empirical findings.

New trends are signaled regarding the international aid channelled during the 1980s to refugee and displaced populations. The author constructs an estimate of the magnitude of development-related population displacements on a global scale, which is increasing; yet in many countries domestic policies and legal frameworks to guide involuntary dislocation and resettlement continue to be lacking.

The differences between providing relief to refugees and the income restoration strategies for resettling displaced people are examined. Examples from programs in Uganda, Mozambique, Tanzania, Ethiopia, Romania, China, and Indonesia are analyzed. The paper emphasizes the responsibility of the state in the case of development-displaced people and the obligation incumbent upon governments to allocate adequate resources for reestablishing the groups uprooted by development programs to full self-sustainability.

10.6 Cernea, Michael M. "African Population Resettlement in a Global Context." In C. Cook, ed. *Involuntary Resettlement in Africa*. World Bank Technical Paper no. 227. Washington, D.C. 1993.

Africa is the scene of massive resettlement processes of all types. The largest forced displacements are those triggered by social and political upheavals (wars, civil unrest, ethnic or religious persecution), and by natural causes (droughts, famines, and so on). Planned land settlement schemes have been an additional cause of population movements in Burkina Faso, Ethiopia, Ghana, Kenya, Senegal, Sudan, and Tanzania.

Involuntary or forced resettlement is distinct from voluntary or assisted settlement. Some government financed development programs have generated, and continue to generate, population displacements of a significant magnitude on the African continent, particularly the construction of major dams in Africa during the 1960s and 1970s.

From 1981 to 1993, the urban development sector became the sector with the largest number of projects entailing resettlement in Africa. During this period, twenty-two Bank-assisted urban and infrastructure projects in Africa involved resettlement, followed by the energy sector with seven projects, and the agriculture sector with five projects.

The agricultural projects (primarily irrigation dams) have affected the largest numbers of people. It is seldom realized that displacements by dam projects in Africa, such as those caused by the Akosombo dam in Ghana, the Koussou dam in Cote d'Ivoire, the Nangbeto dam in Togo, or the Kariba dam in Zambia, have affected a much higher proportion of the respective countries' populations than the displacements caused by the biggest dams in Brazil, China, and India in relation to the total populations of those countries. Most forced displacements have proved to be the cause of untold human misery. Converting unavoidable resettlement into a development opportunity is the way to mobilize the resources of the state, the donor agencies, the resettlers themselves, as well as the host communities in relocation areas.

10.7 Cernea, Michael M. "Involuntary Resettlement: Social Research, Policy, and Planning." In M.M. Cernea, ed. *Putting People First: Sociological Variables in Rural Development*. 2nd ed. New York, London: Oxford University Press. 1991.

Forced population displacement is one of a range of adverse, counter-developmental consequences which can result from induced development processes. This paper describes how displacement tears apart the social fabric of existing communities and creates risks of impoverishment. A risk model is outlined to guide the planning of preventive measures.

Population displacement caused by development projects requires national policies and legislation informed by social science research. For the programs it finances, the World Bank has institutionalized an explicit resettlement policy. Analyzing this case of policy formulation, the author argues that transforming social knowledge into the building blocks of development policies is a three-stage process, and documents each one of the stages. An effective approach is one that can use the "culture" of the project cycle to establish a planning framework and processing criteria.

10.8 Cernea, Michael M. *From Unused Social Knowledge to Policy Creation: The Case of Population Resettlement*. HIID Development Discussion Paper no. 342. Cambridge, Mass.: Harvard University. 1990.

Three themes are treated in this discussion paper: the emergence and content of the World Bank's policy regarding forced population displacement caused by development programs; methodological issues pertaining to the translation of academic social science into institutionalized policy and operational procedures; and the modification of public discourse about resettlement inside the Bank.

Involuntary resettlement has been, and often still is, handled as a salvage operation, rather than one pursuing development objectives. In contrast, the paper emphasizes that the grounding of the Bank's resettlement policy in social science findings has led to a substantive change. Because displacement dismantles a previous production system and way of life, all involuntary resettlement programs must be development programs as well. The backbone of any resettlement plan must be a development "package" aimed at reconstructing the production base of those relocated and at reestablishing them as self-sustaining producers.

The author defines key components of resettlement plans and alternative strategies related to resettlers' production base, compensation, habitat and social organization, environmental implications and environmental management. He concludes by discussing sociologically informed operational procedures for resettlement, particularly the need for on-the-ground social work throughout the project process and for social monitoring.

10.9 Cernea, Michael M. "Internal Refugee Flows and Development-Induced Population Displacement." *Journal of Refugee Studies* 3(4):320-39. 1990.

For a more detailed discussion of this subject see entry 10.5 "Disaster-Related Refugee Flows and Development-Caused Population Displacement." In M.M. Cernea and S.E. Guggenheim, eds. **Anthropological Approaches to Involuntary Resettlement: Policy, Practice, and Theory.** *Boulder, Col.: Westview Press. 1993.*

Also available as World Bank Reprint Series no. 462. Washington, D.C. 1990, and as **Internal Refugees and Development-Caused Population Displacement.** *HIID Development Discussion Paper no. 345. Cambridge, Mass.: Harvard University. 1990.*

10.10 Cernea, Michael M. "Anthropology, Policy and Involuntary Resettlement." *BASAPP (British Association for Social Anthropology in Policy and Practice) Newsletter* 4:3-6. November 1989.

Essentially the same issues are discussed in "Development Anthropology at Work." Anthropology Newsletter 29(6). Washington, D.C. 1988.

This article explores the growing role of professional social science research in improving resettlement planning and implementation. New roles go beyond the traditional roles of providing data to policymakers, after-the-fact research, advocacy, or interpretation. The author sees anthropologists working in the area of resettlement formulating policy, designing plans, and sometimes taking on the responsibilities of managers and decisionmakers. These roles become possible when the technical skills of the professional anthropologist are recognized as valid qualification for exercising leadership in resettlement planning.

The author argues that the pattern of progress in the field of resettlement anthropology—from research to policy and from policy to applied work—could be replicated and expanded in other areas of development and anthropology.

10.11 Cernea, Michael M., and Guy Le Moigne. "The World Bank's Approach to Involuntary Resettlement." *Water Power and Dam Construction Handbook.* Surrey, England: Reed Business Publishing. 1989.

Addressed primarily to engineering and technical audiences, this article criticizes the "engineering bias" in planning dam construction, with only scant attention paid to the sociocultural impact of dams and reservoirs on people. Technical consulting firms often omit forced resettlement from their dam feasibility studies; the authors contrast the World Bank's approach to the engineering-biased perspective found in both developed and developing countries.

10.12 Cernea, Michael M. *Involuntary Resettlement in Development Projects: Policy Guidelines in World Bank-Financed Projects.* World Bank Technical Paper no. 80. Washington, D.C. 1988.

Also available in French and Spanish. Translated into Bahasa Indonesia (see entry 10.13), Italian (see entry 10.14), and Turkish.

In this paper the World Bank's resettlement policy was fully described publicly for the first time. It provides an overview of the evolution of World Bank policy and operational guidelines in regard to involuntary resettlement: During the 1960s and 1970s the handling of involuntary resettlement in development projects was often flawed by a lack of social planning and insufficient financial and technical resources. In 1980 the Bank adopted a new policy and guidelines based on lessons learned from previous relocations and sociological and anthropological research. In 1986, after assessing the first six years under its new policy, the Bank issued additional guidelines to deal more comprehensively with involuntary resettlement.

Historically, involuntary resettlement has been, and often still is, approached as a salvage operation, rather than one pursuing development objectives. In contrast with such approaches, the paper emphasizes that because involuntary resettlement dismantles a previous production system and way of life, all involuntary resettlement programs must be development programs as well. The author argues that the knowledge generated by social science research on resettlement is indispensable for addressing the social and economic problems of such relocation effectively.

The backbone of any resettlement plan must be a development package consisting of a set of project funded provisions aimed at reconstructing the production base of those relocated and at reestablishing them as self-sustaining producers or wage earners. The discussion of the general principles for resettlement as planned change emphasizes government responsibility, involvement of resettlers in the choice among available resettlement options, and prevention of adverse impact on host populations and environment.

The operational procedures described in the paper are tailored to each of the different stages of the project cycle in World Bank financed projects. Annex 1 contains a technical checklist for preparing and appraising resettlement plans in projects. Annex 2 contains guidelines for the economic and financial analyses of resettlement project components. Annex 3 contains a technical checklist for monitoring and evaluating resettlement.

10.13 Cernea, Michael M. *Pemukiman Penduduk Secara Terpaksa Dalam Proyek-Proyek Pembangunan: Pedoman Kebijakan bagi Proyek-proyek yang Dibiayai Bank Dunia. (Involuntary Resettlement in Development Projects. Policy Guidelines for World Bank-Financed Projects)*. Jakarta, Indonesia: Cetakan Pertama. 1990.

With a foreword by Professor Abdul Hakim G.N. and an introductory study by George J. Aditjondro. The introductory study discusses involuntary population displacement and resettlement under Indonesia's government-sponsored programs and the relevance of the World Bank's Resettlement Policy to development programs in Indonesia.

This volume is an adapted translation into Bahasa Indonesia of the publication entry 10.12.

10.14 Cernea, Michael M. "Reinsediamento Involontario nei Progetti di Sviluppo." *Forum*. Comitato Internazionale per lo Sviluppo dei Populi (CISP). November 1990.

This study discusses various monitoring and evaluation techniques for assessing progress and outcomes of resettlement operations. It also summarizes the basic principles of the World Bank's policy guidelines for resettlement as described in entry 10.12

10.15 Cernea, Michael M. "Involuntary Resettlement and Development." *Finance & Development* 25(3):44-6. 1988.

Also published in Hari Mohan Mathur, ed. The Human Dimension of Development: Perspectives from Anthropology. New Delhi: Concept Publishing Company. 1990.

The typical pitfalls that occur in the early stages of the project cycle and account for most of the negative results of resettlement are identified and discussed. To avoid these, the Bank's appraisal methods and internal review of projects causing displacement must be tightened. Creative approaches to resettlement must be introduced, including specialized sociological analysis, intensified supervision, and adequate financing through Bank loans and domestic funds.

10.16 Cook, Cynthia, ed. *Involuntary Resettlement in Africa*. World Bank Technical Paper no. 227. Washington, D.C. 1993.

In October 1991, the World Bank, together with the Institute of Social Research at Makerere University in Kampala, Uganda, organized the African Conference on Environment and Settlement. The conference brought together policymakers, planners, social science researchers and practitioners concerned with the implementation of Bank-financed projects involving involuntary resettlement. The participants attempted to contribute their analysis to the improvement of those specific projects and also to draw from their experience more general lessons that might be applicable to environmental and settlement problems in Africa.

Selected papers from the conference are grouped in this technical paper. Those prepared by World Bank staff sociologists or consultant sociologists and anthropologists are annotated individually in this section of the bibliography under the author's name.

- *"African Population Resettlement in a Global Context"* by Michael M. Cernea
- *"Involuntary Resettlement in Bank-Financed Projects: Lessons from Experience in Sub-Saharan Africa"* by Cynthia Cook and Aleki Mukendi
- *"Resettlement of people Displaced by the Manantali Dam"* by Mamadou Mactar Sylla
- *"Dislocation of Settled Communities in the Development Process: the Case of Kiambere Hydroelectric Project"* by Edward K. Mburugu
- *"Resettlement and Rural Development Aspects of the Lesotho Highlands Water Project"* by Mavuso Tshabalala
- *"Resettlement of Displaced People in Connection with the Nylon Urban Upgrading Project in Douala, Cameroon"* by Louis Roger Manga
- *"Involuntary Relocation in Urban Areas of Mozambique"* by Francisco Pereira
- *"Social Impacts of the Creation of Lake Kariba"* by Christopher H.D. Magadza
- *"Long-term Impacts of Resettlement: The Akosombo Dam Experience"* by Martha A. Tamakloe
- *"The Kainji Lake Experience in Nigeria"* by Julius S.O. Ayeni, Wolf Roder, and J.O. Ayanda
- *"Environment and Settlement in Eastern Sudan: Some Major Policy Issues"* by Gunnar M. Sorbo
- *"Resettlement and Integration of Pastoralists in the National Economy: Ranch Restructuring in Uganda"* by David Pulkol

- *"Settlement and Resettlement: Experience from Uganda's National Parks and Reserves"* by Mark A. Marquardt
- *"Development Strategies and Issues for Land Settlement in West Africa"* by Della E. McMillan, Thomas Painter, and Thayer Scudder
- *"Population Trends and Economic Growth in Sub-Saharan Africa"* by Jean-Marie Cour
- *"Environment and Settlement Issues in Africa: Toward a Policy Agenda"* by Cynthia C. Cook.

10.17 Cook, Cynthia, and Aleki Mukendi. "Involuntary Resettlement in Bank-Financed Projects: Lessons from Experience in Sub-Saharan Africa." In C. Cook, ed. *Involuntary Resettlement in Africa.* World Bank Technical Paper no. 227. Washington, D.C. 1993.

The authors review lessons learned from World Bank projects involving resettlement in Africa and present empirical data from various projects. Even with good intentions and an appropriate Bank policy framework, few projects have succeeded in promoting the sustainable economic and social development of the resettled people. Constraints to successful implementation include inadequate or absent national policies, institutional weaknesses, land tenure problems, lack of local participation, and failure to anticipate the social and environmental consequences of resettlement.

10.18 Cook, Cynthia. "Environment and Settlement Issues in Africa: Toward a Policy Agenda." In C. Cook, ed. *Involuntary Resettlement in Africa.* World Bank Technical Paper no. 227. Washington, D.C. 1993.

The author summarizes the discussions held at the 1991 Makerere conference and the proposals that were made for future action. These actions fall into three main areas: first, preparing resettlement policy proposals based on the Bank guidelines and on the lessons of experience, and discussing these proposals with African decisionmakers in the context of policy reform; second, conducting additional research on identified issues with support from the international community; and, third, networking among African professionals and institutions involved in the study of resettlement issues in order for research findings to feed back more rapidly into the policy dialogue. Makerere University's Institute of Social Research offered to spearhead this networking activity.

10.19 Davis, Gloria, and Helen Garrison. *Indonesia: The Transmigration Program in Perspective.* A World Bank Country Study. Washington, D.C. 1988.

Between 1980 and 1986 the Indonesian Transmigration Program supported the movement of more than two million people from the densely populated "inner islands" of Java, Bali, and Lombok to the less populated "outer islands" of Sumatra, Kalimantan, Sulawesi, and Irian Jaya. An equal number of people are believed to have moved on their own, making this program the largest government sponsored voluntary resettlement scheme in the world. This report was initiated in 1985 as a review of resettlement during the third five-year plan (1979-1984).

Among the conclusions emerging from this report are that economic rates of return and initial settler incomes were low and that the program was complex and difficult to implement. Spontaneous migrants were not adequately incorporated into program planning and the scale of the program heightened concern about the environmental impact and potential social problems. Yet, the study also found that economic and social prospects for settlers were superior to those on Java, and transmigration appeared to have contributed significantly to employment generation and regional development.

In light of this analysis, this review, which was written prior to resource constraints in Indonesia which developed in the late 1980s, recommended that (a) the rate of new settlement should be slowed and major emphasis should be placed on the consolidation and improvement of existing sites; (b) new settlements should be based on more productive farming systems; (c) institutions responsible for planning and carrying out the program should be strengthened; (d) increased attention should be given to accommodating spontaneous migrants in productive holdings; and (e) higher priority should be given to social and environmental concerns.

10.20 Davis, Gloria. "The Indonesian Transmigrants." In Julie Sloan Denslow and Christine Padoch, eds. *People of the Tropical Rainforests.* **Washington, D.C. Smithsonian Institute. 1988.**

Indonesia's transmigration program, which resettled over two million people from the overcrowded inner islands to less densely settled outer islands between 1980 and 1986 is the largest voluntary, government-supported resettlement program in the world. The author provides an overview and history of resettlement in Indonesia and evaluates both positive and negative views of the program.

Since 1980, the World Bank has supported the Indonesian government's efforts to identify land suitable for agriculture and to ensure that this land is free of claims by local people. The government has taken steps to strengthen provincial involvement in the selection of sites and to improve forums for the redress of grievances in compensating local people for their land. Problems have occurred, but historically most outer island residents have welcomed settlement because it also brought jobs, schools, and clinics.

In addition to government sponsored settlers, who apply for resettlement voluntarily, there has been a spontaneous flow of people moving without government support who move to be near family or friends. The fact that people move voluntarily in government programs and that large numbers of people move spontaneously provides some evidence that opportunities are better for migrants in the outer islands. Just how much better is a matter of dispute, and several World Bank studies, in which the author participated, have made an effort to evaluate the transmigration program.

On the positive side, the report indicates that transmigration in the third five-year plan created at least five hundred thousand permanent jobs, mainly in agriculture, at a cost of about $3,000 per job; much temporary work was generated by the resettlement process, and it is estimated that nearly one-quarter of a million households have benefitted from jobs created by land development alone. However, there is evidence that incomes are too heavily dependent on off-farm work: nearly half of family income in the larger communities is derived from off-farm wage work, site development, and the establishment of plantation crops.

Concern exists that reductions in the government's development budget may reduce off-farm employment, which leaves outstanding questions about the level of sustainability of the new settlements. The author offers recommendations to reduce pressure on the environment in the outer islands while increasing productivity and accommodating the continuing demand from inner island residents for new land to meet their subsistence needs.

10.21 Guggenheim, Scott E. "Peasants, Planners, and Participation: Resettlement in Mexico." In M.M. Cernea and S.E. Guggenheim, eds. *Anthropological Approaches to Involuntary Resettlement: Policy, Practice, and Theory.* **Boulder, Col.: Westview Press. 1993.**

The Mexico Hydroelectric Development Project, internationally funded and currently in progress, incorporates the construction of two dams, the 960 MW Aguamilpa, and the 280 MW Zimapan, which together are expected to displace about 3,500 people.

The author summarizes the history of involuntary resettlement in Mexico to date and draws comparisons with the resettlement planning process and problems for the above mentioned two dams. He also documents the substantial progress made by Mexico's national power company, the Comision Federal de Electricidad (CFE).

The lessons learned in the course of the as yet ongoing resettlement process are: (a) the necessity of planning resettlement on the context of a resettlement policy framework with legislated standards and systematized mechanisms; (b) the benefit gained from restructuring the CFE, which created a high level resettlement unit;

(c) the strengthening of the CFE's institutional capabilities through the use and acceptance of local participation in planning and managing the resettlement program; and 4)the realization that resettlement researchers have much to contribute by focusing on the middle ground between theories and policies on the one hand, and ground level processes on the other.

10.22 Guggenheim, Scott E. "Resettlement in Colombia: The Case of El Guavio." *Practicing Anthropology* 12(3):14-20. 1990.

This article focuses on the resettlement problems that contributed to the delays and enormous cost overruns of Colombia's Guavio hydroelectric dam. Three planning problems hampered the resettlement component of the project: (a) population estimates seriously undercounted the population to be displaced; (b) widespread illiteracy and people's lack of information were used by dishonest officials to commit compensation fraud; and (c) resettlers who realized they had been left out of the compensation program, defrauded, or left without enough resources to move elsewhere, became politically active and joined forces in strikes with dam workers.

The dam's international funders, particularly the World Bank, assisted with the planning of a corrective action program, tying social and environmental improvements to a subsequent power sector loan needed to finish the project. Fraud has been eliminated, replacement lands have been provided for remaining resettlers, and research and resettlement planning have become more prominent in Colombia's dam planning. As a result, the same organizational structures that initially channeled frustrations into organized resistance are now providing the architecture for developing resettlement procedures and supporting resettlers' reestablishment.

10.23 Le Moigne, Guy, Scott E. Guggenheim, and others. *Dam Planning, People, and the Environment: World Bank Policies and Practices*. 17th Congress on Large Dams. International Commission on Large Dams. Vienna. 1991.

Investments in dams are needed to meet the growing food and energy needs of developing societies. At the same time, increased awareness of the social and environmental implications of large dams has raised serious questions about their adverse impacts. This paper discusses the World Bank's evolving policy and operational methods to ensure that the benefits and potential negative effects of dams are correctly evaluated.

Two matters of particular concern to the World Bank have been: (a) the need for measures to protect populations displaced by dams; and (b) the need to fully internalize the environmental impacts of dam projects. Full-fledged resettlement plans that will improve or at least restore the living standards, production levels, and earning potential of displaced families are required for all projects causing involuntary displacement. The Bank also requires environmental impact assessments prior to approving dam projects.

Converting sound policy requirements into operational practices is a difficult process. Examples of World Bank experiences in Asia, Latin America, and Africa illustrate its role in ameliorating the adverse social and environmental impacts of dam construction. The cases discussed in the paper include dam projects where planning was inadequate as well as cases where better planning resulted in environmentally desirable outcomes.

10.24 Magadza, Christopher H.D. "Social Impacts of the Creation of Lake Kariba." In C. Cook, ed. *Involuntary Resettlement in Africa*. World Bank Technical Paper no. 227. Washington, D.C. Forthcoming.

The resettlement program undertaken in connection with the construction of the Kariba Dam on the Zambezi River between Zambia and Zimbabwe forced river valley cultivators to move to unfamiliar uplands where slopes and soil conditions made farming more difficult and more vulnerable to environmental risks. Fishery and livestock potentials have been developed, but these programs have brought little benefit to the local people.

The project has had a negative effect on the nutritional status of the resettled people and has increased environmental and health risks, without providing the necessary social services. Sociological study of the consequences of the project has not moved policymakers to take remedial action.

10.25 Mathur, Hari Mohan. "Resettling the Development Displaced Population—Issues and Approaches." *Management in Government* 23(2):109-20. Government of India, New Delhi. 1991.

Involuntary resettlement is not a process that will disappear in the foreseeable future. The number of projects that entail the acquisition of land, which is already large, will increase further. Land is the basic requirement for most large infrastructure projects and, owing to population growth, uninhabited land is becoming increasingly scarce.

Displacement is always traumatic for those forced to resettle. However, the effects of displacement are worst for tribal people, whose survival is already at stake, and the poor, who lag behind in sharing the benefits from development.

The author presents an overview of resettlement programs in the past and their flaws, and the evolution of the World Bank's resettlement policy. Resettlement performance has lately begun to improve, however, the very fact that some operations have been more successful than others indicates that further improvements are possible. Those involved in planning and managing resettlement must be willing to adopt new approaches.

10.26 Mburugu, Edward K. "Dislocation of Settled Communities in the Development Process: The Case of Kiambere Hydroelectric Project." In C. Cook, ed. *Involuntary Resettlement in Africa.* World Bank Technical Paper no. 227. Washington, D.C. Forthcoming.

The author reports the findings of a survey of people displaced by the Kiambere Dam in Kenya. The results show that cash compensation was inadequate to replace lost resources and that the displaced population was less well-off following resettlement. Among the problems experienced were inadequate land availability in resettlement areas, disruption of family relations and culture, declines in farm production, deterioration in housing conditions, and an increase in the incidence of water-borne diseases and malaria.

10.27 McMillan, Della E., Thomas Painter, and Thayer Scudder. "Development Strategies and Issues for Land Settlement in West Africa." In C. Cook, ed. *Involuntary Resettlement in Africa.* World Bank Technical Paper no. 227. Washington, D.C. Forthcoming.

This chapter summarizes the study described in greater detail in entry 10.29.

10.28 McMillan, Della E., and others. *Settlement and Development in the River Blindness Control Zone: Case Study, Burkina Faso.* World Bank Technical Paper no. 200. Series on River Blindness Control in West Africa. Washington, D.C. 1993.

The Onchocerciasis Control Programme (OCP) is widely acknowledged as the most successful ongoing disease control program in Africa. One of the primary benefits of the OCP has been the opening up of approximately 25 million hectares of tillable land in previously sparsely populated onchocerciasis endemic river valleys.

This case study is part of the Land Settlement Review (LSR), a regional study examining the phenomenon of land settlement in West Africa resulting from the successful control of onchocerciasis. Burkina Faso has experienced more settlement in the onchocerciasis-controlled areas than any other country in the region. The government of Burkina Faso has been active in promoting settlement over an 18 year period and this study provides important insights into the possibilities for and limits to government action in support of land settlement.

116 *Settlement and Involuntary Resettlement*

10.29 McMillan, Della E., Thomas Painter, and Thayer Scudder. *Settlement and Development in the River Blindness Control Zone.* World Bank Technical Paper no. 192. Series on River Blindness Control in West Africa. Washington, D.C. 1992.

This volume is the summary report of the Land Settlement Review (LSR), a regional study examining the phenomenon of land settlement in West Africa resulting from the successful control of onchocerciasis. It analyzes the process of land settlement, both spontaneous and government sponsored, and recommends operational policy guidelines for promoting viable and sustainable settlement-related activities in the areas where onchocerciasis has been controlled.

The LSR found that government-sponsored programs were too costly and cumbersome to be successful on a large scale, while spontaneous settlements tend to plateau at low levels of productivity and to undertake activities in areas where they may not be environmentally sustainable.

Instead, the authors advocate the adoption of an "assisted spontaneous" approach to settlement, capitalizing on the initiative of settlers, and supporting and structuring their efforts by providing necessary infrastructure and services. They focus on the importance of including host communities and seasonal resource users such as pastoralists in planning for sustainable resource use and management. Secure tenure rights are an important element in sustainable development. These rights should be assigned based on local agreements, taking customary tenure systems as the starting point.

10.30 Morse, Bradford, and Thomas R. Berger (with Donald Gamble and Hugh Brody). *Sardar Sarovar: The Report of the Independent Review.* Ottawa: Resource Futures International (RFI) Inc. 1992.

The Narmada Sardar Sarovar dam and irrigation projects, which will submerge land in the three Indian states of Gujarat, Madhya Pradesh, and Maharashtra, will entail the displacement and resettlement of over 100,000 people. During the late 1980s the projects became the focus of heated controversy regarding their human and environmental impacts. In 1991 the World Bank commissioned an independent review of the measures being taken to mitigate these impacts. The four-member Independent Review team included an anthropologist who has written extensively about the impacts of large-scale development on rural and tribal communities.

In the assessment of the resettlement and rehabilitation components of the projects, the authors first consider the overarching principles of the World Bank's policy that apply generally to resettlement, and then examine in detail the history of the projects' appraisal, the resettlement and rehabilitation policy of each of the three states, and the progress of their implementation.

The Narmada valley is occupied by a mixture of both caste and tribal villages. Over fifty percent of the population potentially affected by the projects consists of tribal people of the Bhil and Bhilala tribal groups. They cultivate land based on customary usage without holding formal title to it. The review criticizes the treatment of these large groups as "encroachers" and the fact that two of the three states in question, Madhya Pradesh and Maharashtra, did not acknowledge their tribal people's right to adequate land for resettlement. Because resettlement is regarded in India as a state responsibility, there is no national policy for resettlement and rehabilitation.

The Independent Review concludes that India and the three affected states have failed to enforce the provisions of the Narmada Water Disputes Tribunal's 1979 decision and the loan agreements with the World Bank. The World Bank originally failed to incorporate its own policies in the agreements and subsequently pursued an inadequate "incremental" approach in an unsuccessful attempt to secure compliance with its resettlement guidelines and with the projects' legal agreements.

10.31 Partridge, William L. "Successful Involuntary Resettlement: Lessons from the Costa Rican Arenal Hydroelectric Project." In M.M. Cernea and S.E. Guggenheim, eds. *Anthropological Approaches to Resettlement*. Boulder, Col.: Westview Press. 1993.

Studies of failed resettlement schemes are abundant, but few successful experiences have been documented. In this chapter, however, the author describes and analyzes a successful resettlement case where advance planning and analysis of social data during the planning process played important roles in avoiding negative consequences and successfully addressing complex social, economic and environmental problems.

The evaluation of Costa Rica's Arenal Hydroelectric Project conducted by the author was based on analysis of census data, project planning documents, participant observation, household surveys, and interview research in the communities of New Tronadora and New Arenal. Economic reconstruction of farming systems and commercial enterprises in the new communities were the subject of special analysis; extensive data were collected regarding land tenure and distribution, subsistence production and consumption, commercial crops and their sale and the role of project planning in supporting reestablishment of the affected families.

The main conclusion of the analysis is that direct participation of the affected families, even in a situation of potential social conflict such as this, acts to provide not only more effective solutions, but also provides a mechanism whereby unanticipated outcomes can be successfully dealt with.

10.32 Partridge, William L., and M. Painter. "Lowland Settlement in San Julian, Bolivia—Project Success and Regional Underdevelopment." In D. Schumann and W.L. Partridge, eds. *The Human Ecology of Tropical Land Settlement in Latin America.* **Boulder, Col.: Westview Press. 1989.**

The authors present results of an anthropological study of factors explaining the relative success and failure of smallholders in a planned colonization scheme, including social, economic and environmental issues which affect decisionmaking in the context of broader regional development processes. The research took place over seven months, in which a team of social scientists were resident in the colonization area called San Julian. The research team employed participant observation, focus group discussion, directed interview, and socioeconomic survey techniques to gather data on the differential performance of some 200 smallholders living in 20 settlements within the zone.

The data were compared with available land records to identify factors associated with frequent sale of farm plots and factors associated with long-term residence in the zone. The data yielded reliable correlations, the strongest of which were the association between long-term residence (over ten years) in the zone and the availability of a reliable drinking water supply, availability of off-farm employment on nearby ranches and plantations, and availability of transport connections with outside markets. The differential success and failure of the colonists directs attention to the vital role played by off-farm income earning opportunities as a key factor in settlement planting, as well as the more generally recognized role of adequate physical infrastructure.

10.33 Partridge, William L. "Involuntary Resettlement in Development Projects." *Journal of Refugee Studies* **2(3):373-84. 1989.**

This article is the text of the first Elizabeth Colson Lecture given at Oxford University in March 1989, which outlines a research agenda for the scholars interested in continuing the work Elizabeth Colson pioneered. Colson's contributions to resettlement research are reviewed and analyzed in relation to the policies and practical applications that have evolved in recent years in the multilateral development agencies.

The author reviews the new lessons learned from the application of these policies and identifies gaps in current understanding of resettlement issues, either by researchers or by governments. Among these are the differential impacts of resettlement (that is, social class, age, occupation, and so on), the institutional failure to accept responsibility for resettlement, the key role of women in all resettlement operations, and the unappreciated social energies for innovation and entrepreneurial action released by the disintegration of traditional authority structures. A challenge is issued for broader research by resettlement scholars to address these issues.

10.34 Partridge, William L. "Reasentamiento de los Comunidates: Los Roles de los Grupos Corporativos en las Relocalizaciones Urbanos." In L.J. Bartolome, ed. *Relocalizaciones: Antropologia Social de las Poblaciones Desplazadas*. Buenos Aires: Instituto de Desarrollo Economico y Social. 1986.

The author urges attention to the role of corporate group formation in the process of involuntary resettlement, whether urban or rural. The cases examined are drawn from much of the "grey" literature on resettlement which remains unpublished, and relates that to the better known work of urban settlement specialists who concentrate on voluntary resettlement processes. Commonalities are documented and analyzed.

10.35 Scudder, Thayer. "A Sociological Framework for the Analysis of New Land Settlements." In M.M. Cernea, ed. *Putting People First: Sociological Variables in Rural Development*. 2nd ed. New York, London: Oxford University Press. 1991.

New land settlement programs have been among the least satisfactory type of development interventions. Many of the problems have been traced to a failure to appreciate the socioeconomic and cultural complexities involved in recreating human communities and building a viable productive basis for them. How social science knowledge can be applied in settlement projects is the subject of this chapter.

The author develops a settlement model drawn from worldwide experience with colonization projects. The chapter is based on the proposition that settler families everywhere pass through regular developmental sequences as they voluntarily move away from the old and adapt to their new environments. Although the length of each stage can vary, their sequence is both similar and predictable. Each stage is marked by distinct attitudes toward risk, innovation, and receptiveness to new opportunities.

The long process of resettlement adaptation described by the author typically extends well beyond the planning horizons of most development projects. One implication of this discrepancy is that evaluations of settlement projects are often carried out too soon, when in fact, the model the author describes suggests that their full benefits are not realized until the later phases of settler development.

The model also predicts that most settlers will develop mixed production systems to reduce risk, rather than relying exclusively on the agricultural endeavors facilitated by the project. This reliance on off-farm income sources should, in theory, be an asset to strategies seeking to stimulate regional development. In practice, however, multiple income source approaches are left out of most settlement planning models.

10.36 Serra, Maria Teresa Fernandez. "Resettlement Planning in the Brazilian Power Sector: Recent Changes in Approach." In M.M. Cernea and S.E. Guggenheim, eds. *Anthropological Approaches to Involuntary Resettlement: Policy, Practice, and Theory*. Boulder, Col.: Westview Press. 1993.

Of the primary sources available in Brazil for the generation of electric power (water, coal, nuclear fuel, petroleum products, and biomass), hydropower is the most important. The available potential is very large and economically attractive. The two chief difficulties limiting hydroelectric development in the long run are related to the formation of reservoirs and difficulties with long-distance electricity transmission.

Forty-six new hydroelectric plants are specified in the Brazilian Power System Planning Coordination Group's 1990-1999 Expansion Plan. Together they will require the relocation of 9,000 Indians, 4 percent of Brazil's total Indian population, and approximately 136,000 non-indigenous people.

The power sector's 1990 Environmental Master Plan has incorporated a broad range of guidelines, including specific ones for population relocation. As a result, there have been serious attempts on the part of the sector's major companies to improve the quality of their resettlement planning and their approach to local participation. The author analyzes the policy shifts and presents three examples of projects undertaken at different times which illustrate the evolution of social and resettlement policy. She concludes with a discussion of the main difficulties of introducing resettlement policy faced by the power sector as it begins to implement the changes.

10.37 Shihata, Ibrahim F. I. "Legal Aspects of Involuntary Population Resettlement." In M.M. Cernea and S.E. Guggenheim, eds. *Anthropological Approaches to Involuntary Resettlement: Policy, Practice, and Theory*. Boulder, Col.: Westview Press. 1993.

A critical issue confronting development organizations is how to conceptualize and manage situations that require involuntary resettlement. The need for involuntary displacement in certain projects raises complex questions about roles and obligations, both in promoting projects that cause displacement and in developing policy, legal, and operational procedures to reconcile national and local interests. Developing policy guidelines translated into operational procedures is the systematic way for large institutions to maximize public benefits and minimize local costs in such situations.

The author argues that the specific development orientation of the World Bank's resettlement policy derives from the Bank's commitment to provide balanced development opportunities. Projects that cause displacement should provide the population adversely affected with clear opportunities to share in tangible project benefits.

The study explores several of the main legal questions that commonly arise during resettlement operations assisted by the World Bank: compensation methodologies and timing; compensation and resettlement eligibility criteria; land acquisition, titling, and transfer; and regulations relating to resettlement agencies. Lessons derived from many Bank-assisted projects involving resettlement underscore the fact that in many countries, the national legal framework for resettlement is incomplete. There is a great need to ensure that the legal issues involved in resettlement and rehabilitation be addressed by legal scholars jointly with sociologists and anthropologists to create the necessary frameworks for countries where resettlement requirements appear.

10.38 Sorbo, Gunnar M. "Environment and Settlement in Eastern Sudan: Some Major Policy Issues." In C. Cook, ed. *Involuntary Resettlement in Africa*. World Bank Technical Paper no. 227. Washington, D.C. Forthcoming.

The author analyzes the long-range impacts of settlement and resettlement in the Sudanese province of Kassala over the last thirty years, related to irrigation development and the resettlement of Nubians from the Aswan High Dam area. Anthropological field research reported in the paper indicates that, while initial agricultural production objectives have not been sustainably achieved, the project did provide a basis for sustainable settlement based on the development of non-farm enterprises and a more diversified pattern of agricultural production than originally envisaged.

The author contends that settlement projects in the past have been overdesigned and too rigid in implementation, thus missing many opportunities to take advantage of changing circumstances. African governments rarely possess the institutional capacity to manage such complex projects successfully. He recommends, therefore, that decisionmakers should focus more on formulating policy frameworks that provide suitable incentives for environmentally sound spontaneous settlement, rather than planning investment programs for over-managed area development.

10.39 Tamakloe, Martha A. "Long-Term Impacts of Resettlement: The Akosombo Dam Experience." In C. Cook, ed. *Involuntary Resettlement in Africa*. World Bank Technical Paper no. 227. Washington, D.C. Forthcoming.

In the course of implementing the Volta River Project at Akasombo in Ghana, changes in government policy orientations had disruptive effects on the lives of the resettlers. Unanticipated social consequences of the resettlement program led to significant changes in the population's age structure, ethnic composition, and economic activities, and in the mechanisms for conflict resolutions in the new villages.

Field research suggests that the introduction of mechanized agriculture as part of the resettlement program may have accelerated environmental degradation around the new man-made lake. Reductions in river flow caused adverse health consequences by facilitating the spread of schistosomiasis below the dam, which recent migrants from this area have brought back into the resettlement villages as well.

10.40 Tshabalala, Mavuso. "Resettlement and Rural Development Aspects of the Lesotho Highlands Water Project." In C. Cook, ed. *Involuntary Resettlement in Africa*. World Bank Technical Paper no. 227. Washington, D.C. Forthcoming.

The author reports on the displacement of several thousand people and compensation activities made necessary by the Lesotho Highland Water Project, a large-scale engineering undertaking that will transfer water from Lesotho to South Africa. He starts with a review of settlement patterns in Lesotho and gives an overview of the project, summarizes the environmental impact assessment within the project, and provides empirical social and economic data about the project area population.

Besides direct compensation in the short term, long-term socioeconomic reestablishment will be facilitated for the affected population through a targeted rural development program. The author concludes with an examination of the implementation of the resettlement program.

10.41 World Bank. "Resettlement and Development: The Bankwide Review of Projects Involving Involuntary Resettlement 1986-1993." World Bank Environment Department. Washington, D.C. 1994.

This study is the most comprehensive social impact assessment carried out in the Bank. It analyzes worldwide experiences with development-induced forced displacements, focussing on some 200 projects financed by the Bank during 1986 to 1993 in over 40 countries which entailed population displacement. A task force led by Michael M. Cernea carried out the review and prepared this report with the cooperation of Bank operational and central units. Many staff and consultant sociologists and anthropologists contributed to this review. The final report was written by Michael M. Cernea and Scott Guggenheim.

The study provides the first estimates of the magnitude of worldwide development-caused displacements, reckoned to affect at least 10,000,000 people each year, as a result of dam construction and urban and transportation development programs.

The impact of the Bank's resettlement policy on national policies is assessed and the actual performance of resettlement programs is analyzed. While it found an overall performance improvement in recent years, particularly from 1991 to 1993, the study also concluded that in a number of earlier Bank-financed projects actual resettlement operations and outcomes were not consistent with the standards defined and demanded by the Bank's resettlement policy. Inadequate social and financial planning has been a major problem in resettlement; the financing of resettlement costs has not been commensurate with the importance and complexity of the resettlement process. The study raises important conceptual, policy and legal issues regarding population resettlement and analyzes strategies for managing relocation processes.

Based on the findings and recommendations of this review, important strategic decisions were taken by Bank management which have strengthened Bank policy and will result in an increase in the institutional and financial resources available for more consistent implementation of the resettlement policy. These strategy changes include: greater emphasis on borrowers' political commitment and on the development of domestic resettlement policies and legal frameworks in borrowing countries; increased Bank financing of resettlement operations in future projects to assist the restoration of resettlers' livelihoods; supplementary financing of resettlement in some ongoing projects to correct existing planning, budgeting, and implementation deficiencies; expanded public participation in the preparation of resettlement plans; diversified project vehicles, with full-fledged projects (as opposed to components) for large resettlement operations; and institutional capacity building.

Additional publications relevant to the topics in this section of the Bibliography can be found in Sections 2, 6, and 17.

Part Four

Social Variables in Environmental Management

Environment and Development

11.1 Brandon, Katrina, and Carter Brandon, eds. "Linking Environment to Development: Problems and Possibilities." Special issue of *World Development* 20(4). 1992.

This volume addresses conceptual issues pertaining to the relationship between development and the environment. It places particular emphasis on the sociological aspects of resource management and on the institutional techniques designed to help reconcile environmental concerns with the need for development. Articles are grouped around five themes: (a) global tradeoffs in linking development and the environment; (b) conceptual critiques of economic decisionmaking; (c) methodological approaches; (d) linking development and the environment in rural settings; and (e) linking development and the environment in international and urban settings. Beyond the topical issues presented, five themes emerge where the papers also show the depth of the current debate on environmental issues. These are: (a) global versus national or local issues; (b) macro versus micro levels of economic analysis; (c) North versus South debates; (d) present versus future tradeoffs; and (e) urban versus rural issues.

What emerges from this issue is that there is no one set of tradeoffs or choices available to policy makers. Just as there is a wide range of development objectives and strategies being pursued by countries around the world, there are many legitimate debates about ways to value and manage the environment and no single consensus on how development and environmental objectives are best made compatible in the induced development process.

11.2 Brandon, Katrina, and Alvaro Umaña. "Inventing Institutions for Conservation: Lessons from Costa Rica." In S. Annis, ed. *Poverty, Natural Resources, and Public Policy in Central America*. Washington, D.C.: Overseas Development Council. 1992.

The agencies responsible for conservation and natural resource management in most Central American countries are institutionally and politically weak; they have little power to promote substantial reforms. This article describes how the Arias administration undertook a major reorganization in Costa Rica to integrate environmental concerns into economic decision making. New institutional arrangements were "invented" and established to reconcile the state's desire to have a unified national strategy for resource management and at the same time decentralize actual decision making, control, and financial responsibility to a network of regional actors.

The explicit institution building requirements in Costa Rica included: (a) research and scientific information as a basis for policy making; (b) a central authority to set and enforce adherence to national priorities; (c) financing to make programs work; and (d) and participatory mechanisms to deal with the complexities of local situations. These requirements were met by consolidating and strengthening disparate environmental agencies and joining them into one ministry; and decentralizing conservation and development at the local as well as the national level.

New and creative financing arrangements such as debt swaps were developed and conservation funding was aggressively sought. The government also created the National Biodiversity Institute (INBIO), which catalogs Costa Rica's biodiversity and identifies ways that it can be used to generate socioeconomic development. The authors recommend steps to be taken in other countries in order to create a similar infrastructure.

11.3 Cernea, Michael M. *The Urban Environment and Population Relocation*. World Bank Discussion Paper no. 152. Washington, D.C. 1993.

Also published in F. Davidson, and others, eds. **Urban Relocation and Policy Practice.** *Rotterdam: Institute for Housing and Urban Development Studies. 1993.*

Urban economic growth and environmental improvement in developing countries often requires the involuntary displacement and relocation of various groups of residents, sometimes of entire established micro-neighborhoods. Yet urban sociology and urban anthropology in these countries have scarcely dealt with this process.

The frequency and magnitude of urban compulsory displacements are likely to increase in the future as the trend towards urbanization grows stronger, as shown by examples from Sudan and Egypt and by statistical projections of urbanization worldwide.

The paper examines the causal mechanisms of involuntary displacement, the typology of displacement processes, and the policy issues involved in executing resettlement. Among the dramatic disruptions caused by displacement are loss of home, often loss of jobs, destruction of income generating assets, and separation from site-related informal network services. Development projects that are oblivious to the perils of impoverishment through displacements are shown to be in conflict with the poverty reduction goals of urban growth strategies. Urban poverty is likely to increase when displacement occurs unless such displacement is guided by correct resettlement policies.

The paper discusses experiences with urban relocation under ongoing World Bank-financed urban development projects. Three cases of major displacements of urban populations—in Indonesia (Jakarta and Bogor), in China (Shanghai), and in the Yacyreta project at the Argentina-Paraguay border—are examined in some detail. The author concludes that population displacement and relocation must be regarded as an integral part of policies for urban socioeconomic development, rather than a mere side-effect. The author argues that, in order to avoid or minimize population dislocation, countries must enact domestic policies and legal frameworks that will explicitly regulate involuntary displacement and relocation.

11.4 Cernea, Michael M. "Environmental and Social Requirements for Resource-Based Regional Development." In P. Hall, and others, eds. *Multilateral Cooperation for Development in the Twenty-First Century: Training and Research for Regional Development*. Nagoya: United Nations Center for Regional Development. 1991.

There is a contradiction between accelerating the pace of development, on the one hand, and protecting the environment, on the other. Finding a practicable solution to this dilemma largely depends on the emergence of self-controlling environmental management systems led by the resource users themselves. Two concepts appear frequently in the environment versus development debate: "local level" and "users' role." As these terms suggest, the characteristics of social organization are paramount in the use of natural resources by people.

Environmental consciousness can be more easily developed through increased awareness of the local and regional issues at stake. Natural resources exist in a local context; they are used, and often abused, at the local level by the primary users. Over many decades, development programs ignored the strategic importance of the local and regional levels in establishing effective resource management systems.

"Localness," however, is not in itself a criterion of quality. The more local a resource management system is, the more vulnerable it is to interference by *supra*local systems. Macro factors are of decisive functional importance for local social organization within a complex society.

The author presents the case of a successful regional development strategy in Senegal, focused on improving rangeland and water use while increasing users' income. This case demonstrates the possibility and the positive effects of combining capacity-building at the users' level with macro-policy tools for environmental management.

11.5 Cruz, Maria Concepcion J. *Economic Stagnation and Deforestation in Costa Rica and the Philippines*. Proceedings of the World Bank's Thirteenth Agriculture Symposium. Washington, D.C. 1993.

This paper presents case studies of rural-to-rural migration in Costa Rica and the Philippines. The author concludes that for countries already experiencing population pressures on resources, worsening economic conditions create additional stress on open access, frontier lands. Pressures from a growing labor force and deepening poverty promote expansion into ecologically sensitive sites.

11.6 Cruz, Maria Concepcion J. *Population Growth and Land Use Changes in the Philippines*. New York: The Rene Dubos Forum on Population, Environment, and Development. 1993.

This paper presents a case study of frontier migration in the Philippines. Mass migration into forest lands is a process that directly links the impacts of economic contraction on deforestation and conversion of forests into agricultural land. The case study utilizes data from a population census completed in the mid-1980s. The urbanward migrations of the 1970s appear to have reversed in the early 1980s, and the shift signifies substantially increased pressures on marginal forest sites.

11.7 Davis, Shelton H., James F. Hicks, Herman E. Daly, and Maria de Lourdes de Freitas. *Ecuador's Amazon Region: Development Issues and Options*. World Bank Discussion Paper no. 75. Washington, D.C. 1990.

When natural resources are of a unique nature and are spatially concentrated, national economic development policy must be informed by specific regional analyses. This is the case with Ecuador's Amazon Region because it has a very fragile renewable natural resource base, rich biological diversity, significant native populations, and large, but diminishing petroleum reserves.

Certain social processes and national trends, especially population growth and migration out of the Sierra and Costa regions, are creating extraordinary pressures on the Amazon Region. These resent significant threats to the region's social stability and environmental integrity, as well as to its potential to make long-term contributions to Ecuador's economic development.

This discussion paper presents the results of a multidisciplinary analysis, that included an anthropological perspective, of the socioeconomic problems of Ecuador's Amazon Region within the framework of the country's overall development. National and regional policy linkages were emphasized in this study in order to clarify how regional natural resource management can contribute to national economic development policy.

11.8 Elmendorf, Mary, and Patricia K. Buckles. *Sociocultural Aspects of Water Supply and Excreta Disposal.* Transportation, Water and Communications Department. The World Bank. Washington, D.C. 1980.

Social and cultural factors influencing people's responses to water supply and excreta disposal technologies were investigated in seven case studies of communities in rural and urban fringe areas of Latin America.

Part 1 of this volume describes the methodology and questionnaire used to investigate how sanitation and water supply problems were perceived and the extent to which people were willing to participate and pay for improved services. Part 2 summarizes each case study, including the technologies introduced and community response to them. Part 3 presents the cross-community findings on perceptions, preferences, related practices, and the use of social science techniques to understand them. In Part 4, the report focuses on the implications of the findings and recommends an approach that can be used by planners to integrate social and cultural factors into project design to ensure the introduction of water supply and excreta disposal technologies that will be accepted, properly used, and maintained.

11.9 World Bank. *Environmental Assessment Sourcebook.* Vols. I-III. World Bank Technical Paper no. 140. Washington, D.C. 1991.

The Sourcebook is designed to assist all those involved in environmental assessment (EA). They include the environmental assessors themselves, project designers, and World Bank task managers. This focus supports an important premise of EA, that sustainable development is achieved most efficiently when negative environmental impacts are identified and addressed at the earliest possible planning stage.

The Sourcebook presents discussions of fundamental environmental considerations (with emphasis on those with relatively more impact); summaries of relevant Bank policies; and analyses of other topics that affect project implementation (for example, financial intermediary lending, community involvement, and economic evaluation). Volume I contains policies, procedures, and cross-sectoral issues; Volume II contains sectoral guidelines; and Volume III contains guidelines for environmental assessment of energy and industry projects.

Chapter 3 of the first volume is devoted to practical discussion of key issues in social analysis related to the environment. It provides a description of specific core concerns (variation among social groups within communities; control over local resources;

variation within production systems; institutions; and use of social information in environmental assessments) and an overview of social issues in ecologically sensitive areas. In addition, five topics of particular significance to Bank projects are discussed: indigenous peoples, cultural property, involuntary resettlement, new land settlement, and induced development.

Chapter 7 of the first volume offers practical guidance on community involvement and the role of nongovernmental associations in environmental assessment. The roles and responsibilities of Bank staff, affected people, local NGOs, and borrowing government officials are specified, and two levels of public consultation, that it, with the affected population, and with organizations that have expertise related to the nature, scope, and particulars of potential environmental effects, are discussed in detail.

Land and Land Tenure

12.1 Bromley, Daniel, and Michael M. Cernea. *The Management of Common Property Natural Resources. Some Conceptual and Operational Fallacies.* World Bank Discussion Paper no. 57. Washington, D.C. 1989.

The concept of common property has been largely misunderstood and falsely interpreted by many development practitioners and government officials. Common property regimes are not free-for-all systems, as socially uninformed policy makers and planners believe. In their classic form, common property regimes are structured ownership arrangements within which management rules exist, group size is known and enforced, and values an sanctions encourage co-owners to follow accepted arrangements. Cases of misinterpretation of property regimes or of good resource management are discussed in light of projects in Botswana, Morocco, Senegal, Somalia, and Thailand.

Resource degradation in developing countries, while incorrectly attributed to "common property systems," actually originates in part in the dissolution of local level institutional arrangements. Without the establishment of adequate substitute regimes, the erstwhile common property regimes are gradually converted into *open access, in which each person is driven to take as much as possible before others do.* While this has been referred to as "the tragedy of the commons," it is actually "the tragedy of open access." Natural resource deterioration is also occurring widely outside the boundaries of common property systems, under private property and state property regimes.

Development assistance for natural resource management will succeed only if programs and projects become more concerned with the people using natural resources, rather than with the particular commodities around which projects have often been organized. The notion that national or even regional governments in the developing countries can effectively manage local natural resources is largely without empirical support.

Interventions aiming to generate sustainable development must explicitly address the social arrangements among people as they interact with each other and the natural resource base, and help build forms of social organization conducive to sustainable use of resources. Essential for project execution is the system of incentives and sanctions to influence individual and group behavior.

12.2 Cernea, Michael M. *Land Tenure Systems and Social Implications of Forestry Development Programs*. World Bank Staff Working Paper no. 452. Washington, D.C. 1981.

This paper examines some of the social, cultural, and behavioral variables associated with the design and implementation of forestry projects. The Hill Farming Technical Development Project undertaken in 1978 in Azad Kashmir, Pakistan is a case in point, notably with respect to the role of land tenure systems and their sociological implications. It is analyzed by the author together with relevant experience gained from other forestry projects.

The operational difficulties confronted in the Azad Kashmir pilot forestry program are relevant to similar situations elsewhere in the developing world. Particular attention is paid to the lack of congruity between project-assumed and actual land tenure systems.

The author reviews the social and economic issues involved in the basic policy question of whether or not to subsidize reforestation programs. He suggests alternative approaches involving the mobilization of small and possibly also larger farmers, with sociological consideration of farmers' self-help strategies, forestry cooperatives, and other modes of achieving partial cost recovery of forestry plantations.

12.3 Feder, Gershon, and Raymond Noronha. "Land Rights Systems and Agricultural Development in Sub-Saharan Africa." *World Bank Research Observer* 2(2):143-69. 1987.

Links between land rights and agricultural development provide a conceptual framework to analyze land rights systems in Sub-Saharan Africa. The discussion demonstrates that land rights in Sub-Saharan Africa evolved in response to changing political, social, and economic conditions, often the results of governmental interventions that may not have been conducive to efficiency or equity.

The evidence dispels some popular misconceptions about land rights systems in Sub-Saharan Africa. There is increasing individualization of ownership, and in many areas possession has always been individual. Even in areas where communal ownership has been dominant, cultivation and use remain with individual households and an increasing range of rights to land are appropriated by the individual household. Existing and indigenous systems are not inherently equitable. Land sales and mortgaging by individuals are observed frequently in many areas where such transactions are not recognized under the formal legal system.

If efficiency ultimately requires formal recognition of individual land rights, that stage has not been reached yet in many parts of Sub-Saharan Africa. In some parts the justification for changing land rights already exists; the practical problem in such cases is the careful analysis of benefits and costs, including equity considerations.

12.4 Hecht, Robert M. "Immigration, Land Transfer, and Tenure Changes in Divo, Ivory Coast, 1940-1980." *Africa* 55(3):319-36. 1985.

The connection between changes in land tenure patterns in Africa and the transformation of agriculture throughout most of the continent during the twentieth century, from subsistence farming to a market economy and crop exportation, is of major importance for agricultural policy makers.

This article traces the change in land tenure patterns from communal rights to individual rights in the province of Divo in Ivory Coast between 1940 and 1980. The changes in the system have been underscored by the process of land transfers to immigrant farmers, a subject which has received little attention until now.

The author describes the general economic development of Divo from 1940 to 1980 and analyzes important changes in the system of land transfers in two villages, Ghebiri and Brabore. He concludes that the changes in land tenure and land use patterns have caused a degree of social conflict, but have not seriously obstructed agricultural development in the region. He also recommends that authorities should formalize arbitration procedures in cases of land tenure disputes.

12.5 Migot-Adholla, Shem E., and others. "Indigenous Land Rights Systems in Sub-Saharan Africa: A Constraint on Productivity?" *The World Bank Economic Review* 5(1):155-75. 1991.

There is considerable debate about whether indigenous land tenure systems are a constraint on agricultural transformation. Some researchers see the indigenous tenure systems as static constraints on agricultural development, providing insufficient tenure security to induce farmers to make necessary land improving investments. Others contend that the indigenous tenure arrangements are dynamic and tend to evolve in response to changes in factor prices.

This study reports empirical findings on the relationship between indigenous land tenure systems and agricultural productivity in Sub-Saharan Africa. Data was collected from farming households in several regions of Ghana, Kenya, and Rwanda during 1987-88. The authors find that, in general, agricultural productivity is unresponsive to the individual rights held over land, suggesting that factors other than land tenure are more constraining for agricultural development. Therefore, ambitious land registration and titling programs would appear to be inappropriate at this time for the surveyed regions in Sub-Saharan Africa.

12.6 **Noronha, Raymond. "Common Property Resource Management in Traditional Societies." In P. Dasgupta and K.G. Maler, eds.** *Environment and Emerging Development Issues*. Oxford: Oxford University Press. 1993.

The author analyzes the management of natural resources under common property regimes among traditional societies and the nature of common property systems. Several explanations are proposed for the decline of the ability of traditional societies to control the use and exploitation of grazing lands and other resources through this type of property regime.

Water and the Sociology of Irrigation

13.1 Bagadion, Benjamin U., and Francis F. Korten. "Developing Irrigators' Organizations: A Learning Process Approach." In M.M. Cernea, ed. *Putting People First: Sociological Variables in Rural Development.* 2nd ed. New York, London: Oxford University Press. 1991.

Examination of development projects worldwide indicates that social and institutional issues are often not adequately addressed. In recognition of this failing, many implementing agencies are giving greater attention to social issues and adding trained sociologists and anthropologists to project design and implementation teams.

Quite often, however, a wide gap remains between the needs that are identified by social scientists and the actual implementation of programs that address those needs. In many cases this is because the implementing agency is not oriented to deal with those needs.

Addressing social issues often involves building new capabilities among the people at the community level. But many government agencies assigned to implement large projects provide little support for building such capabilities.

The agency first has to learn how to address social needs effectively at the village level, then develop support systems appropriate to the required field-level actions. This learning process must allow for trial and error on a small scale, continuous examination of the village-level work to identify problems, issues and successful approaches, and adjustments in agency policy, procedures, and structures to accommodate responses to the field-level needs.

The authors describe and discuss the development of a participatory approach by the National Irrigation Administration in the Philippines, and illustrate with it the learning process required to enhance the agency's capacity to support community participation. The authors recommend steps to be taken at the agency level to allow it first to recognize and then use local capabilities, and to adjust its policies and procedures accordingly.

13.2 Byrnes, Kerry J. *Water Users' Associations in World Bank-Assisted Irrigation Projects in Pakistan.* World Bank Technical Paper no. 173. Washington, D.C. 1992.

The field study described in this paper examines the growing organizational capacity of the local social actors over the course of three successive World Bank-financed irrigation projects in Pakistan. The creation of some 14,000 water users' associations (WUAs) represents a leap forward in asserting users' roles and participation in water management, in purposively creating a new social fabric intended to endure and support the cost-effective use of the new physical infrastructure for irrigation, and in mobilizing human and material resources for immediate activities of mutual benefit.

The author reconstructs and examines the development of these new social patterns and explores how the three main WUA functions (water allocation, infrastructure maintenance, and management of the irrigators' group) are performed. He also identifies areas in which further assistance could overcome persistent institutional weaknesses and increase the returns on investments in WUAs.

13.3 Cernea, Michael M., and Ruth Meinzen-Dick. "Design for Water User Associations: Organizational Characteristics." In Guy Le Moigne, Shawki Barghouti, and Lisa Garbus, eds. *Developing and Improving Irrigation and Drainage Systems*. Selected Papers from World Bank Seminars. World Bank Technical Paper no. 178. Washington, D.C. 1992.

This paper analyzes how Bank-financed irrigation development projects approved between 1976 and 1990 deal, in their design and implementation strategies, with the basic organizational features of water user associations (WUAs). It assesses whether or not these organizational characteristics are taken into account during the appraisal of Bank projects and what project staff must do to strengthen and support WUAs.

The contextual and organizational characteristics examined include: preexistence of water user organizations; new organizations; membership criteria; size of the base units; federation of base units; role specialization: accountability; and linkages with irrigation agencies. The paper also discusses the relative benefits of relying on organizations that already function among water users versus establishing new ones.

Although the research and conclusions presented in this paper derive from irrigation systems, many of the same organizational issues apply to other resource management projects in which local resource users could create their own organizations and increase their bargaining power when working with outside government or private agencies.

13.4 Coward, E. Walter, Jr. "Planning Social and Technical Change in Irrigated Areas." in M.M. Cernea, ed. *Putting People First: Sociological Variables in Rural Development*. 2nd ed. New York, London: Oxford University Press. 1991.

Financially induced irrigation development programs have often focused only on technical and physical components. Institutional concerns, when present, are limited mostly to strengthening central water agencies.

However, it is being increasingly recognized now that major institutional weaknesses frequently undermine the operation and maintenance of physical infrastructure, causing irrigation schemes to perform below expectation, and even resulting in serious adverse environmental impacts. These unintended effects often result not from technical causes, but from inattention to the social organization of the water users.

This chapter is concerned with the correlation between technical and social changes, especially when projects aim to rehabilitate or improve already existing irrigation systems. All too often, planners ignore locally developed irrigation systems and self-management techniques in the rush to provide improved alternatives.

Particularly interesting are the author's recently discovered examples of indigenous social mechanisms for water allocation shared by groups of villages. The author argues convincingly that a more careful incorporation of existing social, technical, and managerial arrangements into irrigation project designs would make for higher success rates, avoid undermining existing grassroots institutions, and lower the maintenance costs of irrigation systems.

13.5 Freeman, David M., and Max K. Lowdermilk. "Middle-Level Farmer Organizations as Links between Farms and Central Irrigation Systems." In M.M. Cernea, ed. *Putting People First: Sociological Variables in Rural Development.* 2nd ed. New York, London: Oxford University Press. 1991.

The authors examine the human networks which are required to organize and manage irrigation systems. Their structural-functional model looks at the different organizational levels needed to coordinate the tasks involved in making irrigation infrastructure meet farm requirements.

The authors argue that their task-focused model can be usefully applied at three different levels: the farm, the command (irrigation) area, and the state bureaucracy. They emphasize that the mid-level organizational structures, located between local and national management, are the most neglected in the design of irrigation projects.

The contribution of this framework lies in using a sociological perspective to understand irrigation organizations, both formal and informal. This chapter underscores the need to rely on fieldwork-based descriptions of the customary rules in order to understand how irrigation systems work. By clarifying the possible ways to better involve the users in system operation, and the social principles that explain why a system is operated in a particular way, the social analyst can determine how to make system improvements more effective.

13.6 Migot-Adholla, Shem E. "Irrigated Agriculture in Africa: Past Accomplishments and Future Directions." In Derick Thron, ed. *Proceedings of the Forum on the Performance of Irrigated Agriculture in Africa.* WMS Report no. 86. Logan Utah: Utah State University. 1988.

13.7 Schuh, G.E., Guy Le Moigne, Michael M. Cernea, and Robert J.A. Goodland. "Social and Environmental Impacts of Dams: The World Bank Experience." In *Transactions of the Sixteenth Congress on Large Dams, San Francisco, June 13-17, 1988* vol. I. Paris: International Commission on Large Dams. 1988.

Also available as World Bank Reprint Series no. 438. Washington, D.C. 1988.

This article discusses the nature of large dam projects and provides an overview of the World Bank's experience with this class of projects, particularly the evolution of Bank policy and operational guidelines in regard to involuntary resettlement and environmental issues typically raised by dam construction. The Bank has financed over 400 dam projects in the course of four decades.

The authors describe the World Bank project cycle, which encompasses the Bank's procedures for incorporating sociological and environmental considerations into project planning and implementation. In addition to the general policies concerning the social and environmental impacts of dams, three specific policy areas have been identified for special attention: indigenous people, wildlands conservation, and protection of cultural property.

The authors summarize lessons learned and identify several areas, particularly social and environmental, where further improvements in project design and execution are desirable. They conclude with a note of caution: while there is much that the Bank can do to improve the social and environmental impact of dams, there are limits to the Bank's influence on the policies and practices of member countries. Informed public opinion is needed to command and redirect the attention of decision makers. The authors invite readers to offer their advice, expertise and imagination to help ensure that social and environmental aspects of dams are handled adequately, so that potential harm is minimized and benefits gained outweigh the costs.

Forests and Social Forestry

14.1 Barnes, Douglas, and Julia Allen. "The Causes of Deforestation in Developing Nations." *Annals of the Association of American Geographers* 75(2):163-84. 1985.

14.2 Cernea, Michael M. "The Social Actors of Participatory Afforestation Strategies." In M.M. Cernea, ed. *Putting People First: Sociological Variables in Rural Development.* 2nd ed. New York, London: Oxford University Press. 1991.

The practice of social forestry demands the formation of patterns of social organization propitious for afforestation activities. The author calls for a break with the stereotype that tree growing is the business of professional foresters alone, or of mother nature alone. He recommends strategies to engage the rural consumers of fuelwood into organized activities for producing trees and managing forests, and suggests a variety of organizational models for creating production-oriented user groups.

The author reports on his case study of a reforestation intervention in Azad Kashmir in which project planners sought to promote reforestation on traditional common property land called *shamilat*. His field study found that *shamilat* no longer worked on genuine corporate management principles. Instead, the commons in Azad Kashmir have become privatized through a process of three historical stages: (a) informal partitioning; (b) incremental appropriation; and (c) formal privatization. During this process, considerable amounts of *khalsa* (crown land) and *shamilat* land were gradually converted to *malkiat* land.

Broadening the analysis to a number of recent projects that promoted "community woodlots" but largely failed, the author argues that these projects were socially ill-conceived and predicated on improperly selected or defined units of social organization. Lacking a correct understanding of the kind of social process required for such programs, financial investments in the technical process far outpaced the investment in human and institutional processes.

The author recommends specific options for replacing the diffuse "community woodlot" approaches with two basic strategies for social forestry, relying on clearly identified social actors: (a) family-centered strategies for tree planting and (b) group-centered strategies (farmers' groups, associations of landless tree growers, age groups, women's groups, and other groups), both supported by sound organizational and distributional arrangements.

14.3 Cernea, Michael M. "A Sociological Framework: Policy, Environment, and the Social Actors for Tree Planting." In N.P. Sharma, ed. *Managing the World's Forests*. **Iowa: Kendall/Hunt Publishing Co. 1992.**

Also published as HIID Development Discussion Paper no. 319. Cambridge, Mass.: Harvard University. 1989.

One section of this study was published in the Overseas Development Institute's Social Forestry Network series under the title Beyond Community Woodlots: Programmes with Participation. *London: Overseas Development Institute. 1990.*

An earlier version, which addressed other issues in addition, was published as User Groups as Producers in Participatory Reforestation Strategies. *World Bank Discussion Paper no. 70. Washington, D.C. 1992.*

This study discusses policy options and operational strategies for improving social forestry programs. Analysis of social forestry approaches, often called "community" forestry or "village" woodlots, reveals that many programs genuinely intended to be participatory are formulated in fuzzy terms, are not designed around well identified social actors, and do not ensure clear benefit distribution arrangements and incentives.

The author argues that the profound behavioral change to be elicited on a gigantic scale among farmers through social forestry strategies is tantamount to a historic shift from simple gathering behavior to cultivation behavior. Trees and forests are to be produced by people.

The first part discusses the prerequisites for achieving such a shift and focuses on land tenure variables in forestry. It includes a historical analysis of the privatization of the commons in Azad Kashmir which reveals why the World Bank-financed community forestry project which attempted to stimulate farmers' communal tree planting failed.

The second part broadens the analysis to the whole category of "community based" forestry interventions and concludes that their failures are largely traceable to the misconceptions embedded in their design about communities' capacity for coordinated collective action in planting and managing trees. The author identifies seven basic sociological reasons for which communities, which are resident but non-homogenous population clusters, should not be regarded as willing and able corporate actors in afforestation programs.

The author argues that social forestry strategies (a) must be conceived starting with the definition of the adequate units of social organization capable of translating the strategy into practice; (b) must ensure a match between the sylviculture technologies they promote and the social groups they aim to involve; and (c) must carry out a certain amount of social engineering (group formation and maintenance, establishing incentives and penalties, and setting up authority arrangements and communication channels).

The author recommends options to replace the elusive and diffuse "community" approaches with two basic strategies for social forestry: family-centered strategies or group-centered strategies. The latter relies on units of social organization larger than the family. Evidence from many social forestry projects is examined to compare the results of these two approaches. The study concludes that such alternative structures need not pre-date the project: while those already in existence must be strengthened, new group structures can be created through the very programs that call for collective action.

14.4 Cernea, Michael M. "Alternative Units of Social Organization Sustaining Afforestation Strategies." In M.M. Cernea, ed. *Putting People First: Sociological Variables in Rural Development*. New York: Oxford University Press. 1985.

This study has been reprinted in several readers and anthropology books, including: M. R. Dove and C. Carpenter, eds. Sociology of Natural Resources in Pakistan and Adjoining Countries. Lahore, Pakistan: Vanguard Books. 1992.; J. Yves and D. C. Pitt, eds. Deforestation: Social Dynamics in Watershed and Mountain Ecosystems. London: Routledge. 1988; and Louise Fortmann and J. Bruce, eds. Whose Trees? Proprietary Dimensions of Forestry. Boulder, Col.: Westview Press. 1988. (For content, see annotations for titles 14.2 and 14.3).

14.5 Cook, Cynthia C., and Mikael Grut. *Agroforestry in Africa: A Farmer's Perspective*. World Bank Technical Paper no. 112. Washington, D.C. 1989.

A summary of this study is published in Finance & Development. December 1990.

Agroforestry, is broadly defined as the integration of trees and shrubs in farming systems, which offers promising technological options for reversing soil degradation, restoring tree cover, and improving agricultural productivity. The authors have reviewed the literature on agroforestry in order to identify a limited number of successful experiences for further field study. Seven case studies were conducted by an interdisciplinary team, covering indigenous and innovative systems found in the highlands of East Africa, the semi-arid zone, and the humid lowlands of West Africa.

Key findings include the importance of understanding the economics of agroforestry systems from the farmer's point of view as well as from the broader perspective of the benefits to society. Project evaluation should take into account local markets and opportunities for off-farm employment offered by tree products, as well as the opportunity costs perceived by farmers in making adoption decisions.

Farm households are not homogeneous, and project designs should allow for differences in the socioeconomic level, age and gender of the people expected to adopt the proposed technology. In Africa, trees are integral parts of agro-sylvo-pastoral farming systems and should be considered in this sociocultural context, with attention to the implications of customary and formal legal rules regarding land and tree tenure. The institutional framework for project implementation should be selected and developed with a view to long-term sustainability.

14.6 Davis, Gloria, and Richard Ackermann, eds. *Indonesia: Sustainable Development of Forests, Land, and Water.* A World Bank Country Study. Washington, D.C. 1990.

This document was prepared by a multidisciplinary group of Bank staff and consultants, including economists, agriculturalists, foresters, anthropologists, and others, as an input into the Bank's Economic Report, presented at the 31st meeting of the Inter-Governmental Group on Indonesia in June 1988. It was also intended as a background analytical resource for the preparation of Indonesia's fifth five-year development plan (1989-1994).

The report focuses primarily on issues related to land and forest management in the outer islands and land and water resource management in Java. The main audience for the report was intended to be Indonesian economic planners, and for this reason the main objective of the report was to demonstrate that increased attention to the environment was necessary to achieve the Government's development objectives.

To take account of more recent developments in Indonesia, the executive summary was updated for this publication in 1990. The main report was not revised and provides a snapshot of the situation at the end of the fourth five-year plan. Many of the issues raised in this report are being addressed in the fifth 5-year plan.

14.7 Dyson, Mary. "West and Central African Rain Forest Conservation Conference." *World Bank Environmental Bulletin* 3(1):5. Washington, D.C. 1991.

The first major regional conference on tropical forestry to be held in Western or Central Africa took place in Abidjan, Côte d'Ivoire, in November 1990, cosponsored by the World Bank and the IUCN. Participants discussed the various issues related to conservation and rational utilization of West and Central African rainforests, the emerging strategies of African governments, and the World Bank's new forestry policy.

The conference's search for solutions to rapid deforestation included calls to reduce Sub-Saharan Africa's population growth rates and to help farmers intensify agricultural production. African countries were urged to reassess their forestry and conservation policies in light of their national, regional, and global importance. Consultation with local communities on the design of national forest programs and their empowerment to help implement them were strongly urged.

14.8 Dyson, Mary, Robert Goodland, and others. "Tropical Moist Forest Management: The Urgency of Transition to Sustainability." *Environmental Conservation* 17(4):303-18. 1990.

Also published in R. Costanza, ed., Ecological Economics: The Science and Management of Sustainability. New York: Columbia University Press. 1990.

An increasing number of citizens, foresters, and environmentalists realize that most current use of tropical moist forest is unsustainable. Tropical moist deforestation benefits exceedingly few people while it permanently impoverishes, uproots or sickens millions of people, impairs local or global environmental services, and exacerbates global environmental risks. Commercial logging is recognized as one of the top causes of deforestation.

The authors argue the case for a transition to sustainability by improving forest management at least to "best practice," by deflecting logging from primary to secondary forests, and by beginning a phased transition to plantations, especially rehabilitating degraded lands. The transition should be rapid in countries where forests are rapidly disappearing and where logging is a main cause (Côte d'Ivoire, Ghana, Nigeria, Papua New Guinea). The transition is less urgent where tropical moist forests are extensive and stable.

14.9 Guggenheim, Scott E., and John Spears. "Sociological and Environmental Dimensions of Social Forestry Projects." In M.M. Cernea, ed. *Putting People First: Sociological Variables in Rural Development*. 2nd ed. New York, London: Oxford University Press. 1991.

Forestry policies and programs face two major tasks: slowing down deforestation and intensifying tree planting both inside and outside forests. Rural populations must become more involved in tree planting activities, for without their massive participation afforestation activities cannot possibly make headway against the current rates of tree consumption and destruction. To address the social and cultural issues involved in forestry projects, particularly in social forestry, this chapter proposes a sociological framework for designing forestry strategies and programs.

Concerned with how to provide effective incentives for smallholders to grow trees, the authors present three arguments. First, policy makers must recognize the pivotal role of small farmers in both environmental preservation and tree production. National policies span a range of legal, financial, and institutional areas, setting a macroscopic context that can encourage, as well as constrain, smallholder tree production. At present, few countries have policy frameworks designed to stimulate small farm tree production.

Second, development projects must adapt their means to local situations. The authors use a large body of evidence to show how some projects still compete with and undermine local approaches to natural resource management.

Third, on the positive side, local level institutions governing land tenure, labor availability, production orientation, technical innovation, and access to capital must be brought into project planning through good social research and participatory project approaches.

14.10 Molnar, Augusta, and Janice Alcorn. "Deforestation and Forest-Human Relationships in India." In Les Ponsel, ed. *Tropical Forest Ecology: The Changing Human Niche and Deforestation.* **Forthcoming.**

14.11 Noronha, Raymond J. "Why Is It So Difficult to Grow Fuelwood?" *Unasylva* **33:3-12. 1981.**

The Korean model of community fuelwood projects, which was widely acclaimed in the mid-1970s, could not be easily transferred to other countries and cultures because of differences in local community structures. This article stresses the need to assess sociocultural factors before designing forestry projects.

14.12 World Bank. *The Forest Sector.* **A World Bank Policy Paper. Washington, D.C. 1991.**

Since the late 1970s, increased knowledge of the ecological aspects of forests has been parallelled by a better understanding of human behavior with regard to trees—and why this behavior is often not in accord with national and global interests.

A wide range of analyses and research over the past decade has shed light on the determinants of the effective demand for land and wood (the cause of deforestation), the importance of tenure arrangements, and the links between government policies and the forest sector. The use of government policies to influence behavior in the sector is a principal theme of this paper.

This policy paper, defining the issues and approaches to investing in the forest sector, was prepared by a multidisciplinary group of World Bank specialists, including sociologists and anthropologists as well as foresters, economists, environmentalists and agriculturalists. Chapter 1 describes the two most important challenges in the sector—excessive deforestation and inadequate reforestation—and highlights the causes and extent of the problem. Drawing on the analysis of the causes of excessive deforestation and inadequate planting, Chapter 2 discusses policies and programs directed toward overcoming these underlying causes. Strategies for investing in social forestry are outlined, focusing on two approaches: family centered approaches and group centered approaches. Chapter 3 discusses the role of the World Bank in supporting governments' efforts to implement forestry-related policies and programs.

Rangelands and Pastoralism

15.1 Bonfiglioli, Angelo Maliki. *Agro-Pastoralism in Chad as a Strategy for Survival: An Essay on the Relationship between Anthropology and Statistics*. World Bank Technical Paper no. 214. Washington D.C. 1993.

This paper is a multi-disciplinary study of the system within which Sahelian agropastoral groups in Chad live and work. It examines the key features of a traditional rural society, describing the Chadian agropastoral universe as a coherent whole, governed by an internal dynamic that operates according to its own rationalities within an environment of uncertainty.

To assess the impact of national macroeconomic decisions on Chad's pastoral groups, statistical measurements and reports are not enough. Only an anthropological analysis can help to capture and understand the reactions of households to these decisions and to account for the ultimate social costs or benefits of these decisions to particular population subgroups within this society. In a traditional society like that of the Sahelian agropastoralists in Chad, behavior cannot be modified except within the framework of already existing conventional social constraints.

Accurate knowledge of the mechanisms of this society facilitates definition of appropriate analytical concepts and design of suitable tools for the observation, measurement and analysis of economic behaviors. Using a cultural and sociological description of a traditional society, the investigator develops a twofold perspective: that of economic analysis, which attempts to explain behaviors, and that of statistical observation, which attempts to measure them. The detailed description of Chadian agropastoral society is used to explain the link between microeconomic behaviors and what occurs at the mesoeconomic or market level.

15.2 Cernea, Michael M. "Pastoralists' Organizations for Resource Management: An African Case." In P. Daniels, and others, eds. *Proceedings of the International Conference on Livestock Services for Smallholders*. Yogyakarta, Indonesia. November 1993.

For good environmental management, considering the environment's physical characteristics alone is insufficient. Sociological variables, particularly the presence or absence of forms of social organization capable of assuming natural resource management, are of paramount importance.

The author illustrates this argument with a description of the Eastern Senegal Livestock Development Project, an example of a successful regional development strategy which created a user-based system of managing resources. A total area of 1.3 million hectares was divided into 53 sub-areas and long-term user rights over each were assigned to an individual grazing association. This project helped local communities establish self-managed grazing associations, and facilitated legal protection of the new organizations by the Government. The project also combined technical assistance to support the user associations in improving productive use of rangelands and water sources, with human resource development in the form of literacy classes and veterinary training for some graduates of the literacy classes (see also entry 11.4).

The most important factor accounting for overall success was the presence of a clearly conceptualized operational strategy for building organizations at the local level. These local level organizations proved to be a crucial social tool for adjusting and monitoring the balance between the users' interest to productively consume, and at the same time preserve, the natural resources that are the basis of their economic existence.

15.3 Dyson-Hudson, Neville. "Pastoral Production Systems and Livestock Development Projects: An East African Perspective." In M.M. Cernea, ed. *Putting People First: Sociological Variables in Rural Development*. 2nd ed. New York, London: Oxford University Press. 1991.

Livestock development projects attempt to address the extraordinary environmental and socioeconomic pressures that have beset pastoral societies by improving animal husbandry, and in the course of doing so, modifying traditional pastoralism. They have probably been the least successful subgroup among agricultural projects.

The author bases his interpretation on a sociological analysis of the social organization pastoralists have developed to adapt to an inhospitable environment. He argues that the pressures on pastoralists clash with their complex and delicately balanced systems, which often cannot rapidly absorb the changes promoted through financially induced development projects. By misunderstanding the intricacy of the pastoral socio-ecosystem and failing to develop projects compatible with its structural characteristics, development planners themselves often add to the causes of failure.

Defining the social and cultural features of East African pastoralist societies, the author highlights the social organizational variables that must be considered if planned interventions are to be effective in gradually modifying existing social systems.

The author presents a case analysis of the rather unsuccessful Kenya Range Livestock Project, for which he served as anthropologist-consultant, first as a member of the project appraisal team and years later as an evaluation analyst. As he readily recognizes, the presence of social anthropologists on the project design team is by no means a guarantee of project success. Sociocultural input in project design is indeed indispensable but, as the case proves, other factors are also required to ensure the project's effective implementation.

In light of this experience, the author proposes five additional guidelines for the new generation of livestock projects in the 1990s. These include the need for longer-term financial commitments, a deconstruction of the "integrated approach, attention to the new family units within pastoralist populations, the promotion of smaller-scale experimental interventions, and the need to decentralize and localize development projects.

15.4 Jowkar, Forouz. *Nomadism, Nomadic Support, and Settlement in the Islamic Republic of Iran: The Rangelands and Livestock Development Project*. Working Paper. Institute for Development Anthropology. Binghamton, NY. 1993.

The paper analyzes the potential for assisting the settlement of seminomadic herders in Iran in the context of a project proposed by the Government of Iran for World Bank co-financing. Loss of rangelands in Iran has contributed to a decline in the herd productivity of nomadic pastoralists and to an intensifying conflict between herders and farmers. Faced with shrinking grazing lands and inflationary prices of commodities, many herders spontaneously settle in rural and peri-urban areas under undesirable conditions.

To avoid problems associated with spontaneous settlement, Iran is launching a program of planned nomadic settlement as a component of a larger project that aims to simultaneously rehabilitate the rangelands, improve herd productivity, and increase herder income. The paper makes several recommendations based on field analysis to increase the effectiveness of the settlement component of the project.

The recommendations include involvement of both herders and farmers in land rehabilitation programs; rigorous enforcement of laws banning encroachment on grazing lands; provision of affordable fuel to avoid deforestation; financial and administrative improvement of herder cooperatives; flexible land allocation to accommodate varying family sizes; time-bound legal guarantees for settlers wishing to resume transhumance; improvement of marketing systems for both farm and non-farm products; family planning; improvement of women's income generating activities in culturally accepted areas such as dairying, farming, and weaving;

provision of gender sensitive extension services; and adoption of a monitoring system using indicators of costs and benefits of both settlers and host communities.

Parks and Biosphere Reserves

16.1 Brandon, Katrina. "Basic Steps toward Encouraging Local Participation in Nature Tourism Projects." In K. Lindberg and D. Hawkins, eds. *Ecotourism: A Guide for Planners and Managers*. North Bennington, Vt. The Ecotourism Society. 1993.

Ecotourism has been heavily promoted as a way of providing substantial benefits to both conservation and local communities. Yet there is ample evidence that tourism, even small-scale, is not structured to meet local needs and that benefits often flow outside the area. There is a serious lack of integration of local needs and preferences into the planning process.

This chapter deals with ecotourism activities for which providing benefits to communities is a major objective. It summarizes some of the basic issues in working with local communities to ensure that ecotourism development is consistent with local social, ecological, and economic objectives, including: (a) the role of local participation; (b) empowerment as an objective; (c) participation in the project cycle; (d) creating stakeholders; (e) linking benefits to conservation; (f) distributing benefits; (g) involving community leaders; (h) using agents for change; (i) understanding site-specific conditions; and (j) monitoring and evaluating programs.

16.2 Brandon, Katrina, and Michael Wells. *People and Parks: Linking Protected Area Management with Local Communities*. World Bank. Washington, D.C. 1992.

New approaches to national parks that combine conservation with development may offer the best chance to protect threatened wildlands and the valuable biological reserves they contain. But while the concept—introduced in this study as "integrated conservation-development projects"—sounds simple and highly promising, the practice so far has often been difficult and sometimes disappointing.

The findings presented in this study are based on site assessments of twenty-three projects in nineteen protected areas in Latin America, Asia, and Africa. Despite the diversity of the sites examined, the authors found several common reasons why some efforts to combine development with conservation succeeded while others failed. They offer practical ideas for increasing success rates by modifying or changing the approaches taken so far.

The study highlights the critical importance of launching projects in a supportive policy environment. Another important factor in successful projects is a mix of organizations with complimentary skills and resources—including development agencies and nongovernmental organizations—working together with governments and local people in the design and implementation of ICDPs. Brief case studies of each of the twenty-three projects are included.

16.3 Brandon, Katrina, and Michael Wells. "Planning for People and Parks: Design Dilemmas." *World Development* 20(4):557-70. 1992.

Integrated Conservation-Development Projects (ICDPs) attempt to link biodiversity conservation in protected areas with social and economic development in surrounding communities. Unless such linkages are created, surrounding social pressures will hamper the protection of biodiversity.

As documented by the authors, the performance of ICDPs thus far has been undercut by numerous difficulties, many of which are strikingly similar to those encountered in rural development programs. While many of these difficulties can be traced to specific social implementation weaknesses or technical design flaws, more fundamental issues of a social nature pose policy and conceptual challenges to the ICDP approach. This paper highlights the evolution of these projects thus far and identifies the tradeoffs inherent in linking conservation and development at the field level.

16.4 Brandon, Katrina, and Alvaro Umaña. "Costa Rica's Real Riches." *Americas Magazine.* August 1991.

This article describes the creation of Costa Rica's megapark system, and how it attempts to involve local people in the design of large, integrated conservation and development areas. It includes brief descriptions of each of Costa Rica's megaparks.

16.5 Wells, Michael, and Katrina Brandon. "The Principles and Practice of Buffer Zones and Local Participation in Biodiversity Conservation." *Ambio* 22(2-3):157-62. 1993.

Recognition is growing that the successful management of protected areas ultimately depends on the cooperation and support of local people. As a result, there has been a dramatic increase in financial support for projects attempting to link the conservation of biodiversity in protected areas with local social and economic development. Drawing on the analysis of twenty-three integrated conservation-development projects (ICDPs) in fourteen developing countries, the authors explore the challenges which have arisen in operationalizing two key concepts which lie at the heart of community-based conservation.

The first is buffer zones; the second is greater participation of local people in conservation and development. The authors describe important practical constraints which have so far limited the effective implementation of these two concepts. Despite some critical constraints operating outside individual projects' sphere of influence, they conclude that innovative, well designed projects that constructively address local people-park relationships are essential to the conservation of biodiversity.

*Part Five*

Social Policy in Sectoral Analysis

Housing and Urban Development

17.1 Bamberger, Michael, and Alberto Harth. "Can Shelter Projects Meet Low-Income Needs? The Experience of El Salvador." In Geoffrey Payne, ed. *Low Income Housing in the Developing World*. Chichester: John Wiley and Sons, Ltd. 1984.

This paper summarizes the main findings and conclusions of the evaluation of the El Salvador Sites and Services Housing Projects and proposes some general lessons for the provision of affordable low-cost housing in other countries.

17.2 Bamberger, Michael. "The Role of Self-Help Housing in Low-Cost Shelter Programs for the Third World." *Built Environment* 8(2):95-107. 1982.

The author reviews the lessons to be drawn from World Bank housing projects with respect to the potential contribution of self-help in providing affordable and socially acceptable housing to low-income groups.

17.3 Campbell, Tim. "Environmental Dilemmas and the Urban Poor." In H. Jeffrey Leonard, ed. *Environment and the Poor: Development Strategies for a Common Agenda*. New Brunswick, N.J. and Oxford: Transaction Books. 1989.

This chapter examines in detail some of the assumptions related to urban environmental decay. It is divided into three parts: the first demonstrates the magnitude of the urban environmental challenge in terms of the scale of urbanization and the degree of poverty in developing country cities. The second section examines the forms of environmental trade-offs facing policy makers into the next century, subdivided by scale. This discussion of environment-development trade-offs at the household level is followed by consideration of the environmental city at large. The third part of the chapter contains policy prescriptions and suggested areas for action.

The author invokes the notion of an "urban ecosystem" which makes it possible to visualize the city as a place in which a wide variety of resources—natural, human, and social—are intertwined, some created, some consumed, some left as wastes. Among the most important environmental resources for the urban poor are informational resources in the form of social ties and networks that help sustain the survival strategies of low-income populations.

In light of this view, the widely observed costs of giant cities must be weighed against the environmental benefits that form much of the attraction of cities for the poor. This does not diminish the serious toll that degradation has taken on the health and safety of all residents, as well as on the future development prospects for urbanized developing countries.

17.4 Cernea, Michael M. "Urban Development and Compulsory Population Displacement." *Practicing Anthropology* 12(3):10-19. 1990.

The paper examines the social and economic issues raised by population displacement in urban settings, their causal mechanisms, the typology of displacement processes, and the policy issues involved in improving the outcomes of involuntary resettlement.

17.5 Keare, Douglas H., and Scott Parris. *Evaluation of Shelter Programs for the Urban Poor: Principal Findings*. World Bank Staff Working Paper no. 547. Washington, D.C. 1982.

The paper reports on the evaluation of four shelter projects for urban poor in El Salvador, the Philippines, Senegal, and Zambia conducted between 1975 and 1980. This evaluation confirmed that the first generation of Bank-supported urban shelter projects had been remarkably successful. Self-help construction methods were relatively efficient. The impacts of projects on the housing stock were generally greater than anticipated. The projects were affordable and generally accessible to the target populations. Measurements indicate that the impacts on the socioeconomic conditions of the participants fulfilled expectations without negative impacts on expenditures for food and other basic necessities.

Notwithstanding this general record of success, the projects encountered some problems and produced some unexpected results: most projects experienced delays in implementation; materials loan components were not as successful as expected; support packages for small businesses encountered problems; and two of the first three projects experienced cost recovery problems.

In addition, the use of family labor in construction was less than expected and the demand for rental accommodations and credit greater than expected. The analysis of successes and shortcomings supports recommendations that future projects include explicit provisions and opportunities for rental arrangements and incorporate credit provisions more nearly tailored to the needs of targeted families.

17.6 Moser, O. Caroline. "Housing." In L. Ostergaard, ed. *Gender and Development: A Practical Guide*. London: Routledge. 1991.

17.7 Moser, O. Caroline. "The Urban Context: Human Settlements and the Environment." In S. Sontheimer, ed. *A Reader on Women and Environment*. Rome: Italian Association for Women and Development. 1991.

17.8 World Bank. *Urban Policy and Economic Development: An Agenda for the 1990s*. A World Bank Policy Paper. Washington, D.C. 1991

Donor assistance to the urban sector in developing countries since the early 1970s has concentrated on the public provision of shelter and residential infrastructure and only more recently on municipal development and housing finance. While these efforts have succeeded in physical terms, they have not achieved citywide or sectorwide policy or institutional impacts. Rather, they tended to "projectize" the city at the neighborhood level.

External assistance has not addressed the major constraints on the urban economy and the need for policy reform. What is needed is a change in the objectives of external assistance in the urban sector. Such assistance should focus on the policy and institutional requirements for improving the productivity of the urban economy.

This paper, of which the principal author was a Bank political scientist, outlines a policy framework and strategy for improving urban economies' productivity, alleviating urban poverty, and improving the management of the urban environment. Chapter 1 defines the economic basis for continuing urban growth and assesses the legacy of government and donor efforts. Chapter 2 focuses on the key constraints to urban productivity, the persistence and increase of urban poverty, and the growing crisis of the urban environment. Chapter 3 proposes an agenda of policy reform and action for the developing countries, and Chapter 4 presents a broadened strategy for the World Bank.

Additional publications relevant to this topic can be found in Sections 2, 3, 6, 8, and 22.

Rural Development

18.1 Barnes, Douglas. *Electric Power for Rural Growth: How Electricity Affects Rural Life in Developing Nations*. Boulder, Col.: Westview Press. Rural Studies Series. 1988.

This book is a comprehensive empirical investigation of the recent public policy controversy over rural electrification in developing nations and is based on surveys in India, Colombia, and Indonesia. In separate chapters the book examines the major policy issues in the controversy, particularly the impact of rural electrification programs on (a) agricultural development; (b) small scale industrialization; (c) patterns of social life; (d) rural equity; and (e) the benefits and costs of rural electrification.

The author weighs both the direct and indirect benefits and costs of electrification. The comparative aspect of his research helps counteract the country-specific nature of most energy project evaluations, and the scope of the analysis provides a broad picture, rather than focusing on the impact on households alone.

18.2 Barnes, Douglas. "The Impact of Rural Electrification and Infrastructure on Agricultural Changes in India, 1966-1980." *Economic and Political Weekly* 21(1):26-34. 1986.

Questions have been raised concerning the vast capital investments in rural electrification and whether they have had the desired impact on rural areas. This study empirically examines what agricultural impact electricity and other infrastructure improvements have had on 108 villages in three state in India.

The conclusion is that electrification has had a direct impact on agricultural productivity, in addition to other social impacts, by encouraging private investment in electric pumps. However, farmers have also made substantial investments in diesel pumps, although at a somewhat slower rate. In villages first receiving electricity a trend to substitute electric pumps for diesel ones was found. Although the impact of rural electrification on agriculture has been significant, there has been no explosive agricultural growth as was anticipated by many of the early planners.

18.3 de Wilde, John C., Thayer Scudder, and others. *Experiences with Agricultural Development in Tropical Africa* vol. I. Baltimore: The Johns Hopkins University Press. 1967.

Undertaken with the participation of Dr. Thayer Scudder, this book is one of the earliest World Bank studies with an anthropological input.

18.4 Hall, Anthony, and others. *Brazil: An Interim Assessment of Rural Development Programs for the Northeast.* A World Bank Country Study. Washington, D.C. 1983.

This study is the work of a multi-disciplinary team, including a rural sociologist, who synthesized the economic and operational experience gathered by the World Bank during six years of assistance to rural development projects in Brazil's Northeast. The analysis focuses on the federal programs for rural development and water resource management in use, or considered for use, as of 1983 to help small farmers in the region.

The results of public interventions during the 1950s-1970s were modest. Both inter- and intra-regional disparities continued to exist. Per capita income in the Northeast in 1979 was about US$800, or 40 percent of the national average. Regional health, nutrition, and education indicators were also below national levels, even though progress in reducing poverty in the region occurred, especially in the 1970s. Within the region, the rural population had lower earnings on average than the urban population, even after adjusting for income in kind, and also ranked lower on most social indicators.

Yields of export and basic food crops in the Northeast were lower than the yields prevailing in other parts of Brazil. Average yields also declined or exhibited little improvement during the decade preceding the report. The region had a highly skewed land tenure structure, with many small subsistence farms coexisting with large farms devoted mainly to plantation agriculture or cattle raising. Over the two decades preceding the study, the distribution of land worsened and land formerly available to sharecroppers and tenants was put to other uses.

18.5 Mehta, Shiv R. *Social Development in Mauritius: A Study on Rural Modernization in an Island Community.* New Delhi: Wiley Eastern Limited. 1981.

The author contends that the roots of the severe social problems and economic contradictions in Mauritius lie in the land tenure system and terribly skewed land distribution. Attempting to illuminate the potential for social development, this book focuses on the value systems, education, aspirations held for children, and political knowledge of the poor. The author, a sociologist who created and headed the Monitoring and Evaluation Unit of the World Bank financed Rural Development Project in Mauritius for several years during the 1970s, conducted several sociological field studies on which this book is largely based.

The author presents, among other data, the findings of a sample survey of twenty-nine village council areas of Mauritius, qualified by his own warning about the inherent limitations of the questionnaire-survey approach. Two main points are made: an accelerating homogenization of the ethnic-cultural differences between various groups is at work in Mauritius; and, while the much emphasized racial and cultural divisions are becoming less pronounced, the cleavages of a strict socioeconomic and class nature within the society are deepening and becoming potentially more explosive. These are crucial issues to be addressed by Mauritian development strategies.

Topics addressed in this book, which date from the author's research in Mauritius, are also addressed in the following articles:

- "Role Analysis of the Village Development Office in Mauritius." *Indian Journal of Social Work* VIII (1) (April 1981)
- "Maternal and Child Health and Family Planning Status in and Island Village Community." *Journal of Family Welfare* XXVII (4) (June 1982)
- "Setting up a Fishermen's Cooperative in Mauritius." *Indian Cooperative Review* (October 1982)
- "Women's Organizations in Rural Development: A Case Study of Their Role in Mauritius." *Man and Life. Journal of the Institute of Social Research and Applied Anthropology.* (Calcutta) 9(3-4) (1983).

Additional publications relevant to the topics can be found in Sections 2, 3, 12, 13, 14, and 19.

Agricultural Extension

19.1 Adisak Sreensunpagit. "Monitoring and Evaluation of Extension: Experience in Thailand." In M.M. Cernea, J.K. Coulter, and J.F.A. Russell, eds. *Agricultural Extension by Training and Visit: The Asian Experience.* World Bank. Washington, D.C. 1983.

This paper discusses the experience accumulated in Thailand with the monitoring and evaluation of the national Training and Visit (T&V) system of agricultural extension. The paper first describes the organizational structure of the Monitoring and Evaluation Unit (MEU), next outlines the methodology employed in monitoring and evaluation, and then summarizes some of the specific studies carried out by the unit.

The two main forms of monitoring and evaluation are the surveys carried out periodically for both monitoring and impact evaluation purposes, and the in-depth sociological case studies on special topics. Each is described in some detail, and several findings generated by these studies are summarized. A brief discussion follows on the project management's use of monitoring and evaluation findings. Finally, some of the difficulties encountered are also highlighted. Several recommendations on how to improve future monitoring and evaluation activities in Thailand are suggested in the concluding section (see also related entry no. 19.6).

19.2 Cernea, Michael M., John K. Coulter, and John F.A. Russell, eds. *Research-Extension-Farmer: A Two-Way Continuum for Agricultural Development.* World Bank. Washington, D.C. 1985.

The volume focuses on the sociological and institutional issues of the complex communication processes between farmers and agricultural researchers. The linking mechanism between these two sets of actors is the extension organization, created because without it the necessary communication would be much diminished.

Starting from this premise, most papers in this volume analyze why, in various countries, there is often little close collaboration between agricultural research and agricultural extension even though they have a common ultimate objective. The underlying technical, sociological, institutional, and economic implications of building up such linkages are analyzed in detail, and specific recommendations are made for action programs, particularly, but not exclusively, under the framework of the training and visit (T&V) system of extension.

The editors, who also organized the international symposium, of which this volume is the result, have grouped the issues of research-extension linkages into four main areas: (a) policy and institutional issues in the improvement of research and extension linkages (contained in five chapters on Bangladesh, India, and Indonesia); (b) identification of farmers' priority production problems; (three chapters on farming systems research); (c) the generation of improved technology and its on-farm validation (the chapters on Bangladesh and Sri Lanka); and (d) the joint identification and formulation of extension messages by extension and research staff (four chapters on IRRI research in Indonesia, Pakistan, and Thailand).

19.3 Cernea, Michael M., John K. Coulter, and John F.A. Russell. "Building the Research-Extension-Farmer Continuum: Some Current Issues." In M.M. Cernea, J.K. Coulter, and J.F.A. Russell, eds. *Research-Extension-Farmer: A Two-Way Continuum for Agricultural Development*. World Bank. Washington, D.C. 1985.

This chapter establishes the conceptual and operational framework for the discussions which follow it within the volume (see entry 19.2). The authors argue that the social mechanisms of the extension organization (T&V) must build a continuum between research stations and their ultimate beneficiary, the farmer. This continuum should be a two-way communication process, not only a one-sided flow from researcher to farmer, since each actor in this continuum can mutually enforce and inform the others.

The paper outlines the main issues of concern for extension practitioners: the causes of the weak links between extension and research; the choices confronting policy makers in deciding on investments for research and extension; the need for response to production problems as perceived by farmers; and the importance but relative neglect of the social science perspective in developing the research-extension-farmer continuum.

19.4 Cernea, Michael M., John K. Coulter, and John F.A. Russell, eds. *Agricultural Extension by Training and Visit: The Asian Experience*. World Bank. Washington, D.C. 1983.

The volume examines the organization and communication processes of agricultural extension from a technical and sociological perspective, based on experiences in Asian countries with the Training and Visit (T&V) system of agricultural extension. Following the success of its first involvement with T&V extension in Turkey and India in the early 1970s, the World Bank became involved in financing over 90 projects that supported the introduction of the T&V system during the 1970s and early 1980s.

Managers of T&V systems from India, Indonesia, Nepal, the Philippines, Sri Lanka, Thailand, Burkina Faso, and Kenya contributed papers and case studies to this volume. It contains the country papers presented by extension system managers and evaluators from Asian countries, together with issue papers and a concluding chapter by the editors (see also entries 19.1, 19.5, 19.6).

19.5 Cernea, Michael M., John K. Coulter, and John F.A. Russell. "Strengthening Extension for Development: Current Issues and Prospects." In M.M. Cernea, J.K. Coulter, and J.F.A. Russell, eds. *Agricultural Extension by Training and Visit: The Asian Experience*. World Bank. Washington, D.C. 1983.

This chapter sums up the major issues discussed in the volume (see entry 19.4). The first set of issues revolves around the relationship between the essential factors of agricultural production—informed farmers, improved technology, available inputs, and attractive markets—and the effectiveness of extension services. Another set of important issues results from the sociological aspects of the knowledge transfer process. Increasing the effectiveness of this process depends on improving the quality of the extension workers' services, not simply increasing their numbers. Because the participation of the beneficiaries in the process is a deciding factor in project success, an understanding of village sociology and face-to-face contact between farmers and village-level workers in agricultural communities which are still emerging from subsistence agriculture are vital.

Maintaining the extension system's dynamism requires good leadership and innovation. Managers need rapid feedback through a monitoring and evaluation system which assesses the relevance of extension messages, the delivery system, rates of sustained adoption of new technology, and overall impact. This requires an appropriate blend of rapid appraisal, surveys, and in-depth case studies.

19.6 Cernea, Michael M. "Evaluation of Farmers' Reactions to Extension Advice: A Comment." In M. M. Cernea, J. K. Coulter, and J. F. A. Russell, eds. *Agricultural Extension by Training and Visit: The Asian Experience*. World Bank. Washington, D.C. 1983.

Monitoring performance and evaluating impact still lag behind the progress in organizing T&V extension services although they are essential to managing extension and in continuously adjusting the service to the needs of farmers. However, there is little quality information generated through empirical evaluation of the agronomic, social, or economic processes triggered by T&V extension, or of farmers' reactions to advice.

An important cause of this information scarcity is excessive reliance on the cumbersome large-scale sample survey approach and neglect of simpler, speedier, more in-depth, and village-focused assessments. Comparing financial costs of different types of monitoring studies experimented with in Thailand and their uneven practical value, the author points out the specific tradeoffs between approaches. No single strategy is perfect. If the design for monitoring and evaluation is overambitious, given the limited resources that are typically available, it will fail. The Thai experience has proven that less expensive, comparable, in-depth sociological case studies are easier to design and carry out and their results can be made available more quickly.

19.7 Cernea, Michael M. "Sociological Dimensions of Extension Organization: The Introduction of the T&V System in India." In B. Crouch and S. Chamala, eds. *Extension Education and Rural Development* vol. 2. Chichester: John Wiley and Sons, Ltd. 1981.

The most significant progress in agricultural extension worldwide in the seventies was the development of a new extension system called the "Training and Visits" (T&V) extension system, and its successful implementation in several large countries in South and East Asia. An identical set of policy principles and organizational rules was used to create similar extension organizations in different countries, including Bangladesh, India, Indonesia, Malaysia, Sri Lanka, and Thailand with financial assistance provided by the World Bank through agricultural projects.

The author discusses the structure of the T&V extension system, its organizational principles and what makes it different from other extension arrangements, in particular its sociological implications. He reports on the introduction of the new system in six Indian states—Assam, Bihar, Madhya Pradesh, Orissa, Rajasthan and West Bengal.

19.8 Epstein, T. Scarlett. "The Training and Visit System and its Socio-Cultural Setting." *Culture and Agriculture*. Issue 20. 1983.

The paper describes elements of the Training and Visit extension system and discusses its strengths and weaknesses. It asserts that extension projects using this approach have often not taken the human element fully into account in extension, particularly the needs of farm women.

Education

20.1 Colletta, Nat J. *Achieving and Sustaining Universal Primary Education: A Review of the International Experience with Relevance to India.* World Bank Policy Planning and Research Working Paper no. 166. Washington, D.C. 1989.

To achieve its goal of full enrollment of children aged six to fourteen by 1995, India will have to have increased its enrollment from less than 80 percent to 100 percent in the space of a decade and must reduce the high dropout rate (over 50 percent by fifth grade) to near zero for eight grades. Funding, local accountability, relevant curricula and instructional materials, emphasizing basic knowledge and reasoning skills, good teacher training, and upgrading poorer schools are all important factors in achieving universal primary education. But promoting female enrollment may also require making special efforts to release young girls from their household responsibilities, particularly child care.

20.2 Colletta, Nat J. "Worker Education: Revolution and Reform." In John N. Hawkins, ed. *Education and Social Change in the People's Republic of China.* New York: Praeger. 1983.

20.3 Colletta, Nat J., and T. Todd. "The Limits to Nonformal Education and Village Development: Lessons from the Sarvodaya Shramadana Movement." In George Papagianis and John Bock, eds. *Nonformal Education and National Development.* New York: Praeger. 1983.

20.4 Colletta, Nat J. *Worker-Peasant Education in the People's Republic of China: Study of Adult Education in Post-Revolutionary China.* World Bank Staff Working Paper no. 527. Washington, D.C. 1982.

The political and economic transformations which have taken place in China since the 1920s have drastically changed the face of Chinese adult education. The most important functions of adult education have been political socialization, the solving of practical problems in industry and agriculture, and the raising of the basic educational level of the masses. The relative priority of these aspects has shifted over the past few decades with ideological shifts.

At the time this study was conducted, the educational pendulum was swinging toward the institutionalization of adult education programs with emphasis on quality and access. While success has been marked, many problems such as rural-urban inequities and the potential risk of losing the relevance of programs to local needs through an emphasis on the formalization of adult education, among others, still remain.

The author offers recommendations for more empirical evaluation of adult education programs, particularly focusing on such studies as the comparative cost-effectiveness of on-job versus vocational school training and the differential impact of various forms of mass media.

20.5 Colletta, Nat J. "Assessing the Impact of Nonformal Education Programs on National Objectives." In D. Windham and L. Anderson, eds. *Education and Development: Issues in the Analysis and Planning of Post-Colonial Societies*. Boston: Dr. Heath and Co. 1982.

20.6 Colletta, Nat J., and Ross Kidd, eds. *Tradition for Development: Indigenous Structures and Folk Media in Non-Formal Education*. Bonn: The German Foundation for International Development. 1982.

The central thesis of this paper is that a culture-based nonformal education development strategy enables new knowledge, skills and attitudes to be introduced within the framework of existing knowledge, cultural patterns, institutions, values, and human resources. That the indigenous culture is the fabric within which development can best be woven is based upon three assumptions: indigenous elements have traditional legitimacy for participants in development programs; these elements contain symbols that express and identify various valid perceptions of reality; and they serve multiple functions—they can involve, entertain, instruct, and inform.

The author discusses the following indigenous social/cultural forms relevant to culture-based education: (a) traditional leadership and functional roles; (b) traditional communication systems; (c) indigenous organizational forms; (d) indigenous socio-economic processes; (e) indigenous knowledge systems; (f) traditional etiology and belief systems, and (g) indigenous technologies.

20.7 Colletta, Nat J. *American Schools for the Natives of Ponape: Study of Education and Culture Change in Micronesia*. Honolulu: The University Press of Hawaii, East-West Center. 1980.

20.8 Colletta, Nat J., and David Radcliffe. "Nonformal Education: An Educological Approach." *Canadian and International Education* 9(2). 1980.

20.9 Fuller, Bruce, and Aklilu Habte, eds. *Adjusting Educational Policies: Conserving Resources While Raising School Quality.* World Bank Discussion Paper no. 132. Washington, D.C. 1992.

African governments and donor agencies have realized in recent years that development programs can only succeed if built upon sound policy and institutional foundations. Since the mid-1980s, several educational policy adjustment programs have been initiated in Sub-Saharan Africa.

This volume explores these early policy efforts, drawing on reports from government leaders and donor representatives in Ghana, Malawi, and Senegal. Three specific questions are addressed: What types of policy and budget changes have been attempted? What lessons have been learned regarding local school and community effects, stemming from central policy adjustments? How can policy programs better complement long term efforts to strengthen institutions?

The papers in this volume were presented at a conference attended by government officials and donor agencies, co-sponsored by the World Bank and USAID. Highlights of the conference debate are reported.

20.10 Fuller, Bruce. *Raising School Quality in Developing Countries: What Investments Boost Learning?* World Bank Discussion Paper no. 2. Washington, D.C. 1986.

Low levels of student achievement and school quality persist in developing countries. The importance of school quality in raising literacy and influencing economic development is reviewed in this paper. Some of the lessons learned in how best to improve the quality and efficiency of schools are discussed within four areas: school quality and development; defining school quality; improving school quality; and increasing school efficiency,

20.11 Heyneman, Stephen. "Protection of the Textbook Industry in Developing Countries: In the Public Interest?" *Book Research Quarterly.* Winter 1990. 3-11.

Many developing countries protect their textbook industries to safeguard national image, local jobs, infant industries, and foreign exchange. Yet, as this article points out, protection has costs, and these costs have become excessive. Reducing protection for textbooks production, the author argues, would benefit both education and economies in developing countries.

20.12 Heyneman, Stephen. "Economic Crisis and the Quality of Education." *International Journal of Educational Development* 10(2/3):115-29. 1990.

At a time when the education system has expanded in size to a point unprecedented in history, a crisis of similar proportions has affected the ability of the system to operate. This crisis has deeply hurt the quality of education in developing countries. It has been particularly devastating to the non-salary category of the recurrent budgets, that is, resources available for reading materials, chalk, furniture, and the like.

Countries are attempting to adjust their education systems in an effort to control the impact of the economic crisis, but the changes in policy are not benign. Such adjustments might affect teachers' salaries and their conditions of service, the balance between public and non-public responsibilities in educational management and finance, and the number and kinds of roles the education system is expected to perform.

The financial crisis may, however, have some positive results. It may increase the professional capacity to manage the education system based upon what is feasible rather than upon precedent. With that, considerably greater professional credibility may develop within the education sector than would otherwise exist.

The crisis may clarify to the world that many policy dilemmas in education—the structure of teacher rewards, diversification of financial resources for higher education, and non-governmental responsibilities in vocational education—are not specific to developing countries, but are policy dilemmas from which lessons can be drawn across categories of economic development.

Nevertheless, no matter how serious and successful education sector adjustment may be, education systems in developing countries will remain impoverished in terms of physical resources by comparison to OECD countries. That problem may require multilateral solutions based on new international agreements on the necessity of basic education. Before a discussion of new solutions can be meaningful, the story must commence where it began—at the time of hope and quantitative expansion.

20.13 Heyneman, Stephen. "The World Economic Crisis and the Quality of Education." *Journal of Education Finance* 15:456-69. 1990.

Universal education as a public right, an incontestible social obligation, and a sound economic investment is an outgrowth of the post-World War II era. Throughout the 1950 and 1960s, newly independent countries in Asia and Africa identified universal education as one of the highest public priorities. By the mid-1970s the developing world contained the majority of the world's school-age population and was facing an economic crisis that affected its ability to pay its own bills and to meet its external and internal obligations.

The author examines the effects of debt servicing, budget reductions, and adjustment on education expenditures, as well as the managerial challenge of providing a quality basic education under different adjustment options.

20.14 Heyneman, Stephen, and Bernadette Etienne. "Higher Education in Developing Countries: What, How and When?" *Institute of Development Studies (IDS) Bulletin* 20(1):41-8. 1989.

Higher education in developing countries no longer resembles the object of hope and public aspiration that it did in the 1960s. Expanding enrollments, limited financing, and changing expectations of students and the marketplace require higher education institutions to make difficult choices about three levels of academic quality: Should the university attempt to disseminate existing knowledge? Should the university participate in a dialogue that contributes to the production of new knowledge? Should be university seek to be recognized as a contributor to new knowledge?

The author examines how the economy, the language of instruction, and the comparative advantages of the different levels of academic quality affect the planning, financing and management of universities.

20.15 Heyneman, Stephen, and Bruce Fuller. "Third World School Quality: Current Collapse, Future Potential." *Educational Researcher* 18(2):12-9. 1989.

Eager to boost literacy, economic growth, and national institutions, developing country governments and international aid agencies have greatly expanded schooling since the 1950s. Enrollments have quintupled since the late 1950s—from 100 million to more than 500 million children.

The sharp economic decline felt over the past decade throughout the developing world, however, has led to deep cuts in education budgets. Child populations are doubling every twenty years in many countries. Popular demand for primary schooling, as manifest in enrollment rates, continues to skyrocket. This conflict between ever-rising enrollments and falling resources is severely eroding school quality.

The authors detail and illustrate this collapse of educational quality, calling on North American educators to recognize this quiet crisis and to contribute to its remedy. In addition, they map out a strategy for attacking the problem, drawing on the growing body of developing country research and new initiatives coming from international organizations.

20.16 Heyneman, Stephen. "Multilevel Methods for Analyzing School Effects in Developing Countries." *Comparative Education Review* (November 1989): 498-504.

One important problem in predicting academic achievement is how to handle the "location" from which the sample is drawn since it varies considerably—different classrooms, schools, districts, states, and occasionally, different countries. Pupils in the same "units" tend to share common experiences (and educational inputs) that make their results more like each other than would be the case if pupils were to be drawn from a random population.

How should this unit of analysis problem be handled? Many studies in the 1970s used ordinary least squares (OLS), which assumed that the variability of each variable was identical. This assumption was clearly a problem since variance within one level was naturally very different from other levels. For example, mother's educational background will differ within the sample as a whole, but it will differ differently according to the classroom, the state, or the country.

The same may be true of educational inputs, textbooks, and the like. Now there is a way to incorporate such differences using a statistical technique called multilevel analysis (MLA). The author comments on the results (and the tone) of one recent experiment using MLA.

20.17 Heyneman, Stephen, and Ingemar Fagerlind, eds. *University Examinations and Standardized Testing—Principles, Experience, and Policy Options.* World Bank Technical Paper no. 78. Washington, D.C. 1988.

As countries today renew their use of educational testing, new concerns have arisen about how better to manage such testing. China provides one example of the new emphasis on purposefully managing the policies toward educational testing. In September 1984, the Chinese government asked the Economic Development Institute of the World Bank to assist the officials of the Ministry of Education in thinking through some of the policy options for examinations and standardized testing.

This book summarizes the descriptions of testing systems in selected Organization for Economic Co-operational Development (OECD) countries and the advice given to the government officials following the April 1985 meeting. The attention devoted to problems of logistics and to economies of scale are perhaps more pertinent to large, heterogeneous countries such as China. However, this book contends that many of the principles discussed at the meeting and presented here are applicable to other developing countries.

20.18 Heyneman, Stephen, and Joseph P. Farrell. "Textbooks in Developing Countries: Economic and Pedagogical Choices." In Philip G. Altbach and Gail P. Kelly, eds. *Textbooks in the Third World: Policy, Content and Context*. New York: Garland Publishing, Inc. 1988.

Reading materials strongly determine the kind of educational experience a nation is able to provide for its students. The paper examines the issues and choices made by governments in textbook provision—market size, state versus private sector production and distribution, local versus international publishing, copyright provisions, textbook fees, curriculum and textbook content, and textbook provision as part of a package of interventions.

The author concludes that before discussing options to generate additional resources for textbook provision by instituting savings elsewhere, or by seeking savings within the budget category at risk, a government must define a clear and comprehensive textbook policy.

20.19 Heyneman, Stephen. "Curricular Economics in Secondary Education: An Emerging Crisis in Developing Countries." *Prospects* 8(1):63-74. 1987.

20.20 Heyneman, Stephen. "Uses of Examinations in Developing Countries: Selection, Research, and Education Sector Management." *International Journal of Educational Development* 7(4):251-63. 1987.

In September 1984, the Chinese government asked the Economic Development Institute of the World Bank to assist officials in the Ministry of Education to think through various policy options for examinations and standardized testing. In response, a meeting was held in April 1985 in Beijing. The meeting was attended by all provincial and national officials in charge of examinations, technicians and psychometricians in charge of designing examination items, and senior university officials and planners in the Ministry of Education.

Attending from outside the country were the chief executive officers of examination agencies in three OECD countries; directors of the National Assessment of Educational Progress and the International Association for the Evaluation of Educational Achievement; and experts on the examination systems in Sweden, Australia and Kenya.

The article summarizes the comments given to the Chinese Government on three areas: specific testing issues such as aptitude versus achievement tests, multiple choice versus other formats, and so on; management issues within the system of selection, such as whether government agencies or universities should make the selection decision, and whether a testing agency should be autonomous from government control; and the uses of testing to perform necessary research and education sector management functions.

20.21 Heyneman, Stephen, and Daphne White. *The Quality of Education and Economic Development*. A World Bank Symposium. Washington, D.C. 1986.

The two studies presented in this volume were originally prepared for a conference on school quality sponsored by the World Bank's Research Committee and held in May 1983. The first study relates to the economic growth that might result from expenditures on the quality of education. The second study concerns the best way to implement changes intended to improve the quality of education. For many years the educational systems of developing countries placed emphasis on growth and on the need to provide more schools and more classrooms for students. Attention has been shifting toward the quality and the value of education being received.

20.22 Heyneman, Stephen. "The Nature of a Practical Curriculum." *Education with Production* 4(2):91-104. 1986.

Curricular equity is central to equal educational opportunity. Expensive mistakes are made when educational planners polarize themselves with primary school curriculums that either prepare students to continue in school or enter the marketplace. What then should educational planners do to design an equitable curriculum that instills the knowledge most effective for productivity on the part of all those who attend school? The paper examines four sources of evidence that can provide information to educational planners—the complexity of the skills to be taught for the age group; the nature of public and parental demand; the monetary and cognitive costs; and the economic benefits.

20.23 Heyneman, Stephen. "Diversifying Secondary School Curricula in Developing Countries: An Implementation History and Some Policy Options." *International Journal of Educational Development* 5(4):283-88. 1985.

This paper describes the history of the diversified curriculum debate. The first section briefly refers to the precedents for such discussions during the colonial era. A second section describes the institutional environment behind the beginning of bilateral and multilateral assistance to diversified curricula in 1960. The third section summarizes the changes in thinking about diversified curricula that have occurred in the World Bank over the last 20 years.

The third section is divided into three subsections: the original World Bank rationales for diversified education (1960-70); the implementation history (1970-80); and post-

1980 strategies, including financing research. The paper concludes with a fourth section which refers to the options on diversified education ahead.

20.24 Heyneman, Stephen, and others. "Textbooks in the Philippines. Evaluation of the Pedagogical Impact of a Nationwide Investment." *Educational Evaluation and Policy Analysis* 6(2):139-50. 1984.

Also available as World Bank Reprint Series no. 335. Washington, D.C.

20.25 Heyneman, Stephen. "Research on Education in the Developing Countries." *International Journal of Educational Development* 4(4):293-304. 1984.

Developing countries are in a major educational crisis. Educational opportunity has expanded but quality has been sacrificed. In some instances the quality of education has become so low that one might do well to question whether the costs of expansion do not outweigh the benefits. Research on education has not prepared the developing countries to meet the crisis at hand.

The article mentions three examples—in pedagogy, in curriculum, and in "deschooling" theory—where educational research has not been helpful. On the other hand, the article points to several areas where there has been useful work, and where new work might make a substantial contribution in the years ahead.

20.26 Heyneman, Stephen. "Educational Investment and Economic Productivity: Evidence from Malawi." *International Journal of Educational Development* 4(1):9-15. 1984.

Tracer study data on the destination and earnings of a sample of nearly 1,000 secondary school graduates were used to estimate the returns to investment in the Malawi Certificate of Education. Even when adjustment is made for the possibility of unemployment among graduates, the social rate of return is estimated to be in the order of 20 percent and the private rate 50 percent. These results are used to explain the strong private demand for entry into secondary education and to support the case for further expansion of such schools in Malawi.

20.27 Heyneman, Stephen, and William Loxley. "The Distribution of Primary School Quality within High- and Low-Income Countries." *Comparative Education Review* 27(1):108-18. 1983.

20.28 Heyneman, Stephen, and William Loxley. "The Effect of Primary School Quality on Academic Achievement Across Twenty-nine High- and Low-Income Countries." *The American Journal of Sociology* 88(6):1162-94. 1983.

Also available as World Bank Reprint Series no. 268. Washington, D.C.

Most previous research on effects of schooling has concluded that the effect of school or teacher quality on academic achievement is less than that of family background or other student characteristics that predate entry into school. However, the evidence is derived mainly from a few of the world's school systems (mostly in Europe, Japan, and North America). This paper explores diverse influences on pupil achievement in Africa, Asia, Latin America, and the Middle East.

Children who attend primary school in countries with low per capita incomes have learned substantially less after similar amounts of time in school than pupils in high-income countries. At the same time, the lower the income of the country, the weaker the influence of pupils' social status on achievement. Conversely, in low-income countries, the effect of school and teacher quality on academic achievement in primary school is comparatively greater.

From these data, which are more representative of the world's population of schoolchildren than those used in previous studies, it is possible to conclude that the predominant influence on student learning is the quality of the schools and teachers to which children are exposed.

20.29 Heyneman, Stephen, guest ed. Special Issue: "Education and the World Bank." *Canadian and International Education* 12(1). 1983.

This journal edition contains five papers. "Summary of the 1980 World Bank Sector Policy Paper," by Wadi D. Haddad, analyses the relationship between education as an investment in the social and cultural resources of a nation, and education as an investment in economic development. The paper also relates this view of education to the lending policy and program of the World Bank.

"The World Bank and Education: Reflections of a Partner," by Sippanondha Ketudat, examines the risks and advantages of the cooperation between the World Bank and developing countries in education and human resources development. "World Bank Lending in Education: One View of How It Happens," by Laurence Wolff, describes the stages whereby the World Bank, working with a national government, develops and funds a specific project. "Overview of the World Bank's Research on Education," by Peter R. Moock and Robin S. Horn, describes how educational research in the Bank is organized and financed and how research outputs are disseminated. "Where the Bank Is Going in the Field of Education," by Aklilu Habte, examines the diverse pattern of World Bank lending in education.

20.30 Heyneman, Stephen. "Improving the Quality of Education in Developing Countries." *Finance & Development*. March 1983. 18-21.

20.31 Heyneman, Stephen. "Education during a Period of Austerity: Uganda, 1971-1981." *Comparative Education Review* 27(3):403-13. 1983.

20.32 Heyneman, Stephen, and William Loxley. "Influences on Academic Achievement Across High- and Low-Income Countries: A Re-Analysis of IEA Data." *Sociology of Education* 55(1):13-21. 1982.

Previous international studies of science achievement put the data through a winnowing process to decide which variables to keep in the final regressions. Variables were allowed to enter the final regressions if they met a minimum beta coefficient criterion of 0.05 averaged across rich and poor countries alike. The criterion was an average across all countries because the original idea was to identify the variables thought to be "important" across all societies taken together.

The question is whether this process tended to omit school variables that may have had strong effects within one country but not across the average of many countries. The authors re-entered variables for each country separately, using the same minimum entry criterion of 0.05, but within each country separately. Using only variables that have been found to be "important" in that particular society, they obtained different results, and the changes were of two sorts: they tended to increase significantly the variance explained by school effects, and this increase tended to be greatest in the "poorer" countries.

20.33 Heyneman, Stephen, and others. "Improving Elementary Mathematics Education in Nicaragua. An Experimental Study of the Impact of Textbooks and Radio on Achievement." *Journal of Educational Psychology* 73(4):556-67. 1981.

Also available as World Bank Reprint Series no. 391. Washington, D.C.

Because widespread availability of textbooks in the United States preceded research on the effectiveness of instructional materials, there has been little systematic study of their impact on student achievement. The developing world provides an appropriate setting for such studies. This article reports an experimental study of the impact of textbook availability on mathematics achievement of students in Nicaraguan first-grade classes.

This intervention is compared with control classes in which textbooks are relatively rare, and with a radio-based instructional program that uses student worksheets but no other textual material. Classes were assigned at random to the three conditions.

The control and two treatment groups scored similarly on a pretest of mathematical readiness.

Both the textbook and the radio treatments had significant positive effects on achievement. Availability of textbooks increased student posttest scores by about 3.5 items correct, approximately 0.33 of a standard deviation. Availability of the radio instructional program increased student posttest scores 14.9 items, about 1.5 standard deviations. Both interventions reduced the achievement gap between urban and rural students. However, the question remains whether either radio or textbook use is sufficiently powerful to close the substantial achievement gap that exists between the schools of high- and low-income societies.

20.34 Heyneman, Stephen. "Instruction in the Mother Tongue: The Question of Logistics." *Canadian and International Education* 9(2):88-94. 1980.

Three factors must be weighed before an investment is made in instructing students in the language spoken at home—the economic cost of materials, teacher training, and so on; the cognitive cost, if any, of using the mother tongue versus one of the other linguistic choices; and the logistical feasibility. This paper discusses logistical feasibility.

Drawing upon a representative sample of primary schools in an East African country it is discovered that only 22 percent of the classrooms are monolingual; 47 percent of the classrooms contain four or more languages. The average number/classroom is 3.8. The problems of intra-classroom linguistic heterogeneity must be overcome if mother tongue instruction, as policy, is to be realistic.

20.35 Heyneman, Stephen. "Differences between Developed and Developing Countries: Comment on Simmon and Alexander's Determinants of School Achievement." *Economic Development and Cultural Change* 28(2):403-6. 1980.

20.36 Heyneman, Stephen. *The Evaluation of Human Capital in Malawi.* World Bank Staff Working Paper no. 420. Washington, D.C. 1980.

Malawi has the same portion of its total population in elementary school as it had in 1911. Despite the fact that students attend school longer and are expected to absorb a wider variety of information and skills, the degree of efficiency by which this is accomplished suggests that improvements could be made.

The average 16-year old (eighth grade) Malawian student has attained approximately half the level of reading skills attained by the average 10-year old (fourth grade) student in North America, Western Europe or Japan. This is so because, among other reasons, the schools in Malawi have only one-hundredth the level of reading materials, equipment and pedagogical supplies available to schools in high-income areas of the world. Malawian students are also likely to be learning with significantly lower health and nutrition statuses, with over half reporting bouts with malaria, one in five with bilharzia, one in ten with trachoma and/or hookworm.

Despite a tenfold increase in the number of students since independence, the chance of attending secondary school is still only three out of one hundred. This is typical of education and training in general: it is scarce, and its scarcity helps to determine its profitability as an investment—to the society and the individual. The rate of reported unemployment among males who pass their MCE examinations is 0.7 percent and the economic social rate of return to secondary education at the very least is 14 percent. In sum, despite recent unprecedented expansion, international investments in Malawi's secondary education appear solid.

Suggestions that educational investment might act to cement social inequalities between one generation and the next should be put aside in the case of Malawi. Students from family backgrounds of relative poverty—on the average—perform equally well on selection examinations as do students from privileged family backgrounds. Moreover, earnings are determined not by an individual's family economic position but by education and ability. There is, in essence, no reason to suspect that investments in education would adversely affect social equality; and there is very good reason to suspect that new investments in education and training are badly needed.

Precisely what level of investment should be available for specific skill training, educational research, higher education and management should await more focused studies of these areas. But the available evidence would suggest a minimum level of new investment of approximately $3.5 million a year in primary education and $7.9 million a year in secondary education. Between 1980 and the year 2000 approximately $228 million (at 1978 prices) should be added to the current amount of investment in these two levels of basic education.

20.37 Heyneman, Stephen. "The Career Education Debate: Where the Differences Lie." *Teachers College Record* 80(4):660-88. 1979.

20.38 Heyneman, Stephen. "Why Impoverished Children Do Well in Ugandan Schools." *Comparative Education* 15(2):175-85. 1979.

20.39 Heyneman, Stephen. *Investment in Indian Education: Uneconomic?* World Bank Staff Working Paper no. 327. Washington, D.C. 1979.

In a country where the literacy rate is three in ten, it is often assumed that, economically, there is a surplus of education. This paper reviews the arguments. The case of India reflects a circumstance in which the existence of unemployment has led to the unjustified assumption that external productivity due to education is low.

The paper illustrates new ways to use equity in educational planning: in the distribution of per pupil expenditures, examination pass-rates, literacy, trade training and the availability of books. It also adds two new mechanisms for estimating the economic potential of educational investments: the amount of knowledge acquired in schools, and the degree of impact of school resources on academic achievement. From each source the paper concludes that there is reason to question the widely-held belief that additional investment in Indian education would be uneconomic.

20.40 Heyneman, Stephen, and others. *Textbooks and Achievement: What We Know.* World Bank Staff Working Paper no. 298. Washington, D.C. 1978.

Also published in Journal of Curriculum Studies 13(3):227-46. 1981.

This paper reviews the published evidence from less industrialized societies on the relationship between textbook availability and academic achievement. From the evidence so far, the availability of books appears to be the most consistent school factor in predicting academic achievement.

The paper discusses four areas for future research and evaluation: analysis of existing sets of survey information; collection of new data from intervention experiments; studies of book production and use in classrooms; and the exploration of distribution, equity and costs. If we had more knowledge on these subjects, the coming increase in textbook investments would be all the more secure. Given the inconsistent results from other pedagogical variables, the findings imply that investments in reading materials hold a distinct advantage when maximizing cognitive achievement.

20.41 Jamison, Dean T., Marlaine E. Lockheed, and others. "Education, Extension, and Farmer Productivity." In M. Akin, ed. *Encyclopedia of Educational Research.* New York: MacMillan. 1992.

20.42 Jamison, Dean T., and Marlaine E. Lockheed. "Participation in Schooling: Determinants and Learning Outcomes in Nepal." *Economic Development and Social Change* 35(2):279-306. 1987.

Also available as World Bank Reprint Series no. 408. Washington, D.C.

Based on data on three generations of members of 795 rural households, this article examines the determinants of adult cognitive competencies and of child school participation in Nepal. A number of results were consistent across analyses. Among these results were the following: attitudinal modernity was a significant determinant of attitude toward school; school availability had no effect on child school participation; and third-generation child school participation was determined jointly by second-generation landholdings, caste, schooling and numeracy, attitudinal modernity, and the child's sex.

20.43 Jimenez, Emmanuel, and Marlaine E. Lockheed, eds. "Private versus Public Education: An International Perspective." Special Issue of *International Journal of Educational Research*. 15(5). 1991.

20.44 Jimenez, Emmanuel, Marlaine E. Lockheed, and others. "School Effects and Costs for Private and Public Schools in the Dominican Republic." *International Journal of Education Research* 15(5):393-410 1991.

Also published informally as "School Effects and Costs for Private and Public Schools in the Dominican Republic." World Bank PPR Working Paper no. 288. Washington, D.C. 1989.

This study assesses the relative efficiency of urban public and of two types of private schools using methodological advances to correct for observed selection bias. A random subsample of 2,472 students in seventy-six schools was drawn from a 1982-83 national study of mathematics achievement in the Dominican Republic; independently gathered data was used for cost analysis.

Two-step methodology was employed to correct for background variables by estimating determinants of the choice of type of school and by using the results to correct for selection bias in achievement regression equations. Peer group characteristics and school inputs were included in the equations as independent variables that are positively correlated to achievement levels.

Selection bias was found to be significant. With bias corrected for and non-school factors held constant, the results indicate (a) students on average learn more in private schools than in public schools; (b) non-elite private schools are the most cost-effective; (c) private schools generate increased economic efficiency by taking advantage of peer group effects and market demands that are not satisfied by the public school system.

20.45 Jimenez, Emmanuel, Marlaine E. Lockheed, and others. "The Relative Efficiency of Public and Private Schools in Developing Countries." *The World Bank Research Observer* 6(2):205-18. 1991.

Also published informally as "The Relative Efficiency of Public and Private Schools in Developing Countries." World Bank PPR Working Paper no. 72. Washington, D.C. 1988.

On the basis of recent World Bank studies of secondary level data in Colombia, the Philippines, Tanzania, and Thailand, this paper suggests that private schools can be a cost-effective option for expanding secondary education in some developing countries. Private school students generally outperform public school counterparts on standardized tests, even when their slightly more advantaged backgrounds are taken into account. In addition, unit costs for private schools are dramatically lower than those for public schools. The paper discusses lessons that private schools provide for improving the efficiency of public schools.

20.46 Jimenez, Emmanuel, and Marlaine E. Lockheed. "Enhancing Girls' Learning through Single-Sex Education: Evidence and a Policy Conundrum." *Educational Evaluation and Policy Analysis* 11(2):117-42. 1989.

Also available as World Bank Reprint Series no. 453. Washington, D.C.

A key consideration in the policy debate on the appropriate role of single-sex education in predominantly coeducational school systems is relative benefit for male and female students. This paper analyzes the relative performance of single-sex education and coeducation in Thailand in enhancing eighth-grade male and female student scores on standardized mathematics tests, holding constant student background, peer, and school characteristics.

The main conclusions are that (a) single-sex schooling is more effective for female students and coeducational schooling is more effective for male students in improving student performance in mathematics; and (b) these differentials are largely due to peer effects rather than to specific characteristics of single-sex and coeducational classrooms or schools.

20.47 Jimenez, Emmanuel, Marlaine E. Lockheed, and others. "The Relative Efficiency of Private and Public Schools: The Case of Thailand." *The World Bank Economic Review* 2(2):139-64. 1988.

Also available as World Bank Reprint Series no. 436. Washington, D.C. 1988.

Cost-effectiveness is a key consideration in the policy debate on the appropriate role of private schools in predominantly public school systems. The article analyzes the relative performance of public and private schools in Thailand in enhancing eighth grade student scores in standardized mathematics tests, given student background and school characteristics. The authors' main conclusion is that private schools on average are more effective and less costly than public schools in improving student performance in mathematics.

20.48 Lee, Valerie E., and Marlaine E. Lockheed. "Single-Sex and Coeducational Education in Developing Countries." *International Encyclopedia of Education: Supplementary Volume Two*. Oxford: Pergamon Press 1991.

20.49 Lee, Valerie E., and Marlaine E. Lockheed. "The Effects of Single-Sex Schooling on Student Achievement and Attitudes in Nigeria." *Comparative Education Review* 34(2):209-231. 1990

Also published informally as The Effects of Single-Sex Schooling on Student Achievement and Attitudes in Nigeria. World Bank PPR Working Paper no. 206. Washington, D.C. 1989.

This study of 1,012 Form Three (ninth-grade) students in Nigeria indicates that single-sex schools improve girls' mathematics achievement and engender less stereotypic ideas about mathematics—even after extensive statistical adjustments for family background and school characteristics. Males in single-sex schools, however, achieve at a lower level and hold more stereotypic views of mathematics than boys at coeducational schools.

Background differences by sex, as well as differences between girls' schools and coeducational and boys' schools, were found to contribute to differences in student achievement. However, a significant residual effect for single-sex schools remained after adjustments were made, suggesting that other organizational or student background factors account for observed differences in effects.

20.50 Levin, Henry M., and Marlaine E. Lockheed, eds. *Effective Schools in Developing Countries*. Falmer Press. 1993.

This collection of papers, prepared for a 1989 World Bank conference describes initiatives in effective education strategies in eight countries and draws conclusions about their features. Included are: (a) "Creating Effective Schools" by Marlaine E. Lockheed and Henry M. Levin, which sets the framework for the subsequent chapters; (b) "The Condition of Primary Education in Developing Countries" by Marlaine E. Lockheed; (c) "How Can Schooling Help the Lives of the Poorest: The

Need for Radical Reform" by Nicholas Bennett; (d) "The New School Program: More and Better Education for Children in Rural Areas in Colombia" by Jairo Arboleda, Clemencia Chiappe, and Vicky Colbert; (e) "CIIEP: A Democratic School Model for Educating Economically Disadvantaged Students in Brazil" by Ana Leonardos; (f) "Improving Educational Effectiveness in a Plantation School: The Case of the Gonakelle School in Sri Lanka" by Angela Little and R. Sivasithambaram; (g) "Local Initiatives and Their Implications for a Multi-Level Approach to School Improvement in Thailand" by Mun C. Tsang and Christopher Wheeler; (h) "Providing Quality Education When Resources Are Scarce: Strategies for Increasing Primary School Effectiveness in Burundi" by Thomas Owen Eisemon, and others; and (i) "Accelerated Schools in the United States: Do They Have Relevance for Developing Countries?" by Henry M. Levin. Each paper provides references and statistical data in the form of tables, figures, and graphs.

20.51 Lockheed, Marlaine E. "Enrollment, Facilities and Finances: International Differences." In M. Akin, ed. *Encyclopedia of Educational Research*. New York: MacMillan. 1992.

20.52 Lockheed, Marlaine E., and Qinghua Zhao. "The Empty Opportunity: Local Control and Secondary School Achievement in the Philippines. *International Journal of Educational Development* 13(1). 1992.

20.53 Lockheed, Marlaine E., and Alastair G. Rodd. *World Bank Lending for Education Research, 1982-89*. World Bank Working Paper Series 583. Washington, D.C. 1991.

This paper reviews the progress of studies included in the World Bank education projects, 1982-89. The methodology employed to identify research components and studies is discussed, as are the volume, type, and budgeted cost of studies, and the determinants of study completion and availability. The authors find that (a) of 146 education projects initiated since 1982, 116 include research components with 436 identifiable, planned studies; (b) these projects are supported with loans and credits of about $4.5 billion, of which $98 million (2 percent) is allocated for research; (c) only 184 (42 percent) of the planned studies are complete, of which only 84 (46 percent) are available at Bank repositories, and eleven studies (6 percent) assess educational outcomes; and (d) research as a percentage of total loan commitment declined sharply from 1982 to 1989.

These data are significant since few countries have efficient monitoring systems, and since studies serve to provide qualitative information relating to areas of possible education policy change. Annex 1 includes a list of available documents and of project and research components with comments by regional staff; annex 2 lists the status of projects incomplete as of 1982.

20.54 Lockheed, Marlaine E., and Nicholas T. Longford. "School Effects on Mathematics Achievement Gain in Thailand." In S.W. Raudenbush and J.D. Willms, eds. *Schools, Classrooms, and Pupils: International Studies of Schooling from a Multi-Level Perspective*. New York and London: Academic Press. 1991.

Longer version is available as A Multi-Level Model of School Effectiveness in a Developing Country. World Bank Discussion Paper no. 69. 1989.

Results of a multi-level analysis which examines determinants of growth in eighth grade mathematics achievement in Thailand showed that schools in Thailand differed in their pretest-adjusted eighth grade mathematics scores, but there were no statistically significant differences in the relationship between pre-test and post-test grades across schools. Schools and classrooms contributed 32 percent of the variance in post-test scores.

Higher levels of achievement were associated with a higher proportion of teachers qualified to teach mathematics, an enriched curriculum, and frequent use of textbooks by teachers. Individual characteristics contributed 68 percent of the variance, with achievement higher for boys, younger students, and children with higher educational aspirations, less perceived parental encouragement, higher self-perceptions of ability, greater interest in and perceived relevance of mathematics.

The model developed in the paper was able to explain most of the between-school variance, but substantially less of the within-school variance. The implication of these results is that schools in Thailand are much more uniform in their effects than previous research in developing countries would have suggested.

20.55 Lockheed, Marlaine E., and Adriaan M. Verspoor, and others. *Improving Primary Education in Developing Countries*. New York: Oxford University Press. 1991.

For excerpt article of book see "Improving Primary Schools in Developing Countries." Finance & Development 27(1):24-6. 1990.

Also available in video in English, French, and Spanish.

How can the quality of and access to primary education in developing countries be improved and how should the improved quality be paid for? Improving primary education in developing countries requires efforts on at least five fronts: (a) bettering conditions for learning in class; (b) improving the preparation and motivation of teachers; (c) strengthening the institutional capacity of the education system; (d) increasing equitable access; and (e) strengthening financial support. In each of these areas, the book synthesizes research and state-of-the-art knowledge and outlines the key issues. Because significant differences among countries necessitate variations in policy responses, an array of policy options is presented. The central message is that resources spent on inputs directly related to student learning will be recovered through reductions in grade repetition and dropout. The book includes an extensive bibliography and twenty-three statistical annexes.

20.56 Lockheed, Marlaine, E., and Eric Hanushek. "Concepts of Educational Efficiency and Effectiveness. *International Encyclopedia of Education: Supplementary Volume Two*. Oxford: Pergamon Press. 1991.

20.57 Lockheed, Marlaine E., and Andre Komenan. "Teaching Quality and Student Achievement in Africa: The Case of Nigeria and Swaziland." *Teaching and Teacher Education* 5(2):93-111. 1989.

Also available as World Bank Reprint Series no. 449. Washington, D.C.

This paper reports the results of the first comparable cross-national comparison of school/classroom effects in Africa. Multi-level analyses showed that differences between schools accounted for substantial variance in eighth grade mathematics scores in Nigeria and Swaziland. However, conventional school and teacher quality variables, such as class size, length of school year, and teacher education and experience, had no effect on student achievement. Rather, it was teaching practices that were related to student achievement. The effect of specific practices differed in the two countries; for instance, in Nigeria time spent doing seat work or blackboard work had a negative impact on achievement, but in Swaziland such work had a positive effect.

20.58 Lockheed, Marlaine E., Bruce Fuller, and others. "Family Effects on Students' Achievement in Thailand and Malawi." *Sociology of Education* 62:239-56. 1989.

Also available as World Bank Reprint no. 451. Washington, D.C.

In analyzing the effects of family background on student's achievements in developing countries, this article used social class measures that are broader than in previous work, as well as more valid for developing countries. Study 1 examined panel data on 4,000 eighth grade students from 99 schools in Thailand. Family background and prior mathematics achievement were found to affect students' educational expectations, perceptions of ability, and effort, which, in turn, influenced subsequent math achievement.

Study 2 examined cross-sectional data on 103 students from twenty-one schools in Malawi and assessed the effects of country-specific family background measures. Family background was found to affect the language and mathematics performance of students in grades four and seven. The article suggests that prior work may have underestimated the influences of family background on achievement in developing countries.

20.59 Lockheed, Marlaine E., and Eric Hanushek. "Improving Educational Efficiency in Developing Countries: What Do We Know?" *Compare* 18(1):21-38. 1988.

The paper defines education efficiency as a ratio of learning to the costs of educational inputs. The authors report the effects of six educational inputs (instructional materials, teacher training, interactive radio, technical-vocational schools, peer tutoring, and cooperative learning) based on studies in various countries, and relate these effects to cost data to determine efficiency. On average, across several countries and a variety of student learning outcome measures, the more cost-effective interventions are textbooks, interactive radio, peer tutoring and cooperative learning. Less cost-effective are teacher training and technical-vocational schools.

20.60 Lockheed, Marlaine E., and Kathleen S. Gorman. "Sociocultural Factors Affecting Science Learning and Attitude." In Audrey B. Champagne and Leslie E. Hornig, eds. *This Year in School Science 1987: Students and Science Learning*. Washington, D.C: American Association for the Advancement of Science. 1987.

Also available as World Bank Reprint Series no. 426. Washington, D.C.

The literature on empirical evidence that links sociocultural factors to children's science learning is quite limited. Screening over 300 studies since 1975, the authors found that fewer than 70 reported sociocultural factors related to science learning, and most of these were conducted above the elementary level. Moreover, a wide assortment of measures have been used, with no consistent definition of science achievement or cultural factors.

The limited available evidence focused on group achievement differences (by gender, race, socioeconomic status) without addressing underlying explanatory mechanisms. However, student motivation appears to be a key factor. Identifying salient elements of culture and adapting science curricula to reflect these elements may be promising areas for future research and development.

20.61 Lockheed, Marlaine E., Stephen Vail, and Bruce Fuller. "How Textbooks Affect Achievement in Developing Countries: Evidence from Thailand." *Education Evaluation and Policy Analysis* 8(4):379-92. 1987.

Also available as World Bank Reprint Series no. 425. Washington, D.C.

For the past decade, researchers have documented the effects of textbooks on achievement in developing countries, but no research has explored the mechanisms that account for this contribution. This paper analyzes longitudinal data from a national sample of eighth grade mathematics classrooms in Thailand and explores the effects of textbooks and other factors on student achievement gain. The results indicate that textbooks may affect achievement by substituting for additional post-secondary mathematics education of teachers and by delivering a more comprehensive curriculum.

20.62 Lockheed, Marlaine E. "Farmers' Education and Economic Performance." In G. Psacharopoulos, ed. *Economics of Education: Research and Studies*. Oxford: Pergamon Press. 1987.

20.63 Lockheed, Marlaine E., and Jane Hannaway, eds. *The Contribution of the Social Sciences to Educational Policy and Practice, 1965-1985*. Berkeley, Cal.: McCutchan Publishing Company. 1986.

20.64 Maas, Jacob van Lutsenburg, and Geert Criel. *Distribution of Primary School Enrollment in Eastern Africa*. World Bank Staff Working Paper no. 511. Washington, D.C. 1982.

This paper examines the distribution of primary school enrollments within and among the countries of the Eastern African region. First, the study makes inter-country comparisons that indicate which countries and which areas in the Region lag in terms of educational opportunities. Thereafter, the focus of the paper shifts from the Region as a whole to the individual countries.

Two basic questions are asked: (a) what is the overall degree of inequality in the distribution of primary school enrollments across the districts and between the sexes within a country? and (b) which specific districts and urban versus rural locations, or sex groups within these areas fall below or above the national average in their enrollments and by how much? Two countries, Lesotho and Sudan, representing the full range of relatively equal and unequal cases, are reviewed in more depth. Finally, the paper attempts to determine how and where to allocate educational investments in order to reduce both inter-country and intra-country inequities. The study draws exclusively on the large amount of routine annual statistics gathered by countries and emphasizes the use of simple, computer generated indicators to reduce the data into readable form.

20.65 Ross, Kenneth, Marlaine E. Lockheed, and others. "Improving Data Collection, Preparation, and Analysis Procedures: A Review of Technical Issues." In K. Ross and L. Mahlck, eds. *Planning the Quality of Education.* **Oxford: Pergamon Press. 1990.**

20.66 Serageldin, Ismail, M.R. Khater, M.E. Mawgood, I. Werdelin, S. Ibrahim, and others. *The Kingdom of Saudi Arabia: Accelerated Literacy Program.* **Fifteen volumes designed for the experimental program (in Arabic). World Bank. 1978/79.**

This vast and unusual experimental program was designed and carried out by the World Bank and national specialists for Saudi Arabia's Ministry of Education. The program was based on a sociological assessment of the composition and literacy needs of various population groups, and involved the preparation of books and manuals specially tailored to different social categories of illiterate adults.

A separate three-volume set was prepared for each of four target groups from four distinct milieus: (a) rural/agrarian; (b) industrial; (c) services sector; and (d) that of young adults who had dropped out of school and regressed into illiteracy. One three-volume set was designed for instruction of numeracy and problem solving skills and was common to each of the streams. Thus, each of the four target groups had six volumes of manuals. The materials were prepared by multidisciplinary teams of international experts working closely with national authorities and specialists, including sociologists and other social scientists.

The program started with a detailed study of the milieu of each of the target groups; their prevalent vocabulary was identified and then subjected to a linguistic analysis. This formed the basis for the elaboration of "modules" that built up skills incrementally using material of immediate relevance to the learners, thereby allowing their social milieu to facilitate and reinforce the learning process. The complexity and phasing of the materials were pretested under real conditions and refined into the final books, which were handsomely produced and illustrated. Detailed training manuals were produced and training was undertaken for teachers as well.

The experimental program was tested under rigorous field conditions in thirty-five schools throughout Saudi Arabia, using comparisons with control classes which used a conventional syllabus. The results were very compelling; the Ministry of Education adopted the results and built on this experimental program to develop an improved accelerated literacy program in the country.

20.67 Serageldin, Ismail, E. Mawgood, I. Werdelin, and M. Youssef. *Remaining Literate in Egypt: Study Findings and Recommendations for Action.* Final Report of the Study on Literacy and Numeracy Retention. RPO 671-55. World Bank. 1984.

This final report, which addressed the methodological and data set issues of the massive Study on Literacy and Numeracy Retention, is a companion to the statistical and econometric volumes produced in the course of the study and published by Michael J. Hartley and Eric V. Swanson. It provides an abbreviated review of the methodology and analyses and draws out the policy conclusions for the benefit of educators and decision makers in Egypt and the Arab world.

The report draws on vast quantities of materials and unpublished working papers (many in Arabic) prepared by teams of international and national experts over a period of four years. It was the basis for seminars organized by M. E. Mawgood in Egypt, and some of its recommendations were later adopted by the Ministry of Education when Mr. Mawgood left the bank to become Deputy Minister of Education in Egypt.

Detailed objective tests were designed, focussing on families of skills, to test literacy and numeracy skills without reference to specific syllabus materials. These tests were then used to establish performance levels for boys and girls in rural and urban schools in Egypt. Dropouts from the same schools from each of the preceding four years were then tracked and tested using the same battery of tests.

In addition, detailed sociological profiles of the students and dropouts were made on the basis of detailed interviews that tracked their family circumstances and the possible influence of their social milieu since dropping out of school on their retention of literacy and numeracy skills. A second year of follow up testing was undertaken to address concerns about longitudinal versus cross-sectional data sets. In all, over 17,000 students and dropouts were tested and interviewed, each subjected to no less than six different instruments, making this one of the most extensive and rigorous studies ever implemented in this domain.

20.68 World Bank. *Primary Education.* A World Bank Policy Paper. Washington, D.C. 1990.

This policy paper, to which Bank sociologists contributed, presents options for improving the effectiveness of primary schools in developing countries. The recommendations are based on a broad program of research on the sociology of education that takes into account various country conditions and experiences. The text focuses on problems common to most developing countries and presents an array of low-cost policy alternatives that have proved useful in a variety of settings.

Of the paper's six sections, the first describes the importance of primary education and the present inability of many education systems to meet their objectives. The second section discusses three areas for improvement in order to meet these objectives: enhancing the learning environment, improving the preparation and motivation of teachers, and strengthening educational management. The topic of the third section is increasing equitable access. The fourth section presents strategies for strengthening the financial base for primary education. The fifth section discusses international assistance to education, and the sixth addresses implications for World Bank action. A summary of policy recommendations concludes the report.

Health

21.1 Hecht, Robert M. *Zimbabwe: Financing Health Services.* World Bank Country Study. Washington, D.C. 1992.

This report identifies options for improving efficiency and equity in the provision of health services in Zimbabwe, and recommends more effective ways to mobilize additional resources for the country's rapidly evolving health system. The context of the report is one of rising personal incomes (and demand for health care), increasingly severe budgetary constraints, and an epidemiological pattern that includes both "traditional" childhood and communicable diseases and new challenges in the form of adult chronic disease and AIDS.

The authors conclude that while Zimbabwe has made enormous strides during its first decade of independence (1980-1989) in expanding health services, continuing to improve access and enhance efficiency are especially important for Zimbabwe at this critical juncture, with the country about to embark on an economic adjustment program that will entail fiscal austerity and could have adverse effects on the poor, if countervailing measures are not adopted. The report also concludes that, with the cash-strapped public sector now providing more than half the health services and health financing in Zimbabwe, non-governmental actors (including church missions, private doctors and nurses, commercial enterprises, and traditional practitioners) will need to play an increasingly important role in the future.

21.2 Moser, Caroline, and P. Sollis. "Did the Project Fail? A Community Perspective on a Participatory Health Care Project in Ecuador." *Development in Practice* 1(1):19-33. 1991.

This article examines a UNICEF/Ministry of Health primary health care program in Ecuador from a community perspective. It contributes to the debate concerning the way in which the relative "success" or "failure" of participatory projects is measured. It argues for evaluators to distinguish between the perceptions of the different actors involved, and to extend their inquiries beyond the actual lifespan of the project. It also provides lessons for the future by discussing the contribution that technical projects can make to capacity building and to the empowerment of community-level organizations.

Roads

22.1 Cook, Peter D., and Cynthia C. Cook. "Methodological Review of Analyses of Rural Transportation Impacts in Developing Countries." *Transportation and Economic Development 1990*. Transportation Research Record no. 1274, 167-78. Washington, D.C.: Transportation Research Board, National Research Council.

This study examines the development of rural transportation impact studies over the last twenty years and the results of rural mobility and migration research carried out during the last ten years. Present impact assessment methodologies focus too narrowly on agricultural effects. They fail to predict significant increases found in nonfarm traffic and related economic benefits. Contrary to common assumptions, rural residents place a high value on travel time. This value reflects the importance of nonfarm employment and the benefits of increased mobility and access to services, which are crucial to adequate impact evaluation. A causal model of impacts is proposed, defining the relationships between access change and rural socioeconomic development.

22.2 Cook, Cynthia C. "Social Analysis in Rural Road Projects." In M.M. Cernea, ed. *Putting People First: Sociological Variables in Rural Development*. 2nd ed. New York and London: Oxford University Press. 1991.

This chapter presents the case for incorporating social analysis into the planning and implementation of rural road projects. Infrastructure projects traditionally have been designed according to economic and engineering criteria. These criteria do not always fully meet the needs of the intended beneficiaries, nor do they take full advantage of local social, cultural, and technical resources. Social analysis is needed at all stages of the project cycle, although the skills of the professional social scientist are particularly essential during project identification, preparation, and evaluation. Taking a social perspective in the design of rural roads projects and programs can help develop community capabilities for self-directed and self-sustained growth.

22.3 Cook, Cynthia C. "Evaluating Alternative Maintenance Strategies for Low-Volume Roads in Sub-Saharan Africa." *Fourth International Conference on Low-Volume Roads, Transportation Research Record no. 1106*. Washington, D.C.: Transportation Research Board, National Research Council. 1988.

Applications of the Bank's Highway Design and Maintenance (HDM) model in Sub-Saharan Africa indicate that periodic maintenance is generally justified only on paved roads with traffic levels of more than 100 vehicles per day and on earth roads with traffic levels of more than 50 vehicles per day. However, road rehabilitation in potentially productive areas is often justified at lower traffic volumes, based on the increase in agricultural production that occurs when road access is provided. These benefits may be lost if a rehabilitated road is allowed to deteriorate due to lack of maintenance. Timely periodic maintenance is generally justified if the initial road construction was justified. However, deferring periodic maintenance for two to four years may be the economically optimal strategy. In any case, routine road maintenance must be regularly carried out in order to preserve road access, the key to the developmental effects of road investments.

22.4 Cook, Cynthia C., and others. *Institutional Considerations in Rural Roads Projects.* World Bank Staff Working Paper no. 748. Washington, D.C. 1985.

This paper explores institutional issues that frequently arise in rural roads projects. It is based upon a review of experience with some fifty Bank-financed projects with rural road components. First, the paper considers rural roads within the broader policy environment for rural development and the issues which may need to be addressed at this level. Second, the paper identifies structural alternatives, interagency coordination, and implementation issues relating to project execution. The third part of the paper deals in greater detail with the role of local participation in rural roads projects.

Energy Use

23.1 Barnes, Douglas, and others. "The Design and Diffusion of Improved Cooking Stoves." *The World Bank Research Observer* 8(2):119-41. 1993.

Essentially the same material is published as What Makes People Cook With Improved Stoves? World Bank Industry and Energy Department Working Paper. Washington, D.C. 1993.

The poorer half of the world's people have long relied for their energy needs on woodfuels. Since the oil shocks of the 1970s, pressure on forest resources has increased and the costs of traditional use of woodfuels have been growing—to the householder, in cash or collection time, and to society in inefficient energy use, deforestation, and local and global harm to health and the environment. Modern, efficient stoves can alleviate some of these problems; programs to design and disseminate them would seem a worthwhile pursuit for development activity.

But do such programs in fact warrant the investment? Why have so many failed to catch on as expected? The authors find that programs have been most successful when targeted to specific areas where woodfuel prices or collection times are high. Field testing, consumer surveys, and involvement of local artisans from the outset have been critical to the ultimate adoption of the stoves. With these elements in place, external support from governments and donors can be useful; lacking them, subsidies may succeed only in distributing stoves that ultimately molder away unused. This article's review of what makes for success and failure is instructive for the design of stove programs in particular, and of development projects that propagate improved methods and technologies in general.

23.2 Barnes, Douglas, and Liu Qian. "Urban Interfuel Substitution, Energy Use, and Equity in Developing Countries." In James Dorian and Fereidun Fesharaki, eds. *International Issues in Energy Policy, Development, and Economics*. Boulder, Col.: Westview Press. 1992.

Also published informally as World Bank Industry and Energy Department Energy Series no. 53. Washington, D.C. 1992.

The findings in this paper are a beginning attempt to answer some fundamental policy questions concerning urban interfuel substitution in developing countries. From the preliminary evidence we can say that government policy plays a very important role in influencing households to choose one fuel over another. Secondly, policies to promote LPG for households with incomes that are less than about US$25 per capita per month are likely to lead to disappointment. Apparently electricity can be promoted at much lower levels of income because of the high value urban households assign for lighting, although this will require substantial capital costs by the electricity industry.

In developing countries, wood fuels do not disappear completely as incomes rise since many high income households still use wood, reflecting the utility of these fuels for urban households. However, they do seem to disappear from urban households in large metropolitan areas with over one million population, where wood apparently is very hard to obtain. The urban poor are probably affected most by urban fuel policies, since they spend a significant proportion of their incomes on energy. Obviously, there is much work to be completed before we fully understand the dynamic patterns affecting urban interfuel substitution in developing countries.

23.3 Barnes, Douglas, and others. "Interfuel Substitution and Changes in the Way Households Use Energy: Estimating Changes in Cooking and Lighting Behavior in Urban Java." *Pacific and Asian Journal of Energy 1(1):21-49. 1992.*

Also informally published as World Bank Industry and Energy Department Energy Series no. 29. Washington, D.C. 1991.

The main shortcoming of standard methods for estimating household fuel demand as a function of fuel choice is that these treat end-use services as constants and do not account for behavioral changes that accompany such a switch as from wood to kerosene for cooking or from kerosene to electricity for lighting.

A statistical procedure has been developed to quantify the effects of such changes based on the actual behavior of households. The procedure was applied to data from a recent household energy survey in urban Java to arrive at precise estimates of fuel substitution ratios for cooking.

The analysis of fuel use for cooking by urban households on Java in general confirmed that estimates of technical efficiency are a sound basis for projections of the potential of LPG (liquified petroleum gas) and wood to replace kerosene. It also showed that wood is used more effectively and LPG less effectively in urban households than would be expected purely on the basis of technical efficiencies of the stoves.

A comparison of kerosene and electricity for lighting indicated that electricity is not only a cheaper option for the country and for households, but that households that use electricity for lighting enjoy roughly six times more light than those using kerosene. This result calls into question previous evaluations of the benefits of electrification based only on the consumer's willingness to pay.

23.4 Barnes, Douglas. "Population Growth, Wood Fuels, and Resource Problems in Sub-Saharan Africa." In G.T.F. Acsadi, G. Johnson-Acsadi, and R.A. Bulatao, eds. *Population Growth and Reproduction in Sub-Saharan Africa.* **A World Bank Symposium. Washington, D.C. 1990.**

Also informally published as Population Growth, Wood Fuels, and Resource Problems in Sub-Saharan Africa. World Bank Industry and Energy Department Energy Series no. 26. Washington, D.C. 1990.

Rapid population growth has resulted in deforestation and wood fuel shortages in many regions of sub-Saharan Africa. In many urban areas rapid growth of urban demand for wood fuels has caused the expansion of deforested rings around cities in a radius of up to 100 kilometers. Shortages in some rural areas have caused women and children to walk further for collecting wood or substitute lower quality fuels such as dung and agricultural waste.

The most serious deforestation and fuelwood problems in sub-Saharan Africa are in the sparsely populated Sahel. Here, rapid population growth is the main problem, since it leads to the simultaneous increase in demand for food and fuels. The increased demand for food is often met by expanding agriculture to new lands. The need for more fuelwood is met through harvesting wood from common lands.

Deforestation has been a significant problem in savanna regions with high population densities, in highly populated mountainous regions, in the dry regions such as the Sahel where tree regrowth is very slow, and around rapidly growing urban centers. The regions in sub-Saharan Africa where deforestation has not been much of a problem include areas where fallows are long and significant land is still available for cultivation. In between these two extremes are areas with a wide range of conditions. For instance, the price of wood energy may rise, land may begin to erode, and women and children may spend more time collecting wood fuels. These less dramatic consequences can gradually become more serious over time, if the population growth is not diminished or if incentives are not in place for the land use system to adjust to the need for both increased food production and tree protection.

23.5 Campbell, Tim. "Social Feasibility of Densified Fuel for Rural Households of Pakistan." In C. Carpenter and M. Dove, eds. *Sociology of Natural Resources in Pakistan and Adjoining Countries*. Honolulu: East West Center. 1993.

This report examines the economic and environmental costs of proposed alternative fuels for household cooking in Pakistan and the sociocultural factors relevant to the acceptability and use of densified biomass in Pakistani households. The author argues that a review of cost, ownership, transportation, acceptability, and social and environmental impacts are necessary in connection with the introduction of new fuels from densified biomass. The report is based on fieldwork carried out during May and June of 1985 among rural and urban households in three provinces of Pakistan.

Part Six

Social Research and Methodologies

Social Research Methods

24.1 Bamberger, Michael. "Methodological Issues in the Evaluation of Community Participation." *Sociological Evaluation Practice* 8:208-25. 1990.

If advocates of participatory approaches wish them to be used more widely in mainstream development projects, argues the author, it will be necessary to introduce more rigor into the way these approaches are evaluated. This raises methodological questions about how to integrate quantitative and qualitative methods into the evaluation of social development programs.

24.2 Cernea, Michael M. "Re-Tooling in Applied Social Investigation for Development Planning: Some Methodological Issues." In N.S. Scrimshaw and Gary Gleason, eds. *Rapid Assessment Methodologies for Planning and Evaluation of Health Related Programs.* Boston, Mass.: INFDC. 1992.

The invention of rapid assessment procedures (RAPs) represents a retooling process in applied social research. Their introduction does not reject traditional methods but, when used correctly, complements and enriches them. Progress in refining RAPs is contributing to the reduction of the costs of using social sciences in development project planning.

However, the author warns, recent trends in the advocacy and application of rapid assessment procedures also reveal risks of superficiality and haste, under the guise of innovation and cost cutting. The paper calls for prudence and a critical analysis of the strengths, weaknesses, and methodological risks of the new procedures. Professional training and an understanding of the place of RAPs within broader research strategies is of paramount importance in order to avoid the risk of misuse of RAPs and distortion of field research and findings.

24.3 Cernea, Michael M. "The 'Production' of a Social Methodology." In E.M. Eddy and W.L. Partridge, eds. *Applied Anthropology in America.* 2nd ed. New York: Columbia University Press. 1987.

Also published in Y. Levi and H. Litvin, eds. **Community and Cooperatives in Participatory Development.** *Aldershot, Hants., England, and Brookfield, Vt.: Gower Publishing Company. 1986.*

Available as World Bank Reprint Series no. 430. Washington, D.C.

A ubiquitous challenge for social scientists is raised by the call for the participation of beneficiaries in the planning and design of development programs. Yet the social sciences are underdeveloped in terms of their capacity to provide concrete, systematic, and tested methodologies whereby beneficiaries can be meaningfully involved as participants in such activities. This essay presents an analysis of the PIDER development project in Mexico, which made a serious attempt to address this problem. The Mexican government established the project in order to achieve development goals by facilitating the participation of the benefiting rural communities in investment planning.

The author documents the steps by which the social scientists who worked on this project systematically evolved a social methodology to implement project objectives. He emphasizes the chronology of actions taken to develop the methodology of community participation and discusses the institutional, cognitive and cultural barriers that had to be overcome.

The key elements of this process included a conceptual framework that required local information and action as well as outside expert opinion; a series of activities that involved local people and outside experts in debate about technical issues; the sustained support of high-level leadership within the agency that initiated the conceptual framework and financed the activities; and continued support during the long period of experimentation, adjustment, and learning needed to develop and institutionalize participatory methods. The example of PIDER can be extended to other contexts; action research can develop innovative social methodologies for program implementation.

24.4 Cernea, Michael M., and Scott E. Guggenheim. "Is Anthropology Superfluous in Farming Systems Research?" In *Farming Systems Research*. Kansas State University Research Series 4(9):504-17. 1985.

Also Available as World Bank Reprint Series no. 367. Washington, D.C. 1985.

This paper refutes an explicit denial of the role of social sciences in farming systems research (FSR) contained in a state-of-the-art review of FSR by Norman W. Simmonds of the Edinburgh School of Agriculture. The authors contend that the treatment of anthropology in the FSR state-of-the-art review is ill-informed; the reviewer does not objectively inform the reader of the considerable body of opinion that differs from his own (mis)judgement and fails to grasp the interplay between the social sciences that jointly inform FSR.

The role of sociology and anthropology in farming systems research (FSR) is being increasingly recognized and FSR is being included in interdisciplinary agricultural research programs. The authors develop the positive argument for recognizing the social and cultural variables that must be studied under the FSR approach and outline reasons why anthropological and sociological concepts and skills are indispensable to FSR teams.

24.5 Cernea, Michael M. *A Social Methodology for Community Participation in Local Investments: The Experience of Mexico's PIDER Program*. World Bank Staff Working Paper no. 598. Washington, D.C. 1983.

The PIDER ("Programa Integral para el Desarollo Rural" or "Integrated Program for Rural Development") program in Mexico included a large-scale effort in the social engineering of beneficiary participation. This paper outlines the history and experience of devising a coherent social methodology for eliciting farmers' participation in identifying priority local investments and implementing them. This methodology was articulated only gradually, with help from sociologists and other social scientists, through a long process of designing, testing, learning, and revising. Action research and social experiments at the community and microregional level were carried out to test and repeatedly refine the participatory approach.

This paper also discusses the constraints on the application of the participatory program, which included the rigidity of the bureaucratic structure, cultural constraints, opposition to peasant participation for political reasons, interagency conflicts over policy and procedural issues, and the weakness of village-based peasant organizations.

24.6 Chambers, Robert. "Shortcut and Participatory Methods for Gaining Social Information for Projects." In M.M. Cernea, ed. *Putting People First: Sociological Variables in Rural Development*. 2nd ed. New York, London: Oxford University Press. 1991.

In putting people first, social information plays a key part. But the methods of eliciting information about people are often too time consuming or badly applied. The author discusses the defects that he identified in the process of generating, analyzing and using social data in rural development and gives an overview of new, refined, time-efficient and cost-effective instruments for eliciting field data.

The author proposes a set of shortcut and participatory procedures to elicit social information. He highlights the progress in molding rapid assessment procedures made during the late 1980s in several developing and developed countries. Advocating new procedures, he indicts what he calls "rural development tourism," characterized by superficial trips to project areas and their easily reached environs. He also criticizes the "quick and dirty" and "long and dirty" approaches to data collection. The middle road is that of rapid rural appraisal or participatory rural appraisal, which attempt to construct a sensitive and relevant picture of the local population and their concerns in a short time.

A wide menu of methods that can be used as alternatives or in combination are described. Among them are various forms of direct observation, "do-it-yourself" methods, imaginative use of key informants, group interviews and chains of interviews, mapping and aerial photographs, diagrams, ethnohistories, ranking procedures, stratifying procedures, stories and portraits, secondary data review, and other methods. Underlying all these procedures is the idea that rural people themselves, although they are the most knowledgeable about their own circumstances, are often the most overlooked resource for information. Therefore, the professional use of these new investigation techniques can make social analysis a much more practical and feasible endeavor in regular project work.

24.7 Cook, Cynthia C. "Demography of the Project Population." In K. Finsterbusch, J. Ingersoll, and L. Llewellyn, eds. *Methods for Social Analysis in Developing Countries*. Boulder, Col.: Westview Press. 1990.

Demographic analysis is one of several methodological tools available to assist in the prediction and evaluation of the social impacts of development projects. The identification and interpretation of demographic data in developing countries presents some particular challenges, but these can be met by taking a creative and pragmatic approach to using whatever data are available. This chapter reviews demographic data sources, common problems in the definition and interpretation of demographic variables, and methods of analysis for the purpose of predicting or assessing social impacts.

24.8 Moser, Caroline, and P. Sollis. "A Methodological Framework for Analyzing the Social Costs of Adjustment at the Micro Level: The Case of Quayaquil, Ecuador." *Institute of Development Studies Bulletin* 22(1):23-30. 1991.

The purpose of this paper is to describe a recently developed research methodology to examine the social dimensions of debt, recession, and structural adjustment policies (SAPs) in terms of their impact on low income urban households. The paper draws on the experience of a research project undertaken during 1988 in the "suburbios," or low income urban areas, of Guayaquil, Ecuador. Since the nature and type of data collected in fieldwork ultimately determines the type and extent of analysis that can be undertaken, the choice of research methodology in social development research is critical. This is a complex question which must take into account such issues as the nature of the research problem, the context of the research, the amount of accessible secondary and background data, and the time available in the field.

24.9 Murphy, Josette, and others. *Farmers' Estimations as a Source of Production Data: Methodological Guidelines for Cereals in Africa.* World Bank Technical Paper no. 132. Washington, D.C. 1991.

Also available in French.

The reliability and timeliness of agricultural production data are insufficient to meet information needs in many African countries. The use of simple data collection methods well adapted to the irregular plots of African traditional agriculture would help improve this situation.

This paper, based on recent evidence comparing the standard crop-cut method and the method based on farmers' estimations, respectively, of the actual weight of harvest, discusses the types of information needs for which the farmers' estimations provide a valid source of production data. It analyzes the advantages, limitations, and requirements of using the farmers' estimation method, and provides guidelines for collecting, analyzing, and interpreting production data from the farmers concerned.

The paper is aimed at management and technical staff in ministries and agricultural service agencies, as well as for survey specialists. It can also be used during training sessions on data collection methodologies. The purpose of the paper is twofold: (a) to inform management and technical staff of the validity and limitations of the farmers' estimations of cereal production as a data source for some information needs; and (b) to provide technical staff and survey specialists with detailed guidelines on the organization, design, and implementation of data collection, as well as verification, interpretation, and utilization of the results in the broader agro-ecological, economic, and cultural context of the country.

24.10 Murphy, Josette. "Farmers' Systems and Technological Change in Agriculture." In M.S. Chaiken and A. Fleuret, eds. *Social Change and Applied Anthropology: Essays in Honor of David Brokensha.* Boulder, Col.: Westview Press. 1990.

In a book of essays in honor of David Brokensha, a pioneer in the field of development anthropology, this chapter discusses the factors which influence farmers' decisions related to technological change and how they should be interpreted into a farmers' system approach. Recent evidence that development agencies understand better the importance of incorporating women and men farmers' perspectives at each phase of program planning, implementation, and evaluation is reviewed.

Suggestions are made on how individuals trained in the social sciences can facilitate this evolution by working within research and development agencies, not only as social scientists, but also in positions where they are involved in the identification, design, supervision, and evaluation of projects, and can influence their colleagues with other disciplinary backgrounds.

Additional publications relevant to the topics in this Section of the Bibliography can be found in Sections 2, 3, and 25.

Social Impact Assessment

25.1 de Kadt, Emanuel. *Tourism: Passport to Development? Perspectives on the Social and Cultural Effects of Tourism in Developing Countries.* A Joint World Bank-UNESCO study. New York, London: Oxford University Press. 1979.

To many developing countries with few resources other than sunny climates, sandy beaches, and exotic cultures, tourism has seemed to offer an opportunity to secure foreign exchange and stimulate economic growth. Critics question, however, whether tourism yields economic returns commensurate with its costs and express concern about its possibly adverse social and cultural effects.

In the five introductory chapters the author addresses this concern in the context of development theory and policy making. He examines tourism planning and decision making at the local, national, and transnational levels. A central issue is how the growth of tourism affects the social and economic welfare of the local people and how the benefits are distributed. Changes in values and attitudes brought about at least in part by encounters with foreign tourists are also explored, as are the effects of tourism on arts, crafts, and cultural activities. The second part of the book contains case studies speaking to the issues discussed by the author. The contributors, from a wide range of disciplines, are concerned primarily with the effects of mass tourism. The general conclusions are relevant to policy makers and others who influence decisions on tourism in developing countries and who seek some direction in making the choices they face.

25.2 de Regt, Jacomina P., and Augustin Reynoso y Valle. "Growing Pains: Planned Tourism Development in Ixtapa-Zihuatenejo." In Emanuel de Kadt, ed. *Tourism: Passport to Development? Perspectives on the Social and Cultural Effects of Tourism in Developing Countries.* A Joint World Bank-UNESCO study. New York, London: Oxford University Press. 1979.

In 1972, under the direction of the Government of Mexico, workers broke ground for a tourist resort near Zihuatenejo, a fishing village on the Pacific coast of Mexico. Beginning with a population of less than 5,000 in 1970, Zihuatnejo was caught up in a swirl of conflicting forces, some introduced by the tourism project itself, others the result of larger social, economic, and political changes in the area. This chapter deals with the reaction of the people of Zihuatenejo to the changes introduced by the development of their community. There is special emphasis on the major problem of land regularization and on the work of the Community Development team in dealing with the disruptions that occurred as a result of growth. The cumulative effects on education, employment, the political scene, and the special impact on the role of women are analyzed in the final section.

25.3 Hecht, Robert M. "The Ivory Coast Economic Miracle: What Benefits for Peasant Farmers?" *Journal of Modern African Studies* 21(1):25-53. 1983.

The pattern of rapid economic growth in the Ivory coast since the early 1950s has been frequently described by foreign experts and Ivorian officials as an economic miracle. This article advances three main arguments that explain the nature and the limitations of this "miracle." First, Ivorian economic development has been characterized by export-led growth, based heavily on two crops, cocoa and coffee, grown by hundreds of thousands of small holders. The government has followed a set of policies designed to encourage expansion of coffee and cocoa production while taxing smallholders heavily for capital accumulation and reinvestment elsewhere in the economy.

Second, Ivorian smallholders have gained only limited benefits from economic growth. Increases in output have been accounted for more by an increased number of farmers rather than increase in output per farmer. As a result of official policies, especially in pricing and marketing, no rural "bourgeoisie" has developed, and peasants are economically blocked and politically impotent. The third argument is that the principle beneficiaries of the Ivorian "miracle" have been government officials and politicians, and foreign, mainly French, private firms.

25.4 Nettekoven, Lothar. "Mechanisms of Intercultural Interaction." In Emanuel de Kadt, ed. *Tourism: Passport to Development? Perspectives on the Social and Cultural Effects of Tourism in Developing Countries.* A Joint World Bank-UNESCO Study. New York, London: Oxford University Press. 1979.

How does tourism affect host societies? In any discussion of the social and cultural implications of tourism, the intercultural relations of the indigenous population with the foreign tourists are undoubtedly of the greatest importance. Also significant are the relations among tourists themselves, because many stereotypes of the indigenous population are formed by tourists and disseminated through intertourist communication. This chapter dispels misconceptions about intercultural encounters, examines intercultural interaction, discusses the roles of those indigenous groups most frequently encountered (hotel employees, entrepreneurs in peripheral tourism areas, young people, and members of the local upper class), and describes the results of intercultural interaction.

25.5 Noronha, Raymond. "Paradise Reviewed: Tourism in Bali." In Emanuel de Kadt, ed. *Tourism: Passport to Development? Perspectives on the Social and Cultural Effects of Tourism in Developing Countries.* A Joint World Bank-UNESCO Study. New York, London: Oxford University Press. 1979.

Bali offers an excellent testing ground of various hypotheses current in the literature on the social impact of tourism. First, it is an island, and it has been suggested that the impact of tourism is greater on islands than in other destination areas. Second, from 1969 to 1975 tourism in Bali grew at an average of 27.5 percent a year, and it has been hypothesized that the rate of growth of tourism is correlated with its impact on a destination area. Third, most tourists visit Bali because of its culture, a situation that has been thought to "commoditize" and debase culture in the eyes of the local populace because cultural manifestations are given a monetary value and performed on demand for tourists.

The author examines these hypotheses in order to determine whether tourism will destroy Balinese culture and lead to a "Waikikianization" of Bali, as the fear is commonly expressed. The author also discusses the question whether a nation should pursue tourism, whatever the social and cultural costs, if there is no other strategy for economic development.

25.6 Noronha, Raymond. *Social and Cultural Dimensions of Tourism.* World Bank Staff Working Paper no. 326. Washington, D.C.: 1979.

Tourism is a viable path to economic development; but many developing countries, by failing to plan, lose control over the development of tourism. Failure to plan reduces the economic gains to the host country, results in loss of local ownership and control of tourist facilities, and may lead to additional adverse consequences (for example, weakening of family ties, loss of land by the local population).

Most of the adverse effects of tourism begin when tourism becomes "institutionalized." Institutionalized tourists are those who travel on packaged tours organized by specialized agencies and do not, to any significant extent, give up their accustomed life style while travelling. They constitute the majority of tourists and the major potential source of foreign exchange from tourism. But they also demand substantial adjustments and expenditures on the part of the host country on Western-style hotels, travel agencies and other familiar tourist trappings. For countries without the capital or the expertise to establish their own such services and facilities, institutionalization becomes the turning point where they lose social, political, and economic control over tourism development.

The World Bank has been slow to take into account the social consequences of tourism; studies of tourism by sociologists themselves are relatively new, and many are unpublished. This paper, therefore, recommends steps the Bank can take to utilize the sociologists' perspective in tourism projects, and mitigate the negative effects of tourism.

Additional publications relevant to this topic can be found in Sections 2, 3, 6, 10, and 24.

General Publications in Anthropology and Sociology

26.1 Cernea, Michael M. "Sociology in Rumania: The View of an American Historian." In John W. Cole, ed. *Society and Culture in Modern Rumania*. Amherst Research Report no. 20. Amherst, Mass.: University of Massachusetts Press. 1984.

In 1929 the Rockefeller Foundation commissioned a report on the state of social sciences in the Balkans and Turkey, which was published in 1930. This article comments on the report's insightful analysis of the state of sociology in Rumania, which, despite difficulties, was flourishing in the 1930s. In contrast, the author points out that after the pre-war period described in the report, the conditions for sociological work in post-World War II Rumania worsened disastrously. He concludes that the gradual suffocation of Rumanian sociology and its unhappy subservience to political impositions was the result of the political, ideological, and economic changes in the country's regime.

26.2 Cernea, Michael M. "Rural Community Studies in Rumania." In J.L. Druand-Drouhin and L.M. Szwengrub, eds. *Rural Community Studies in Europe*. Oxford: Pergamon Press. 1981.

Also published in French as Le Village Roumain. Sociologie des Recherches sur les Communautés Rurales. International Archives of Sociology of Cooperation and Development no. 37. Paris. 1975.

The monographic study of local village communities was the pivotal focus of rural sociological research in Rumania for many decades. In the inter-war period, in particular, this kind of monographic research was pursued more extensively in Rumania than in most other countries. Several remarkable scientists devoted their efforts for decades on end to systematically developing the theory, methodology, and techniques of sociological investigation of village communities and to writing community monographs.

This article surveys a century of rural community research in Rumanian sociology, and identifies characteristics and peculiarities of Rumanian rural sociology. It divides monographic investigations according to historic periods and derives methodological lessons from both the successes and failures of this research.

26.3 Clark, Maria Donoso. "Anthropology at the World Bank." In A.T. Koons, B.N. Hackett, and J.P. Mason, eds. *Stalking Employment in the Nation's Capital: A Guide for Anthropologists*. Washington, D.C: The Washington Association of Professional Anthropologists. 1989.

Employment opportunities for professional anthropologists at the World Bank consist predominantly of consulting assignments, and, less frequently, permanent staff positions. They continue to be concentrated mainly in the sectors of agriculture, population and human resources, and the environment. It is important to focus on the skills and kinds of experience required rather than on position titles. Anthropologists with good hands-on experience dealing with particular development issues and, preferably, with good understanding of economics or another technical field relevant to the Bank's work, may qualify for Bank assignments.

26.4 Colletta, Nat J., and T. Todd. *Social and Cultural Influences on Human Resource Development Policies and Programs: Selected and Annotated Bibliography*. Essex, Conn.: Redgrave Press. 1981.

26.5 Eddy, Elizabeth M., and William L. Partridge, eds. *Applied Anthropology in America*. Rev. 2nd ed. New York: Columbia University Press. 1987.

This textbook consists of original essays on anthropological theory, practice and policy work. The volume provides a historical analysis of the emergence of modern anthropology at approximately the same time as the surge in interest and experience in applying social science to practical human problems. The early pioneers of applied anthropology were in fact leaders of modern business in the United States before and during the second world war.

Contributors to the volume include Conrad Arensberg, Ward Goodenough, Frederick Richardson, Jacquetta Hill-Burnett, Ronald Cohen, William Foote Whyte, Thayer Scudder, William Partridge, Michael Cernea, John H. Peterson, Beatrice Medicine, Paul A. Miller, Thomas M. Johnson, David M. Fedderman, Henry F. Dobyns, Solon T. Kimball, George L. Hicks, Mark J. Handler, Paul L. Doughty, Robert H. Heighton, Cristy Heighton, Michael V. Angrosino, Linda M Whiteford, Perrti J. Pelto and Jean J. Schensul.

26.6 Gross, Daniel R. *Discovering Anthropology*. Mountain View, Cal.: Mayfield Publishing Company. 1992.

This book is a comprehensive introductory textbook for college-level anthropology students. Major topics covered: social and cultural anthropology, biological anthropology, archaeology, anthropological linguistics.

26.7 Gross, Daniel R. *Instructor's Manual for Discovering Anthropology*. Mountain View, Cal.: Mayfield Publishing Company. 1992.

26.8 Partridge, William L., and Elizabeth M. Eddy. "Development of Applied Anthropology in America." In E.M. Eddy and W.L. Partridge, eds. *Applied Anthropology in America*. Revised 2nd ed. New York: Columbia University Press. 1987.
The introductory essay to entry 27.5 places applied anthropology in its historical context and traces its development in America from the early work on reservations of indigenous Americans and among immigrant Europeans, through World War II, the New Deal and Good Neighbor government programs, to present work in international development, health, education and other fields.

26.9 Partridge, William L. "Towards a Theory of Practice." In E.M. Eddy and W.L. Partridge, eds. *Applied Anthropology in America*. Rev. 2nd ed. New York: Columbia University Press. 1987.

The author defines the theory of practice in anthropology and links it to pioneering work of the founders of the Society for Applied Anthropology in the United States in the 1930s and 1940s. The essay examines its theoretical underpinnings, its relationship to other theory building in the field, and its subsequent decline in influence during the 1960s and 1970s. The author documents the resurgence of this theory in the work of a new generation of anthropologists grappling with development and the problems attendant upon economic transformation.

Part Seven

Appendixes

Appendix 1
Informal Papers and Publications

27.1 Bamberger, Michael, and Scott Parris. The Structure of Social Networks in the Zona Sur Oriental of Cartagena. World Bank Water Supply and Urban Development Department Discussion Paper no. WUDD-58. Washington, D.C. 1984.

This paper reports parts of the findings of the study "Income Formation and Expenditure Patterns Among Poor Urban Households in Cartagena, Colombia". The objective of the research was to assess the importance of inter-household transfers as survival and economic development strategies for low-income urban dwellers. This particular paper focuses on anthropological studies of interactions between households in the Zona Sur Oriental of Cartagena and their support networks.

The households' strategies for survival, development, and maintenance of social ties with others are examined in detail. The paper also reviews the functions of transfers in cash, goods, services, information, and effective support between informal networks of households and covers the effects of the Cartagena urban upgrading project on transfers in the Zona Sur Oriental.

In addition to typologizing household strategies and interactions, the report describes the low-income, largely squatter area in which the anthropological research took place, briefly examines the ethnographic literature on inter-household networks among urban poor dwellers, and identifies issues for future analysis and research.

The anthropological research was undertaken in 1981 and 1982 in tandem with the preparation and application of a questionnaire covering demographic and economic characteristics of households and their transfers of money and goods, to a representative sample of 507 households. The two methods of data collection and analysis produced largely complementary results, with each method contextualizing the findings of the other.

27.2 Barnes, Douglas, and others. Accounting for Traditional Fuel Production: The Household Energy Sector and Its Implications for the Development. World Bank Industry and Energy Department Energy Series no. 49. Washington, D.C. 1992.

A fundamental proposition of modern economics is that to the extent that the prices of goods and services are established through exchanges in well-functioning markets, efficient allocations are likely. Conversely, if there are no markets for certain goods and services, allocations may be inefficient not only for the nonmarketed goods but also for marketed goods that may be substitutes for these goods. To the extent that economic development takes place with inefficient allocations, the full potential for growth in societal well-being will not be realized. The notion that GNP does not accurately reflect production in poor developing countries has widespread acceptance. The problem of undermeasuring national production has been well known for decades.

Instead of trying to account for the many areas of informal trade and production, this paper focuses on fuelwood production. In developing countries, the large portion of fuelwood consumed in households and the household labor that is used to collect this fuelwood meet the definition of nonmarketed goods and services. As expected from economic theory, there is evidence of inefficient allocations. Policy makers in certain instances can be misled by the notions that large infrastructure projects are superior to more mundane projects that may deal with informal household production. One of the most important contributions of including household production in the national accounts is not only that the value of household production is more accurately reflected in economic accounts, but the fact that the effect of development can be more fully measured. Such a framework is essential for evaluating the benefits of energy projects, especially in poor developing countries where informal production is a large component of economic activity.

27.3 Barnes, Douglas. Understanding Fuelwood Prices in Developing Nations. World Bank Industry and Energy Department Energy Series. Washington, D.C. 1992.

Several major policy issues emerge from the empirical analysis of wood fuel prices. Wood prices do not rise slowly as wood resources are depleted. There is evidence that prices are volatile and over a period of years may ratchet upward by rising fairly suddenly from low to high levels and back again. They eventually stabilize at levels fairly commensurate with modern fuels.

For cooking fuels, heavy kerosene subsidies are not useful for capping wood fuel prices unless there is a major concurrent shift towards higher or at least more equitable distribution of income to encourage interfuel substitution. However, the countries with heavy kerosene subsidies do have lower wood prices compared to most other countries in the study, but prices are well above the comparable price of kerosene for useful cooking energy.

Growth in income over the short run leads to an increase in fuelwood prices, but over the long run results in a decline in prices as people switch to modern fuels. An equitable growth of income would encourage substitution away from wood over the long run, but problems will remain over the short run.

Few incentives for fuelwood production exist in regions that have low market prices for wood fuels. Likewise, efficient stove and other conservation programs will not be very effective in countries with low prices. On the other hand it is the countries with low prices that are likely to experience the highest future draw down of forest stocks and consequent increases in wood prices.

27.4 Barnes, Douglas. **Sustainable Resource Management in Agriculture and Rural Development Projects: A Review of Policies, Procedures, and Results.** World Bank Environment Department Working Paper no. 5. Washington, D.C. 1988.

This report is based principally on a review of 115 agriculture and rural development projects approved by the Board between 1983 and 1986. The analysis, drawn primarily from the written documentation of the projects, indicates that most of the projects placed a major emphasis on improved production and generation of income for farmers, but relatively few dealt explicitly with long-term resource management issues. Only about 50 percent of projects mentioned resource problems in the project rationale, which means that fully half of the projects addressed sustainable resource management as an implied rather than an explicit part of the project. The projects with sustainable resource management as a significant goal included social forestry, watershed protection, and irrigation and drainage. The projects with greater resource problems included those with large changes in land use or those located in sensitive or marginal environments, including resettlement, livestock credit, and irrigation. Finally, for most projects it was very difficult to determine their implication for resource use, including agricultural extension, research, and many area development projects.

27.5 Barth, Fredrik, and Thomas Rhys Williams. **Report no. 1 of the Environmental and Resettlement Panel for the China Ertan Hydroelectric Project.** Ertan Hydroelectric Development Corporation. Xichang, Sichuan. June 1992.

The construction of the Ertan dam and reservoir will cause the relocation of about 30,000 people from the reservoir submergence area. An international panel consisting of two anthropologists and several Chinese technical experts was appointed to independently monitor the implementation of the project's population resettlement component and environmental mitigation plan. In this first report, the two anthropologists assess the first steps taken in the implementation of the resettlement plan.

The authors evaluate the plans and the actual progress at the Jinghe and Ping Shan sites positively, but criticize the delay in setting up the monitoring and research units required under the project. They call the attention of the project's management to a set of apparently unconsidered socioeconomic consequences likely to occur as a result of the expected flooding and relocation of the town of Yanbian. About 30-40 communities on the north and northwest side of the future lake will be cut off from their connections with surrounding market centers. The report recommends possible solutions for improving the relocation of Yanbian town.

27.6 Barth, Fredrik, and Thomas Rhys Williams. Report no. 2 of the Environmental and Resettlement Panel for the China Ertan Hydroelectric Project. Ertan Hydroelectric Development Corporation. Panzhihua, Sichuan. June 1993.

The report evaluates progress made in the relocation of the farm populations affected by the Ertan reservoir, including the opening of feeder roads to the new resettlement areas, the construction of irrigation facilities, and the preparation of terraced fields and house sites. The resettlers' expectations of enhanced prosperity after resettlement are being secured by innovations with cash crops, such as the introduction of oranges, mangoes, pomegranates, and special crops such as ginger.

The authors note that the criticism expressed in their first report has been taken into account by project officials, and that resettlement plans for Yanbian town have been reconsidered and revised in ways consistent with the concern expressed in the panel's 1992 report. However, the authors report that arrangements for establishing an independent socioeconomic research institution, provided for in the project, have not been carried out. They urge the Ertan Hydroelectric Development Corporation to take immediate action to create this institution as specified in the project design. The authors make specific suggestions for reconceptualizing transport and communication arrangements to effectively serve the needs of the dam catchment basin's residents.

27.7 Bhatnagar, Bhuvan. Non-Governmental Organizations and World Bank-Supported Projects in Asia: Lessons Learned. World Bank Asia Technical Department, Departmental Papers Series no. 2. Washington, D.C. 1991.

This study analyzes the role of NGOs in 39 Bank-supported projects, in twelve sectors in eight Asian countries and describes what has worked and why. It is intended to assist Bank task managers to involve NGOs in future Bank activities in the most effective manner by drawing lessons from past experiences and analyzing current project status.

The analysis is presented in a sequence of answers to nine basic questions about NGOs posed from a task manager's perspective. The first two questions relate to the efficacy of using NGOs in development programs; the next two questions concern categorizing and selecting NGOs for collaboration; two more questions are related to facilitating government-NGO relations and Bank-NGO relations; and the last three questions are procedural, concerning the use of Bank funding, accounting, and evaluation procedures in working with NGOs. The author emphasizes that there are no "right" or universal answers. In using a question-answer format, the study presents and analyzes locally specific approaches which the Bank has taken in relation to NGOs.

27.8   Campbell, Tim, and Mara Morgan. **Achieving Best Practice in Accountability of Local Governance in LAC.** World Bank Latin America Technical Department, Infrastructure and Energy Division (LATIE) Dissemination Note. Washington, D.C. 1992.

In the Latin America and Caribbean Region of the Bank, decentralization, coupled with democratization, is shifting spending and decision making powers to the local level. In these circumstances, local governments become economic decision makers of much greater import than in the past. On grounds of efficiency and stabilization, the Bank must address the essentially political process of economic decision making at the local level.

The purpose of this paper is to define in greater detail the theoretical and practical content of political accountability, defined as mechanisms to hold local officials, elected and otherwise, responsible for their actions in planning, spending, and management. The emphasis on political and institutional matters is a deliberate complement to the Bank's more traditional concern with financial accountability, for which growing experience is leading to standardized good practice. This paper also reviews selected modes of accountability, places them in a policy context, and identifies the most important gaps still to be addressed. On both accounts—what has been done and what is left to do—this paper is designed to assist task managers by identifying the most important principles of, and illustrating typical practice in, accountability in relation to the central mission of the Bank: efficiency in managing resources and equity in social policy, applied at the local government level.

27.9   Campbell, Tim. **Looking Forward and Looking Back on the Urban Sector in LAC: The Transformation of Urban Assistance by the Bank, 1972-1992.** World Bank Latin America Technical Department, Infrastructure and Energy Division (LATIE) Dissemination Note Prepared for the 20th Anniversary of Urban Assistance by the World Bank. Washington, D.C. 1992.

This paper provides an overview of World Bank urban lending during the last twenty years and describes the transition, over the past five years, from projects which emphasized infrastructure and civil works, to projects with a macroeconomic perspective. These new "municipal" projects are aimed at local government in cities, but with linkages to stabilization goals and to intergovernmental transfers or fiscal performance, in addition to physical improvements typical of the old style urban projects. The author points out that decentralization and democratization of the region are additional reasons why lending and assistance in LAC will be required to address questions of intergovernmental balance and accountability.

27.10 Campbell, Tim, and others. Decentralization to Local Government in LAC: National Strategies and Local Response in Planning, Spending, and Management. World Bank Latin America Technical Department, Infrastructure and Energy Division (LATIE) Regional Studies Program Report no. 5. Washington, D.C. 1991.

National decentralization strategies in the nine countries studied have shifted money to local governments in a manner which is out of phase with both expenditure responsibilities and local management capacity. These moves risk macroeconomic instability and decreases in efficiency. However, state reform in most countries is still in transition, and because decentralization is driven to an important degree by political imperatives of power sharing, local public sector empowerment, as opposed to recentralization, is likely to continue over this decade. Therefore, the major challenges for both the Bank and its borrowers lie not only in adjustments of intergovernmental fiscal arrangements, an area in which the Bank has experience and expertise, but also in redefining intergovernmental spending authority and strengthening the accountability and sustainability of local government, areas in which the Bank must increase its knowledge base. To be effective in these newer areas requires revisions in the Bank's present, implicit approach to municipal strengthening, which relies mainly on financial tools to leverage efficiency. A more comprehensive strategy is needed which combines financial tools with an emphasis on allocative efficiency, production efficiency, and equity in local government. To adopt this approach, in turn, implies entering new conceptual and policy terrain— political and legal accountability in governance—and a possible shift in the Bank's Regional skill mix.

27.11 Campbell, Tim, and others. Quasi-Matching Grants and Decentralization in Mexico. World Bank Latin America Technical Department, Infrastructure and Energy Division (LATIE) Dissemination Note. Washington, D.C. 1991.

This paper was prepared as a country report and is a background paper prepared as a part of the LACTD Regional Study on decentralization. The study confirms that many countries require stronger central government incentives to serve such objectives as improvement in poverty and environmental conditions and other areas where local governments are likely to underspend if left to their own preferences.

Matching grants offer a potentially useful tool for bringing local preferences in line with national priorities. The present paper focuses on Mexican matching grants as an example of a potentially useful tool, presently underutilized in LAC, to mediate central-local governmental and financial relationships. Matching grants induce demand for high priority investments in local public goods with spillovers (education, health care, sewage treatment). For the rest of the Region, and in the near term in Mexico, matching grants represent a potentially effective mechanism by which central governments can improve efficiency in resource allocation and project implementation at the local level.

27.12 Campbell, Tim. Social Investment Funds: Decentralization, Local Government and the Poor. World Bank Latin America Technical Department, Infrastructure and Energy Division (LATIE) Dissemination Note. Washington, D.C. 1991.

Social funds have grown increasingly popular as mechanisms to soften the shock of adjustment on low-income populations in the Region. But many of the more than ten funds currently underway or being contemplated do not take sufficiently into account the growing role of local governments—as a result of national decentralization policies—in infrastructure and services vital to the poor. Rather than buttressing new local authority, some funds represent a threat to long term institution building at both national and local levels. This paper addresses these issues and suggests ways to increase the effectiveness of social funds as development tools to strengthen local governments as well as to provide poverty assistance.

27.13 Campbell, Tim, and others. Decentralization in Chile. World Bank Country Report. Latin America Technical Department, Infrastructure and Energy Division (LATIE) Regional Study on Decentralization to Local Government in LAC. Washington, D.C. 1990.

This report is one of four freestanding country reports which form part of a larger comparative analysis of decentralization strategies and local government response in six countries of the Region. Country reports aim to "locate" national strategies in the context of the Region, to relate each country strategy to its macroeconomic objectives, to gauge progress in improving public sector efficiency and service to the poor, and to identify emerging problems and to harvest promising ideas for application elsewhere. The study "normalizes" cross-national observations by focusing on common factors in each country: strategic components of decentralization and local responses in social services and infrastructure. The report begins with a comparative overview of the Chilean strategy, followed by chapters analyzing, in turn, decentralization in fiscal affairs, decision making, and institutional strengthening. The concluding chapter identifies contributions of the Chilean experience, which are applicable to other sectors in the country and other countries in the Region.

27.14 Campbell, Tim, and Guillermo Yepes. Assessment of Municipal Solid Waste Services in Latin America. World Bank Latin America Technical Department, Infrastructure and Energy Division (LATIE) Report no. 8790-LAC. Washington, D.C. 1990.

This survey of solid waste management (SWM) in selected representative cities in the LAC Region was conducted in response to rising concerns about the health and environmental costs of poor solid waste service. The survey documents the policy and service gaps in solid waste management, highlighting the managerial and financial shortcomings of local governments on the one hand, and on the other, the positive experiences recorded so far among private providers of service. The region-wide trend towards decentralization of responsibilities to subnational governments heighten these concerns. It underscores the risks of environmental damage and calls for extensive institution building and improved regulations.

27.15 Cernea, Michael M. The Social Organization of Pastoral Groups and the Sociological Investigation of the Algerian Steppe. World Bank Agriculture and Rural Development Department Working Paper. Washington, D.C. 1975.

This study, which reports the author's findings and recommendations from a sociological investigation of pastoral social organization in Ksar Chellala, Algeria, was carried out for the preparation of the Steppe Development Project. Recent socioeconomic changes, including land reform and a contemplated "sheep reform" are discussed. Since the disruption of the ecological balance of the steppe and its accelerated degradation were the accumulated result of changes in traditional patterns of life (social, political, demographic, technological, and so on), only an integrated approach addressing both social and technical-agricultural needs could lead to effective improvements.

The author outlines the sociological research to be further conducted in the area and discusses the social stratification in the Ksar Chellala zone, the distribution and stratification of the pastoral population (both nomadic and sedentary) and cereal farmers in Ain Oussera, Sidi Ladjel, El Idrissia, and Chahbounia, existing pastoral cooperatives, and their deficiencies. He offers recommendations for making new, cooperative-type institutions socioculturally acceptable to the various tribal pastoral groups, and for overcoming the socioeconomic obstacles to gradual sedentarization.

27.16 Clark, Maria Donoso. Microenterprise Development in Quito, Ecuador: A Case Study of Social, Cultural, and Environmental Factors Affecting Growth. Ann Arbor, MI: UMI Dissertation Information Service. 1991.

This dissertation explores the internal and external dynamics of enterprises owned by microproducers participating in two credit programs: one financed by the Interamerican Development Bank through a non-governmental organization (Fundacion Ecuatoriana de Desarollo) and another by a private commercial bank (Banco del Pacifico). The research sample included 130 microproducers. The main finding of the dissertation is that microproducers in the informal sector resort to a combination of short and long-term strategies to cope with high levels of risk and uncertainty resulting from high monetary and non-monetary costs and from general lack of institutional support.

Short-term strategies help deal with day-to-day risks and opportunities while long-term strategies, termed "anchoring mechanisms" provide stability and growth potential. The three main "anchoring mechanisms are: (1) harnessing nuclear family labor; (2) owning a home; and (3) establishing relationships of trust with other individuals. Ensuring at least one "anchoring mechanism" is a high priority for informal microenterprises, making profit maximization or business expansion frequently a secondary priority. These findings suggest that microenterprise success should be measured not only in terms of profit maximization or business expansion, but in terms of increased standard of living, increased ability of the business owner to provide support to others, or consolidation of the business around the nuclear family. Moreover, microenterprise development programs should focus on the need to reduce transaction costs and facilitate the development of "anchoring mechanisms".

27.17 Clay, Jason W. World Bank Policy on Tribal People: Application to Africa. World Bank Africa Technical Department, Environmentally Sustainable Development Division Technical Note no. 16. Washington, D.C. 1991.

The author considers adaptation of World Bank Tribal Peoples policy to Africa and clarifies the definition of "tribal people" as it applies to social groups in Sub-Saharan Africa, outlining a proposal for treatment of such people in Bank-financed projects.

27.18 Davis, Shelton H. and Alaka Wali, Indigenous Territories and Tropical Forest Management in Latin America. World Bank Environment Department Policy Research Working Paper, Environmental Assessments and Programs. Washington, D.C. 1993.

Indigenous peoples are receiving increased recognition as resource managers of threatened tropical forest ecosystems. Using data from Latin America, the author argues that fundamental changes need to take place in the legal recognition and demarcation of indigenous territories in order to fully use the potential of these social groups.

The author makes a comparison between different national land tenure models which have been applied to forest-dwelling indigenous peoples in Brazil, Venezuela, Ecuador, Peru, Bolivia, Panama, and Colombia and a model proposed by Latin American indigenous organizations. This comparison suggests that not only do indigenous peoples need to be provided with some degree of control over their territories and resources, but there needs to be a new type of partnership among indigenous peoples, the scientific community, national governments, and international development agencies for the management of tropical forests.

27.19 **Dia, Mamadou. Indigenous Management Practices: Lessons for Africa's Management in the '90s.** World Bank Africa Technical Department, Institutional Development and Management Division Concept Paper for Regional Study. Washington, D.C. 1992.

The author argues for the need to adapt development assistance to African local culture, in particular the psychology of economic decision making. He offers new approaches to project management, reconciling traditional values and economic efficiency.

27.20 **Elder, John. The Socio-Economic Determinants of Nutritional Status among Children under Five in Mauritania.** World Bank Africa Technical Department Poverty and Social Policy Series. Washington, D.C. 1991.

The author analyzes the nutritional status of children under five in Mauritania using data collected for the Living Standards Measurement Study. He reviews earlier studies of nutrition in Mauritania, and describes present study methodology and data. He links the presence of malnutrition to various factors (geography, household expenditure, parental education and analyzes the determinants of nutritional status in Mauritania.

27.21 **Fuller, Bruce and Marlaine E. Lockheed. Policy Choice and School Efficiency in Mexico.** World Bank EDT Discussion Paper no. 78. Washington, D.C. 1987.

Little is known about the relative efficiency with which alternative educational policies—set by central governments— actually influence pupil achievement. This study examines the influence of economic wealth and government spending policies on school completion rates among students in Mexico's states over the period 1973-79. Economic factors were found to play a large role in determining a state's school completion rate. In addition, the evidence suggests that providing more places within public preschools is the most cost-effective strategy for raising primary school completion. Reducing the pupil-teacher ratio is related to school completion in the short run but is not an efficient strategy. Increasing the percentage of teachers with paper credentials also yields low returns relative to cost.

27.22 Guggenheim, Scott and Maritta Koch-Weser. Participation for Sustainable Development. Paper prepared for the World Development Report. World Bank. Washington, D.C. 1992

This paper is an overview of the issues related to public participation in environmental development and natural resource management. The authors argue that there are three issues that must be addressed in the discussion of participation in environmental development: (1) the need to separate out participation as a means for improving natural resource management from participation as an end to itself; (2) recognition of the fact that despite the generic concept of participation, in any given country or cultural context participation will have very different meanings; (3) the means by which a philosophy of participation can be turned into usable concepts, strategies, and procedures—the analytic tools of development.

The body of the paper is divided into the following sections: (1) What is Participation? (2) Benefits from Participation; (3) Potential Drawbacks and Costs Associated with Participation; (4) Who Participates? (5) How Participation Can Be Improved; and (6) How Can International Development Assistance Promote Participation? Throughout the text, anecdotal examples are used to illustrate the points made.

27.23 Guichaoua, André, and others. "Les Contraintes Sociales et Institutionnelles du Developpement de l'Agriculture Burundaise Apprehendees au Niveau des Communes." Working paper in preparation for Agricultural Sector Study of Burundi. World Bank. Washington, D.C. 1991.

This paper was created by a multidisciplinary World Bank team which included an economist, a legal expert, an agronomist, a sociologist, and a hydraulics engineer, among others. It analyses social and institutional constraints to agricultural development specifically in a community context.

The study examines community organization, relations between villagers and local authorities, village social services, the tensions and communication constraints between farmers and agricultural officials and extension agents, the growing specialization of rural labor, and community laws and legal structures. The central recommendations of the study concern decentralization of authority, increased community autonomy, greater accountability of providers of public services, clearer specification of scope and responsibilities of government administrators above the community level, and promotion of nongovernmental and cooperative community organizations.

27.24 Kudat, Ayse and Vincy Fong. Gender and Urban Water Supply: A Case Study of Chittagong. World Bank Infrastructure and Urban Development Department, Water and Sanitation Division (INUWS) Working Paper. Washington, D.C. 1991.

27.25 Kudat, Ayse. Women and Reliability of Infrastructure Services. World Bank Infrastructure and Urban Development Department, Water and Sanitation Division (INUWS) Discussion Note. Washington, D.C. 1991.

27.26 Kudat, Ayse. Time for Sharper Focus on Women in Infrastructure. World Bank Infrastructure and Urban Development Department, Water and Sanitation Division (INUWS) Discussion Note. Washington, D.C. 1991.

27.27 Kudat, Ayse. Gender Issues in Transport. World Bank Infrastructure and Urban Development Department, Water and Sanitation Division (INUWS) Discussion Note. Washington, D.C. 1991.

27.28 Kudat, Ayse. Women's Participation in Rural Road Maintenance in Sub-Saharan Africa. World Bank Economic Development Institute (EDI) Working Paper. Washington, D.C. 1989.

27.29 Kudat, Ayse and Helen Abadzi. Women's Presence in Arab Higher Education: Linking School, Labor Markets, and Social Roles. World Bank Economic Development Institute Working Paper. Washington, D.C. 1989.

27.30 Lockheed, Marlaine E., John Middleton, and Greta S. Nettleton, eds. Educational Technology: Sustainable and Effective Use. World Bank PHREE/91/32. Washington, D.C. 1991.

This book reviews research efforts and pilot projects on using technology in general education, distance education, and vocational training in more than fifty developed and developing countries. The editors present (1) an overview entitled "Educational Technology: Toward Appropriate and Sustainable Use," which introduces the purpose and scope of the review and discusses the availability, implementation, and economic efficiency of technologies, as well as barriers to implementation —that is, technological environment, administrative capacity, and political receptivity. The survey chapters are (2) "Educational Technology and the Improvement of General Education in Developing Countries," by Stephen Anzalone; (3) "Uses and Costs of

Educational Technology for Distance Education in Developing Countries: A Review of the Recent Literature," by Greta S. Nettleton; (4) "Uses and Costs of Educational Technology for Vocational Training: Current Research in Canada and the United States, with Implications for developing Countries," by Anna Stahmer (and others). Country case studies are presented in (5) "Pilot Projects in Educational Technology: The Philippine Case", by John Middleton; (6) "A Comparison of Open Universities in Thailand and Indonesia", by David N. Wilson; (7) "Computer Applications in Vocational Training in Norway" by Arvid Staupe; and (8) "Sustainability in Four Interactive Radio Projects: Bolivia, Honduras, Lesotho, and Papua New Guinea," by Thomas D. Tilson.

27.31 **Lockheed, Marlaine E., and Barbara Bruns. School Effects on Achievement in Secondary Mathematics and Portuguese in Brazil.** World Bank PRE Working Paper no. 525. Washington, D.C. 1990.

Determinants of achievement are examined to assess the relative effectiveness of various types of secondary schools in boosting performance and reducing social class differentiation. A stratified random sample of 2,611 students in 62 schools in four cities in Brazil were administered a standardized test of mathematics and Portuguese and a student background questionnaire; a school questionnaire was directed to administrators. While controlling for student-level characteristics, group-level variance in achievement was modeled to explore (1) the percentage of variance attributable to the types of schools attended; (2) influence of school-level factors; and (3) within school differences due to the students' socioeconomic status. Students in federal technical schools outperformed those in general secondary, teacher training, and full secondary schools with technical specializations—in both subject areas. For mathematics only, significant factors included class size (achievement was higher in larger classes) and number of instructional hours. Unrelated variables included teachers' stipends, high tuition fees, enrollment in day-only classes, organizational complexity, and university-educated teachers. These findings suggest that student selection accounted for much of the observed differences.

27.32 **Lockheed, Marlaine E., and others. Effective Primary Level Science Teaching in the Philippines.** World Bank Planning, Policy, and Research (PPR) Working Paper no. 208. Washington, D.C. 1989.

The authors analyzed data from 419 classrooms that participated in the IEA International Science Study. Frequent group work (including peer tutoring), frequent testing, and laboratory teaching were found to improve the achievement of fifth grade science students in the Philippines. Teachers' decisions about whether to test students frequently on the whole were unrelated to their prior education or experience. This suggests that school-level management may be more important in encouraging effective teaching practices than preservice education and training. The three teaching practices identified as effective show promise for application in developing countries because they are low-cost and/or cost-effective.

27.33 Lockheed, Marlaine E. **School and Classroom Effects on Student Learning gain: The Case of Thailand**. World Bank EDT Discussion Paper no. 98. Washington, D.C. 1987.

This paper employs a fixed-effects regression analysis to examine school effects on individual student learning gain during eighth grade in 99 lower-secondary schools in Thailand. Schools accounted for 34 percent of the variance in individual student pretest scores but only 6 percent of the variance in student achievement gain. School factors accounted for approximately 7 percent of the variance in both urban and rural schools. In both rural and urban schools, larger schools and an enriched curriculum were positively associated with learning gain, while higher student-teacher ratios at the school level were negatively associated with learning gain. Other factors, however, operated differently in the two types of schools. An important policy implication is that strategies for improving rural schools should not be derived from research conducted primarily in urban schools in developing countries.

27.34 Molnar, Augusta, and Gotz Schreiber. **Women and Forestry: Operational Guidelines**. World Bank Policy, Planning, and Research (PPR) Working Paper no. 184. Washington, D.C. 1989.

This working paper is a manual for World Bank and borrower staff on ways to involve women in forestry projects. It explains how the involvement of women in forestry can further forestry development and how forestry can better meet the needs of rural women. It includes detailed annexes on planning strategies and types of information to be collected during different phases of the project cycle.

27.35 Murphy, Josette. **Women and Agriculture in Africa: A Guide to Bank Policy and Programs for Operations Staff**. Washington, D.C.: World Bank, Africa Technical Department. 1989.

This document provides agricultural project officers in the World Bank Africa Region with a summary of current Bank strategy regarding its Women in Development Initiative, and with a brief review of gender-related issues which they need to take into consideration when preparing and supervising agriculture operations. Women are key contributors to agriculture and related productive activities throughout Africa, and they are also key decision makers in matters related to income, expenditure, and consumption patterns of the household. These roles make them significant actors in economic development and food security for their countries. Consequently, the World

Bank gives high priority to insuring that its operations encourage and facilitate actions which will enable women farmers to reach their full productive potential and improve their working and living conditions. This objective is to be reached by integrating gender-related issues into normal sectoral and operational work.

27.36 Noronha, Raymond. A Review of the Literature on Land Tenure Systems in Sub-Saharan Africa. World Bank Agriculture Research Unit Paper no. 48. Washington, D.C. 1985.

The author reviews the types of tenurial systems prevalent in Sub-Saharan Africa and concludes that with increasing population and the growth of markets and infrastructure, traditional systems of tenure tend to evolve toward the increasing appropriation of land by smaller units (families and individuals) to the exclusion of the wider unit (extended families, lineages, and clans) and to approximate the western notion of freehold. The introduction of parallel and even conflicting systems of formal law that are based on western models and which are imperfectly implemented leads to growing insecurity of tenure and encourages land grabbing. Another result of the introduction of these formal systems and the theoretical view of tenure in Sub-Saharan Africa (particularly during the colonial regimes) has resulted in the stifling of the evolution of tenure systems to adapt to changing socioeconomic conditions.

27.37 Parris, Scott. Survival Strategies and Support Networks: an Anthropological Perspective. World Bank Water Supply and Urban Development Department Discussion Paper no. UDD-58. Washington, D.C. 1984.

For content, see entry 27.1.

27.38 Shipton, Parker. How Gambians Save—and What Their Strategies Imply for International Aid. World Bank Policy, Research, and External Affairs (PRE) Working Paper no. 395. Washington, D.C. 1990.

International aid interventions in The Gambia have been based mainly on credit and, thus, on debt. Public and private lending institutions have failed dramatically and debts are mounting, but lenders continue extending loans into the countryside.

This paper looks at the saving side of rural finance, internationally the more neglected side. It describes several indigenous and other saving systems, starting with those closest to a rural home and proceeding outward, and shows that farmers resort to both individually and socially devised means of saving, many of them convenient but comparatively costly to them.

Farmers need not just credit, but also more and better opportunities for savings, partly to reduce their dependency on borrowing. A financial policy based only on credit without savings is not only ethically dubious, but also impractical, like walking on one leg.

27.39 Tobisson, Eva, and Anders Rudqvist. "Popular Participation in Natural Resource Management for Development." In vol. *Integrated Natural Resource Management: Report from a Workshop in Francistown, Botswana. 1991.* World Bank Africa Technical Department, Environment Division. Washington, D.C. 1992.

The paper deals with popular participation in natural resource management. Since there are only a few environmental projects with successful popular participation, it is important to examine not only the reasons for the frequent lack of participation, but also the reasons for success in some projects.

Environmental concerns in development are a reflection of a more general environmental debate which is ultimately based on political and economic considerations. The implications of this wider context of practical environmental action are outlined. The authors argue that prevalent natural science and economic bias obscures the essential relationships between local social groups and the natural resources utilized and managed by those groups. Biased notions of what constitutes an "environmental expert" work against the involvement of local groups in project work.

Numerous community aspects must be taken into account in programs professing to take heed of local potential for and constraints on improved natural resource management. The authors have identified several dimensions which they deem of particular significance: ownership, management and control of common property resources, the relationship between gender and the environment, and the usefulness of entities like "village" and "community" as units of social organization in environmental programs.

27.40 World Bank Africa Technical Department, Institutional Development and Management Division Staff. Indigenous Management Practices: Lessons for Africa's Management in the '90s. Work Program and Study Proposal Paper. Washington, D.C. 1992.

This paper is based on Entry 27.14, a concept paper for regional study of the same name. It explores institutional innovations, using case studies to integrate African culture into design and management of programs.

27.41 World Bank Africa Technical Department, Human Resources Division Staff. Women's Crucial Role in Managing the Environment in Sub-Saharan Africa. Technical Note WID/AFTSP. Washington, D.C. 1991.

This paper summarizes the conceptual underpinnings of the connection between the familial and societal functions of women, the constraints and disincentives they face in the socioeconomic system, and the degradation of Sub-Saharan African resources. It provides an overview of World Bank activities in Sub-Saharan Africa linking gender and environmental issues since 1980.

Appendix 2
Index of Works at a Glance

Part One: Social Science and Development

Use of Social Science in Development

1.1 Butcher, David. "Human and Institutional Development." In Czech Conroy and Miles Litvinoff, eds. *The Greening of Aid. Sustainable Livelihoods in Practice.* London: Earthscan Publications Ltd. 1988.

1.2 Cernea, Michael M. "Anthropological and Sociological Research for Policy Development on Population Resettlement." In M.M. Cernea and S.E. Guggenheim, eds. *Anthropological Approaches to Involuntary Resettlement: Policy, Practice, and Theory.* Boulder, Col.: Westview Press. 1993.

1.3 Cernea, Michael M. "The Sociologist's Approach to Sustainable Development." *Finance & Development* 30(4) (December 1993).

1.4 Cernea, Michael M., ed. *Putting People First: Sociological Variables in Development.* 2nd ed., revised and enlarged. New York and London: Oxford University Press. 1991.

1.5 Cernea, Michael M., ed. *Putting People First: Sociological Variables in Development Projects.* (1st ed.). New York: Oxford University Press. 1985.

1.6 Cernea, Michael M. *Mengutamakan Manusia Di Dalam Pembangunan: Variabel-variabel Sosiologi di dalam Pembangunan Pedesaan.* Jakarta: Penerbit Universitas Indonesia. 1988.

1.7 Cernea, Michael M. "Knowledge from Social Science for Development Policies and Projects." In M.M. Cernea, ed. *Putting People First: Sociological*

Variables in Rural Development. 2nd ed. New York, London: Oxford University Press. 1991.

1.8 Cernea, Michael M. "Sociologists in a Development Agency: Experiences from the World Bank." In Michael Schönhuth, ed. *The Socio-Cultural Dimension in Development: The Contribution of Sociologists and Social Anthropologists to the Work of Development Agencies*. Eschborn, Germany: GTZ. 1991.

1.9 Cernea, Michael M. *Using Knowledge from Social Science in Development Projects*. World Bank Discussion Paper no. 114. Washington, D.C. 1991.

1.10 Cernea, Michael M. *Social Science Knowledge for Development Interventions*. HIID Development Discussion Paper no. 334. Cambridge, Mass.: Harvard University. 1990.

1.11 Kardam, Nüket. "Development Approaches and the Role of Policy Advocacy: The Case of the World Bank." *World Development* 21(11):1773-86. 1993.

1.12 Kottak, Conrad Phillip. "When People Don't Come First: Some Sociological Lessons from Completed Projects." In M.M. Cernea, ed. *Putting People First: Sociological Variables in Rural Development*. 2nd ed. New York, London: Oxford University Press. 1991.

1.13 Lethem, Francis J., and Heli Perrett. *Human Factors in Project Work*. World Bank Staff Working Paper no. 397. Washington, D.C. 1980.

1.14 Lipset, Seymour Martin. "The Social Requisites of Democracy Revisited. 1993 Presidential Address." *American Sociological Review* 59(1):1-22. February 1994.

1.15 Rogers, Everett M., Nat J. Colletta, and Joseph Mbindyo. "Social and Cultural Influences on Human Development Policies and Programs." In P.T. Knight, ed. *Implementing Programs of Human Development*. World Bank Staff Working Paper no. 403. Washington, D.C. 1980.

1.16 Serageldin, Ismail. "Public Administration in the 1990s: Rising to the Challenge." In *Public Administration in the Nineties: Trends and Innovations*. Proceedings of the Twelfth International Congress of Administrative Sciences. Brussels: International Institute of Administrative Sciences. 1992.

1.17　Serageldin, Ismail. "The Human Dimension of Structural Adjustment Programmes: World Bank's Perspective." In A. Adedeji, S. Rasheed, and M. Morrison, eds. *The Human Dimension of Africa's Persistent Economic Crisis*. Kent, England: Hans Zell Publishers. 1990.

1.18　Serageldin, Ismail, and Pierre Landell-Mills. "Governance and the External Factor." In *Proceedings of the World Bank Annual Conference on Development Economics 1991*. Washington, D.C.: World Bank. 1992.

1.19　Serageldin, Ismail, and Michel Noël. "Tackling the Social Dimensions of Adjustment in Africa." *Finance & Development* (September 1990): 18-20.

1.20　Uphoff, Norman. "Political Considerations in Human Development." In P.T. Knight, ed. *Implementing Programs of Human Development*. World Bank Staff Working Paper no. 403. Washington, D.C. 1980.

Project Preparation, Design, and Appraisal

2.1　Bamberger, Michael, and Abdul Aziz, eds. *The Design and Management of Sustainable Poverty Alleviation Projects in South Asia*. World Bank Economic Development Institute Seminar Report Series. Washington, D.C. 1993.

2.2　Bennett, Lynn, and Mike Goldberg. *Providing Enterprise Development and Financial Services to Women: A Decade of Bank Experience in Asia*. World Bank Technical Paper no. 236. Washington, D.C. 1993.

2.3　Cernea, Michael M. "Entrance Points for Sociological Knowledge in Planned Rural Development." In H. Schwartzweller, ed. *Research in Rural Sociology and Development*. Greenwich, Conn.: JAI Press. 1987.

2.4　Cernea, Michael M. "The Sukuma: A Socio-Cultural Profile." Working Paper c-1, vol. I, Annex to the Tanzania Mwanza-Shinyanga Rural Development Project Staff Appraisal Report. World Bank. Washington, D.C. 1978.

2.5　Cernea, Michael M., and Scott McLeod. "The Village Self-Help Program in Mwanza-Shinyanga: Socio-Cultural Feasibility Assessment." Working Paper c-9, vol. II, Annex to the Tanzania Mwanza-Shinyanga Rural Development Project Staff Appraisal Report. World Bank. Washington, D.C. 1978.

2.6	Hecht, Robert M. "Land and Water Rights and the Design of Small Scale Irrigation Projects: The Case of Baluchistan." *Irrigation and Drainage Systems*. 4:59-76. 1990.

2.7	Hecht, Robert M. "Salvage Anthropology: The Redesign of a Rural Development Project in Guinea." In M. Horowitz and T. Painter, eds. *Anthropology and Rural Development in West Africa*. Boulder, Col.: Westview Press. 1986.

2.8	Horowitz, Michael M. "Social Analysis Working Paper for the Zimbabwe Rural Afforestation Project." Working Paper no. 20. Binghamton, N.Y.: Institute for Development Anthropology. 1982.

2.9	Molnar, Augusta. "Rapid Rural Appraisal Methodology Applied to Project Planning and Implementation in Natural Resource Management." In Timothy Finan and John van Willigen, eds. *Soundings: Rapid and Reliable research Methods for Practicing Anthropologists*. NAPA Bulletin 10. 1991.

2.10	Molnar, Augusta. Community Forestry: Rapid Appraisal. Community Forestry Note 3. United Nations Food and Agriculture Organization. Rome. 1989.

2.11	Noronha, Raymond J., and Francis J. Lethem. *Traditional Land Tenures and Land Use Systems in the Design of Agricultural Projects*. World Bank Staff Working Paper no. 561. Washington, D.C. 1983.

2.12	Noronha, Raymond, and John Spears. "The Sociological Dimensions of Forestry Project Design." In M.M. Cernea, ed. *Putting People First: 1st ed*. New York: Oxford University Press. 1985.

2.13	Salmen, Lawrence F. "Beneficiary Assessment: Improving the Design and Implementation of Development Projects." In *Evaluation Review* 13(3):273-91. 1989.

2.14	World Bank. Operational Directive 4.01: *Environmental Assessment*. October 3, 1991 (a revision of the former OD 4.00, Annex A. October 1989).

2.15	World Bank. Operational Directive 4.02: *Environmental Action Plans*. July 21, 1992.

2.16	World Bank. Operational Directive 4.30: *Involuntary Re-settlement*. June 29, 1990.

2.17 World Bank. Operational Directive 4.20: *Indigenous Peoples*. September 17, 1991.

2.18 World Bank. Operational Directive 4.00: Annex B. *Environmental Policy for Dam and Reservoir Projects*. April 28, 1989.

2.19 World Bank. Operational Directive 14.70: *Involving Nongovernmental Organizations in Bank-Supported Activities*. August 28, 1989.

2.20 World Bank. Operational Policy Note 11.02: *Wildlands—Their Protection and Management in Economic Development*. June 2, 1986.

2.21 World Bank. Operational Policy Note 11.03: *Management of Cultural Property in Bank-Financed Projects*. September 1986.

2.22 World Bank. Operational Policy Note 10.08: *Operations Issues in the Treatment of Involuntary Resettlement in Bank-Financed Projects*. October 8, 1986.

2.23 World Bank. Operational Manual Statement 2.33: *Social Issues Associated with Involuntary Resettlement in Bank-Financed Projects*. February 1980.

2.24 World Bank. Operational Manual Statement 2.20: *Project Appraisal*. February 6, 1984.

Additional publications relevant to this topic can be found in Section 24.

Project Implementation, Monitoring, and Evaluation

3.1 Bamberger, Michael. "The Politics of Evaluation in Developing Countries." *Evaluation and Program Planning*. 14:325-39. 1991.

3.2 Bamberger, Michael, and Shabbir Cheema. *Case Studies of Project Sustainability: Implications for Policy and Operations from Asian Experience*. Economic Development Institute Seminar Series. World Bank. Washington, D.C. 1990.

3.3 Bamberger, Michael. "The Monitoring and Evaluation of Public Sector Programs in Asia: Why Are Development Programs Monitored but Not Evaluated?" *Evaluation Review* 13(1):223-42. 1989.

3.4 Bamberger, Michael, and Viqar Ahmed. *Monitoring and Evaluating Development Projects: The South Asian Experience*. Economic Development Institute Seminar Series. World Bank. Washington D.C. 1989.

3.5 Bamberger, Michael, and Eleanor Hewitt. *Monitoring and Evaluating Urban Development Programs: A Handbook for Program Managers and Researchers*. World Bank Technical Paper no. 53. Washington, D.C. 1987.

3.6 Bamberger, Michael, and Eleanor Hewitt. *A Manager's Guide to Monitoring and Evaluating Urban Development Programs: A Handbook for Program Managers and Researchers*. World Bank Technical Paper no. 54. Washington, D.C. 1987.

3.7 Bamberger, Michael, and others. *Evaluation of Sites and Services Projects: The Experience from Lusaka, Zambia*. World Bank Staff Working Paper no. 548. Washington, D.C. 1982.

3.8 Bamberger, Michael, and others. *Evaluation of Sites and Services Projects: The Experience from El Salvador*. World Bank Staff Working Paper no. 549. Washington, D.C. 1982.

3.9 Cernea, Michael M. *Measuring Project Impact: Monitoring and Evaluation in the PIDER Rural Development Project—Mexico*. World Bank Staff Working Paper no. 332. Washington, D.C. 1979.

3.10 Cernea, Michael M., and Benjamin J. Tepping. *A System for Monitoring and Evaluating Agricultural Extension Projects*. World Bank Staff Working Paper no. 272. Washington, D.C. 1977.

3.11 Murphy, Josette. "Good Enough, Soon Enough: A User-Oriented Approach to Monitoring and Evaluation in Extension Agencies." *Rural Extension Bulletin 1:4-8*. Agricultural Extension and Rural Development Center, University of Reading, England. February 1993.

3.12 Murphy, Josette, and Timothy Marchant. *Monitoring and Evaluation in Extension Agencies*. World Bank Technical Paper no. 79. Washington, D.C. 1988.

3.13 Murphy, Josette. *Using Evaluations for Planning and Management: An Introduction*. Working Paper no. 2. International Service for National Agricultural Research (ISNAR). The Hague. 1985.

3.14 Narayan, Deepa. *Participatory Evaluation: Tools for Managing Change in Water and Sanitation.* World Bank Technical Paper no. 217. Washington, D.C. 1993.

3.15 Narayan, Deepa. *Workshop on Goals and Indicators for Monitoring and Evaluation for Water Supply and Sanitation in Geneva, Switzerland.* UNDP-World Bank Water and Sanitation Program. Washington, D.C. 1991.

3.16 Perrett, Heli E. *Using Communication Support in Projects: World Bank's Experience.* World Bank Staff Working Paper no. 551. Washington, D.C. 1982.

3.17 Salmen, Lawrence. "Participant-Observer Evaluation of Upgrading Projects in Two Latin American Cities: La Paz and Guayaquil." In Reinhard J. Skinner, and others., eds. *Shelter Upgrading for the Urban Poor: Evaluation of Third World Experience.* Manila: Publishing House Inc. 1987.

3.18 Salmen, Lawrence. *Listen to the People.* New York: Oxford University Press. 1987.

Additional publications relevant to this topic can be found in Section 25.

Part Two: Social Organization and Social Actors

Social Organization and Institutional Development

4.1 Bamberger, Michael, and others. "Resource Mobilization and the Household Economy of Kenya." *Canadian Journal of African Studies* 19(2):409-21. 1985.

4.2 Bouman, F.J.A. "Indigenous Savings and Credit Societies in the Developing World." In J.D. Von Pischke, D.W. Adams, and G. Donald, eds. *Rural Financial Markets in Developing Countries.* Baltimore and London: The Johns Hopkins University Press. 1983.

4.3   Cernea, Michael M. *Nongovernmental Organizations and Local Development.* World Bank Discussion Paper no. 40. Washington, D.C. 1988.

4.4   Cernea, Michael M. "Farmer Organizations and Institution Building for Sustainable Development." *Regional Development Dialogue* 8(2):1-24. 1987.

4.5   Cernea, Michael M. "Modernization and Development Potential of Traditional Grassroots Peasant Organizations." In M. Attir, B. Holzner, Z. Suda, eds. *Directions of Change: Modernization Process in Theory and Reality.* Boulder, Col.: Westview Press. 1981.

4.6   Cernea, Michael M. "The Organization and the Individual: The Economic Rationale of Cooperative Farm Members." *Journal of Rural Cooperation* 3(1). Jerusalem Academy Press. 1975.

4.7   Hecht, Robert M. "The Transformation of Lineage Production in Southern Ivory Coast." *Ethnology* 23(4):261-77. 1984.

4.8   Hussi, Pekka, Josette Murphy, and others. *The Development of Cooperatives and Other Rural Organizations: The Role of the World Bank.* World Bank Technical Paper no. 199. Washington, D.C. 1993.

4.9   Ibrahim, Saad E. and Nicholas Hopkins, eds. *Arab Society: Social Science Perspectives.* Cairo: The American University in Cairo. 1978.

4.10   Partridge, William L. "The Human Ecology of Tropical Land Settlement in Latin America: An Overview." In D. Schumann and W.L. Partridge, eds. *The Human Ecology of Tropical Land Settlement in Latin America.* Boulder, Col.: Westview Press. 1989.

4.11   Pollnac, Richard B. "Social and Cultural Characteristics in Small-scale Fishery Development." In M.M. Cernea, ed. *Putting People First: Sociological Variables in Rural Development.* 2nd ed. New York, London: Oxford University Press. 1991.

4.12   Schumann, D. and William L. Partridge, eds. *The Human Ecology of Tropical Land Settlement in Latin America.* Boulder, Col.: Westview Press. 1989.

Additional publications relevant to this topic can be found in Sections 8 through 15.

Participation

5.1 Bamberger, Michael, and Khalid Shams. *Community Participation in Project Management: The Asian Experience*. Kuala Lumpur: Asian and Pacific Development Centre. 1989.

5.2 Bamberger, Michael. *Community Participation, Development Planning and Project Management*. Economic Development Institute Policy Seminar Report no. 13. World Bank. Washington, D.C. 1988.

5.3 Bhatnagar, Bhuvan and Aubrey Williams, eds. *Participatory Development and the World Bank: Potential Directions for Change*. World Bank Discussion Paper no. 183. Washington, D.C. 1992.

5.4 Bhatnagar, Bhuvan. "Participatory Development and the World Bank: Opportunities and Concerns." In B. Bhatnagar and A. Williams, eds. *Participatory Development and the World Bank: Potential Directions for Change*. World Bank Discussion Paper no. 183. Washington, D.C. 1992.

5.5 Cernea, Michael M. *The Building Blocks of Participation: Testing Bottom-up Planning*. World Bank Discussion Paper no. 166. Washington, D.C. 1992.

5.6 Dichter, Thomas. "Demystifying Popular Participation: Institutional Mechanisms for Popular Participation." In B. Bhatnagar and A. Williams, eds. *Participatory Development and the World Bank: Potential Directions for Change*. World Bank Discussion Paper no. 183. Washington, D.C. 1992.

5.7 Elmendorf, Mary. "Public Participation and Acceptance." In C.G. Gunnerson and J.M. Kalbermatten, eds. *Environmental Impacts of International Civil Engineering Projects and Practices*. New York: American Society of Civil Engineers. 1978.

5.8 Falloux, François, and Lee Talbott. "Political Involvement and Popular Participation." In F. Falloux and L. Talbott, eds. *Crisis and Opportunity: Environment and Development in Africa*. London: Earthscan, Ltd. 1992.

5.9 Narayan, Deepa. *Participatory Materials Toolkit: Training of Trainers and for Community Empowerment*. Washington, D.C.: World Bank. 1994.

5.10 Narayan, Deepa. "Participatory Gender Analysis Tools for the Community and Agency Level." In W. Wakeman, ed. *Gender Issues Sourcebook for the*

Water and Sanitation Sector. Washington, D.C.: Water and Sanitation Collaborative Council. 1994.

5.11 Paul, Samuel. *Community Participation in Development Projects: the World Bank Experience.* World Bank Discussion Paper no. 6. Washington, D.C. 1987.

5.12 Racelis, Mary. "The United Nations Children's Fund: Experience with People's Participation." In B. Bhatnagar and A. Williams, eds. *Participatory Development and the World Bank: Potential Directions for Change.* World Bank Discussion Paper no. 183. Washington, D.C. 1992.

5.13 Rudquist, Anders. "The Swedish International Development Authority: Experience with Popular Participation." In B. Bhatnagar and A. Williams, eds. *Participatory Development and the World Bank: Potential Directions for Change.* World Bank Discussion Paper no. 183. Washington, D.C. 1992.

5.14 Uphoff, Norman. "Monitoring and Evaluating Popular Participation in World Bank-Assisted Projects." In B. Bhatnagar and A. Williams, eds. *Participatory Development and the World Bank: Potential Directions for Change.* World Bank Discussion Paper no. 183. Washington, D.C. 1992.

5.15 Uphoff, Norman. "Fitting Projects to People." In M.M. Cernea, ed. *Putting People First: Sociological Variables in Rural Development.* 2nd ed. New York, London: Oxford University Press. 1991.

Poverty Reduction

6.1 Cernea, Michael M. **Poverty Risks from Population Displacement in Water Resources Development.** HIID Development Discussion Paper no. 355. Cambridge, Mass.: Harvard University. 1990.

6.2 Esman, Milton J. and John D. Montgomery. "The Administration of Human Development." In P.T. Knight, ed. *Implementing Programs of Human Development.* World Bank Staff Working Paper no. 403. Washington, D.C. 1980.

6.3 Grootaert, Christian, and Timothy Marchant. *The Social Dimensions of Adjustment Priority Survey: An Instrument for the Rapid Identification and Monitoring of Policy Target Groups.* World Bank Social Dimensions of Adjustment Working Paper no. 12. Washington, D.C. 1991.

6.4 Grootaert, Christian, Timothy Marchant, and others. *The Social Dimensions of Adjustment Integrated Survey: A Survey to Measure Poverty and Understand the Effects of Policy Change on Households.* World Bank Social Dimensions of Adjustment Working Paper no. 14. Washington, D.C. 1991.

6.5 Safilios-Rothschild, Constantina. "The Role of the Family: a Neglected Aspect of Poverty." In P.T. Knight, ed. *Implementing Programs of Human Development.* World Bank Staff Working Paper no. 403. Washington, D.C. 1980.

6.6 Salmen, Lawrence. *Reducing Poverty: an Institutional Perspective.* World Bank Poverty and Social Policy Series Paper no. 1. Washington, D.C. 1992.

6.7 Salmen, Lawrence. "Reducing Poverty." In *Public Administration and Development* 11(3):295-302. 1991.

6.8 World Bank. *Poverty Reduction Handbook.* Washington, D.C. 1993.

Culture, Beliefs, and Values

7.1 Ardouin, Claude. "What Models for African Museums? West African Prospects." In I. Serageldin and J. Taboroff, eds. *Culture and Development in Africa: Proceedings of an International Conference.* Washington, D.C.: World Bank. 1993.

7.2 Bryant, Coralie. "Culture, Management, and Institutional Assessment." In I. Serageldin and J. Taboroff, eds. *Culture and Development in Africa: Proceedings of an International Conference.* Washington, D.C.: World Bank. 1993.

7.3 Cernea, Michael M. "Culture and Organization: The Social Sustainability of Induced Development." In *Sustainable Development* 1(2):18-29. Australia. 1993.

7.4 Colletta, Nat J., and Umar Khayam. Culture for Development: Toward an Indonesian Applied Anthropology. Jakarta: OBOR Press. 1987.

7.5 Colletta, Nat J. "Cultural Revitalization, Nonformal Education, and Village Development in Sri Lanka." *Comparative Education Review* 26(2):271-86. 1982.

7.6 Colletta, Nat J. "The Fusing of Cultures in Micronesia: Community Learning System Model." *Journal of Asian-Pacific and World Perspectives* 5(2). Winter 1981-82.

7.7 Davis, Shelton H. "The Globalization of Traditional Cultures." *Northeast Indian Quarterly* 8(1):42-3. 1991.

7.8 de Maret, Pierre. "Archaeological Research, Site Protection, and Employment Generation: Central African Perspectives." In I. Serageldin and J. Taboroff, eds. *Culture and Development in Africa: Proceedings of an International Conference*. Washington, D.C.: World Bank. 1993.

7.9 Etounga-Manguellé, Daniel. "Culture and Development: African Responses." In I. Serageldin and J. Taboroff, eds. *Culture and Development in Africa: Proceedings of an International Conference*. Washington, D.C.: World Bank. 1993.

7.10 Goodland, Robert, and Maryla Webb. *The Management of Cultural Property in World Bank-Assisted Projects: Archaeological, Historical, Religious, and Natural Unique Sites*. World Bank Technical Paper no. 62. Washington, D.C. 1989.

7.11 Klitgaard, Robert. "Taking Culture into Account: From 'Let's' to 'How.'" In I. Serageldin and J. Taboroff, eds. *Culture and Development in Africa: Proceedings of an International Conference*. Washington, D.C.: World Bank. 1993.

7.12 Kottak, Conrad Phillip. "Culture and Economic Development." *American Anthropologist* 92(3):723-31. 1990.

7.13 Marc, Alexandre O. "Community Participation in the Conservation of Cultural Heritage." In I. Serageldin and J. Taboroff, eds. *Culture and Development in Africa: Proceedings of an International Conference*. Washington, D.C.: World Bank. 1993.

7.14 McIntosh, Susan Keech. "Archaeological Heritage Management and Site Inventory Systems in Africa: The Role of Development." In I. Serageldin and J. Taboroff, eds. *Culture and Development in Africa: Proceedings of an International Conference*. Washington, D.C.: World Bank. 1993.

7.15 Nyang, Sulayman S. "The Cultural Consequences of Development in Africa." In I. Serageldin and J. Taboroff, eds. *Culture and Development in Africa:*

Proceedings of an International Conference. Washington, D.C.: World Bank. 1993.

7.16 Putnam, Robert D. "Democracy, Development, and the Civic Community: Evidence from an Italian Experiment." In I. Serageldin and J. Taboroff, eds. *Culture and Development in Africa: Proceedings of an International Conference.* Washington, D.C.: World Bank. 1993.

7.17 Ravenhill, Philip. "Public Education, National Collections, and Museum Scholarship in Africa." In I. Serageldin and J. Taboroff, eds. *Culture and Development in Africa: Proceedings of an International Conference.* Washington, D.C.: World Bank. 1993.

7.18 Serageldin, Ismail, and June Taboroff, eds. *Culture and Development in Africa: Proceedings of an International Conference.* Washington, D.C.: World Bank. 1993.

7.19 Serageldin, Ismail. "The Challenge of a Holistic Vision: Culture, Empowerment, and the Development Paradigm." In I. Serageldin and J. Taboroff, eds. *Culture and Development in Africa: Proceedings of an International Conference.* Washington, D.C.: World Bank. 1993.

7.20 Serageldin, Ismail. "Cultural Continuity and Cultural Authenticity: The Architectural Sculptures of Aboudramane and Kingelez." In *Home and the World: Architectural Sculpture by Two Contemporary African Artists.* 1992-1995. Exhibition Catalogue. New York: Museum for African Art. 1993.

7.21 Serageldin, Ismail. "Contemporary Expressions of Islam in Buildings: the Religious and the Secular." In *Expressions of Islam in Buildings.* Geneva: The Aga Khan Trust for Culture. 1991.

7.22 Serageldin, Ismail. "Faith and the Environment," "Islamic Culture and Non-Muslim Contributions," and "Architecture and Society." In I. Serageldin, ed. *Space for Freedom: The Search for Architectural Excellence in Muslim Societies.* Geneva: Aga Khan Award for Architecture and London: Butterworth Architecture. 1989.

7.23 Serageldin, Ismail. "Financing the Adaptive Reuse of Culturally Significant Areas." In Y. Raj Isar, ed. *The Challenge to Our Cultural Heritage: Why Preserve the Past?* Washington, D.C.: Smithsonian Institution Press and Paris: UNESCO. 1986.

7.24 Serageldin, Ismail, and others. "International Labor Migration in the Middle East and North Africa: Current and Prospective Dimensions, 1975-85." In L.O. Michalak and J.W. Solacuse, eds. *Social Legislation in the Contemporary Middle East*. Berkeley, Cal.: University of California. 1986.

7.25 Serageldin, Ismail. "A Unified Approach to the Character and Islamic Heritage of the Arab City." In I. Serageldin and S. Al-Sadek, eds. *The Arab City: Its Character and Islamic Cultural Heritage*. Washington, D.C. and Riyadh, Saudi Arabia: The Arab Urban Development Institute. 1982.

7.26 Stahl, Ann B. "Valuing the Past, Envisioning the Future: Local Perspectives on Environmental and Cultural Heritage in Ghana." In I. Serageldin and J. Taboroff, eds. *Culture and Development in Africa: Proceedings of an International Conference*. Washington, D.C.: World Bank. 1993.

7.27 Taboroff, June. "Bringing Cultural Heritage into the Development Agenda: Summary Findings of a Report on Cultural Heritage in Environmental Assessments in Sub-Saharan Africa." In I. Serageldin and J. Taboroff, eds. *Culture and Development in Africa: Proceedings of an International Conference*. Washington, D.C.: World Bank. 1993.

7.28 Wildavsky, Aaron. "What Cultural Theory Can Contribute to Understanding and Promoting Democracy, Science, and Development." In I. Serageldin and J. Taboroff, eds. *Culture and Development in Africa: Proceedings of an International Conference*. Washington, D.C.: World Bank. 1993.

Women, Family Systems, and Gender Analysis

8.1 Bamberger, Michael. "Gender Issues in Poverty Alleviation in Socialist Economies." In Rita Raj-Hashim and Noeleen Heyzer, eds. *Gender, Economic Growth and Poverty*. Kuala Lumpur: Asian and Pacific Development Centre. 1991.

8.2 Bennett, Lynn. "Expanding Women's Access to Credit in the World Bank Context." *Hunger Notes* 17(3):16-20. 1992.

8.3 Bennett, Lynn. *Women, Poverty, and Productivity in India*. Economic Development Institute Seminar Paper no. 43. World Bank. Washington, D.C. 1992.

8.4   Bennett, Lynn, and others. *Gender and Poverty in India.* World Bank Country Study. Washington, D.C. 1991.

8.5   Bennett, Lynn, and Meena Acharya. *Women and the Subsistence Sector: Economic Participation and Household Decisionmaking in Nepal.* World Bank Staff Working Paper no. 526. Washington, D.C. 1982.

8.6   Cernea, Michael M. "Anthropology and Family Production Systems in Africa." Foreword to Michael M. Horowitz and T. Painter, eds. *Anthropology and Rural Development in West Africa.* Boulder, Col.: Westview Press. 1986.

8.7   Cernea, Michael M. "Macrosocial Change, Feminization of Agriculture and Peasant Women's Threefold Economic Role." *Sociologia Ruralis* 18(2-3):107-24. 1978.

8.8   Cernea, Michael M. "L'Exploitation Familiale des Coopérateurs—Project Social ou Rémanence Economique?" In Placide Rambaud, ed. *Sociologie Rurale.* Paris: Editions Mouton. 1976.

8.9   Cernea, Michael M. "The Large Scale Formal Organization and the Family Primary Group." *Journal of Marriage and the Family* 37:927-36. 1975.

8.10 Dyson, Mary. "Mentor's Mandate: First, Listen! Women's Roles Examined at Global Assembly." *World Bank Environmental Bulletin* 4(1):7. Washington, D.C. 1992.

8.11 Kudat, Ayse. *Women and Human Settlements Development.* Nairobi: United Nations Center for Human Settlements. 1989.

8.12 Molnar, Augusta. "Women and Forestry in the Developing World." *Journal of Society and Natural Resources* 2(4). 1991.

8.13 Moser, Caroline. O. *Gender Planning and Development: Theory, Practice and Training.* London: Routledge. 1993.

8.14 Moser, Caroline. O. "Adjustment from Below: Low-Income Women, Time and the Triple Role in Guayaquil, Ecuador." In H. Afshar and C. Dennis, eds. *Women, Recession and Adjustment in the Third World.* London: Macmillan. 1992.

8.15 Moser, Caroline. O. "Gender Planning in the Third World: Meeting Practical and Strategic Gender Needs." *World Development* 17(11):1799-825. 1989.

8.16 Murphy, Josette, ed. *Women and Agricultural Technology: Relevance for Research*. Proceedings of an Inter-Center Seminar, March 25-29, Bellagio, Italy. The Rockefeller Foundation and ISNAR. The Hague. 1985.

8.17 Safilios-Rothschild, Constantina. "Women's Groups: An Underutilized Grassroots Institution." In *The Long-Term Perspective Study of Sub-Saharan Africa: vol. 3. Institutional and Sociopolitical Issues*. Washington, D.C. 1990.

Indigenous and Tribal People

9.1 Brandon, Katrina. "Integrating Conservation and Development." Research Note in *National Geographic* 7(3):371-72. 1991.

9.2 Cernea, Michael M. "Indigenous Anthropologists and Development-Oriented Research." In H. Fahim, ed. *Indigenous Anthropology in Non-Western Countries*. Durham, N.C.: Carolina Academic Press 1982.

9.3 Davis, Shelton H. *Indigenous Views of Land and the Environment*. World Bank Discussion Paper no. 188. Washington, D.C. 1993.

9.4 Davis, Shelton H., and Jorge Uquillas. "La Cuestion Territorial y Ecologia entre Pueblos Indigenas de la Selva Baja del Ecuador." In Fundacion Gaia and Cerec. *Derechos Territoriales Indigenas y Ecologia en las Selvas Tropicales de America*. Bogota, Colombia. 1992.

9.5 Davis, Shelton H. "The Rainforest Guests." *The Bank's World* 10(6):13-5. 1991.

9.6 Davis, Shelton H. *Land Rights and Indigenous Peoples: The Role of the OAS Inter-American Commission on Human Rights*. Cambridge, Mass.: Cultural Survival, Inc. 1989.

9.7 Davis, Shelton H. *Indigenous Peoples, Environmental Protection, and Sustainable Development*. Sustainable Development Occasional Paper Series. Geneva: IUCN. 1988.

9.8 Davis, Shelton H. "Sowing the Seeds of Violence." In Robert M. Carmack, ed. *Harvest of Violence: The Maya Indians and the Guatemala Crisis*. Norman, O.K.: Oklahoma University Press. 1988.

9.9 Davis, Shelton H. "Agrarian Structure and Ethnic Resistance: The Indian in Guatemalan and Salvadoran National Politics." In Remo Guidieri, Francesco Pellizzi, and Stanley J. Tambiah, eds. *Ethnicities and Nations: Processes of Inter-Ethnic Relations in Latin America, Southeast Asia, and the Pacific*. Houston: The Rothko Chapel and University of Texas Press. 1988.

9.10 Dyson, Mary. "Concern for Africa's Forest Peoples: A Touchstone of a Sustainable Development Policy." In *Conservation of West and Central African Rainforests*. World Bank Technical Paper, Environment Series no. 1. Washington, D.C. 1992.

9.11 Goodland, Robert. *Tribal Peoples and Economic Development: Human Ecologic Considerations*. World Bank. Washington, D.C. 1982.

9.12 Ibrahim, Saad E., and Donald P. Cole. *Saudi Arabian Bedouin: An Assessment of Their Needs*. Cairo Papers in Social Science. Monograph Five. Cairo: The American University in Cairo. 1978.

9.13 Partridge, William L. "The Fate of Indigenous Peoples: Consultation and Coordination Can Avoid Conflict." *The Environmental Forum* 7(5):29-30. 1990.

9.14 Price, David. *Before the Bulldozer: The Nambiquara Indians and the World Bank*. Cabin John, Md.: Seven Locks Press. 1989.

9.15 Warren, D. Michael. *Using Indigenous Knowledge in Agricultural Development*. World Bank Discussion Paper no. 127. Washington, D.C. 1991.

Part Three: Settlement and Resettlement

Settlement and Involuntary Resettlement

10.1 Ayeni, Julius S.O., and others. "The Kainji Lake Experience in Nigeria." In C. Cook, ed. *Involuntary Resettlement in Africa*. World Bank Technical Paper no. 227 Washington, D.C. Forthcoming.

10.2 Bartolomé, Leopoldo J. "The Yacyretá Experience with Urban Resettlement: Some Lessons and Insights." In M.M. Cernea and S.E. Guggenheim, eds. *Anthropological Approaches to Involuntary Resettlement: Policy, Practice, and Theory*. Boulder, Col.: Westview Press. 1993.

10.3 Cernea, Michael M., and S.E. Guggenheim, eds. "Resettlement and Development: The Bankwide Review of Projects Involving Involuntary Resettlement 1986-1993." Environment Department. World Bank. Washington, D.C. 1994.

10.4 Cernea, Michael M., and S.E. Guggenheim, eds. *Anthropological Approaches to Involuntary Resettlement: Policy, Practice, and Theory*. Boulder, Col.: Westview Press. 1993.

10.5 Cernea, Michael M. "Disaster-Related Refugee Flows and Development-Caused Population Displacement." In M.M. Cernea and S.E. Guggenheim, eds. *Anthropological Approaches to Involuntary Resettlement: Policy, Practice, and Theory*. Boulder, Col.: Westview Press. 1993.

10.6 Cernea, Michael M. "African Population Resettlement in a Global Context." In C. Cook, ed. *Involuntary Resettlement in Africa*. World Bank Technical Paper no. 227. Washington, D.C. 1993.

10.7 Cernea, Michael M. "Involuntary Resettlement: Social Research, Policy, and Planning." In M.M. Cernea, ed. *Putting People First: Sociological Variables in Rural Development*. 2nd ed. New York, London: Oxford University Press. 1991.

10.8 Cernea, Michael M. *From Unused Social Knowledge to Policy Creation: The Case of Population Resettlement*. HIID Development Discussion Paper no. 342. Cambridge, Mass.: Harvard University. 1990.

10.9 Cernea, Michael M. "Internal Refugee Flows and Development-Induced Population Displacement." *Journal of Refugee Studies* 3(4):320-39. 1990.

10.10 Cernea, Michael M. "Anthropology, Policy and Involuntary Resettlement." *BASAPP (British Association for Social Anthropology in Policy and Practice) Newsletter* 4:3-6. November 1989.

10.11 Cernea, Michael M., and Guy Le Moigne. "The World Bank's Approach to Involuntary Resettlement." *Water Power and Dam Construction Handbook*. Surrey, England: Reed Business Publishing. 1989.

10.12 Cernea, Michael M. *Involuntary Resettlement in Development Projects: Policy Guidelines in World Bank-Financed Projects*. World Bank Technical Paper no. 80. Washington, D.C. 1988.

10.13 Cernea, Michael M. *Pemukiman Penduduk Secara Terpaksa Dalam Proyek-Proyek Pembangunan: Pedoman Kebijakan bagi Proyek-proyek yang Dibiayai Bank Dunia. (Involuntary Resettlement in Development Projects. Policy Guidelines for World Bank-Financed Projects)*. Jakarta, Indonesia: Cetakan Pertama. 1990.

10.14 Cernea, Michael M. "Reinsediamento Involontario nei Progetti di Sviluppo." *Forum*. Comitato Internazionale per lo Sviluppo dei Populi (CISP). November 1990.

10.15 Cernea, Michael M. "Involuntary Resettlement and Development." *Finance & Development* 25(3):44-6. 1988.

10.16 Cook, Cynthia, ed. *Involuntary Resettlement in Africa*. World Bank Technical Paper no. 227. Washington, D.C. 1993.

10.17 Cook, Cynthia, and Aleki Mukendi. "Involuntary Resettlement in Bank-Financed Projects: Lessons from Experience in Sub-Saharan Africa." In C. Cook, ed. *Involuntary Resettlement in Africa*. World Bank Technical Paper no. 227. Washington, D.C. 1993.

10.18 Cook, Cynthia. "Environment and Settlement Issues in Africa: Toward a Policy Agenda." In C. Cook, ed. *Involuntary Resettlement in Africa*. World Bank Technical Paper no. 227. Washington, D.C. 1993.

10.19 Davis, Gloria, and Helen Garrison. *Indonesia: The Transmigration Program in Perspective*. A World Bank Country Study. Washington, D.C. 1988.

10.20 Davis, Gloria. "The Indonesian Transmigrants." In Julie Sloan Denslow and Christine Padoch, eds. *People of the Tropical Rainforests*. Washington, D.C. Smithsonian Institute. 1988.

10.21 Guggenheim, Scott E. "Peasants, Planners, and Participation: Resettlement in Mexico." In M.M. Cernea and S.E. Guggenheim, eds. *Anthropological Approaches to Involuntary Resettlement: Policy, Practice, and Theory*. Boulder, Col.: Westview Press. 1993.

10.22 Guggenheim, Scott E. "Resettlement in Colombia: The Case of El Guavio." *Practicing Anthropology* 12(3):14-20. 1990.

10.23 Le Moigne, Guy, Scott E. Guggenheim, and others. *Dam Planning, People, and the Environment: World Bank Policies and Practices.* 17th Congress on Large Dams. International Commission on Large Dams. Vienna. 1991.

10.24 Magadza, Christopher H.D. "Social Impacts of the Creation of Lake Kariba." In C. Cook, ed. *Involuntary Resettlement in Africa.* World Bank Technical Paper no. 227. Washington, D.C. Forthcoming.

10.25 Mathur, Hari Mohan. "Resettling the Development Displaced Population—Issues and Approaches." *Management in Government* 23(2):109-20. Government of India, New Delhi. 1991.

10.26 Mburugu, Edward K. "Dislocation of Settled Communities in the Development Process: The Case of Kiambere Hydroelectric Project." In C. Cook, ed. *Involuntary Resettlement in Africa.* World Bank Technical Paper no. 227. Washington, D.C. Forthcoming.

10.27 McMillan, Della E., Thomas Painter, and Thayer Scudder. "Development Strategies and Issues for Land Settlement in West Africa." In C. Cook, ed. *Involuntary Resettlement in Africa.* World Bank Technical Paper no. 227. Washington, D.C. Forthcoming.

10.28 McMillan, Della E., and others. *Settlement and Development in the River Blindness Control Zone: Case Study, Burkina Faso.* World Bank Technical Paper no. 200. Series on River Blindness Control in West Africa. Washington, D.C. 1993.

10.29 McMillan, Della E., Thomas Painter, and Thayer Scudder. *Settlement and Development in the River Blindness Control Zone.* World Bank Technical Paper no. 192. Series on River Blindness Control in West Africa. Washington, D.C. 1992.

10.30 Morse, Bradford, and Thomas R. Berger (with Donald Gamble and Hugh Brody). *Sardar Sarovar: The Report of the Independent Review.* Ottawa: Resource Futures International (RFI) Inc. 1992.

10.31 Partridge, William L. "Successful Involuntary Resettlement: Lessons from the Costa Rican Arenal Hydroelectric Project." In M.M. Cernea and

S.E. Guggenheim, eds. *Anthropological Approaches to Resettlement*. Boulder, Col.: Westview Press. 1993.

10.32 Partridge, William L., and M. Painter. "Lowland Settlement in San Julian, Bolivia—Project Success and Regional Underdevelopment." In D. Schumann and W.L. Partridge, eds. *The Human Ecology of Tropical Land Settlement in Latin America*. Boulder, Col.: Westview Press. 1989.

10.33 Partridge, William L. "Involuntary Resettlement in Development Projects." *Journal of Refugee Studies* 2(3):373-84. 1989.

10.34 Partridge, William L. "Reasentamiento de los Comunidates: Los Roles de los Grupos Corporativos en las Relocalizaciones Urbanos." In L.J. Bartolome, ed. *Relocalizaciones: Antropologia Social de las Poblaciones Desplazadas*. Buenos Aires: Instituto de Desarrollo Economico y Social. 1986.

10.35 Scudder, Thayer. "A Sociological Framework for the Analysis of New Land Settlements." In M.M. Cernea, ed. *Putting People First: Sociological Variables in Rural Development*. 2nd ed. New York, London: Oxford University Press. 1991.

10.36 Serra, Maria Teresa Fernandez. "Resettlement Planning in the Brazilian Power Sector: Recent Changes in Approach." In M.M. Cernea and S.E. Guggenheim, eds. *Anthropological Approaches to Involuntary Resettlement: Policy, Practice, and Theory*. Boulder, Col.: Westview Press. 1993.

10.37 Shihata, Ibrahim F.I. "Legal Aspects of Involuntary Population Resettlement." In M.M. Cernea and S.E. Guggenheim, eds. *Anthropological Approaches to Involuntary Resettlement: Policy, Practice, and Theory*. Boulder, Col.: Westview Press. 1993.

10.38 Sorbo, Gunnar M. "Environment and Settlement in Eastern Sudan: Some Major Policy Issues." In C. Cook, ed. *Involuntary Resettlement in Africa*. World Bank Technical Paper no. 227. Washington, D.C. Forthcoming.

10.39 Tamakloe, Martha A. "Long-Term Impacts of Resettlement: The Akosombo Dam Experience." In C. Cook, ed. *Involuntary Resettlement in Africa*. World Bank Technical Paper no. 227. Washington, D.C. Forthcoming.

10.40 Tshabalala, Mavuso. "Resettlement and Rural Development Aspects of the Lesotho Highlands Water Project." In C. Cook, ed. *Involuntary Resettlement in Africa*. World Bank Technical Paper no. 227. Washington, D.C. Forthcoming.

10.41 World Bank. "Resettlement and Development: The Bankwide Review of Projects Involving Involuntary Resettlement 1986-1993." World Bank Environment Department. Washington, D.C. 1994.

Additional publications relevant to the topics in this section of the Bibliography can be found in Sections 2, 6, and 17.

Part Four: Social Variables in Environmental Management

Environment and Development

11.1 Brandon, Katrina, and Carter Brandon, eds. "Linking Environment to Development: Problems and Possibilities." Special issue of *World Development* 20(4). 1992.

11.2 Brandon, Katrina, and Alvaro Umaña. "Inventing Institutions for Conservation: Lessons from Costa Rica." In S. Annis, ed. *Poverty, Natural Resources, and Public Policy in Central America*. Washington, D.C.: Overseas Development Council. 1992.

11.3 Cernea, Michael M. *The Urban Environment and Population Relocation*. World Bank Discussion Paper no. 152. Washington, D.C. 1993.

11.4 Cernea, Michael M. "Environmental and Social Requirements for Resource-Based Regional Development." In P. Hall, and others, eds. *Multilateral Cooperation for Development in the Twenty-First Century: Training and Research for Regional Development*. Nagoya: United Nations Center for Regional Development. 1991.

11.5 Cruz, Maria Concepcion J. *Economic Stagnation and Deforestation in Costa Rica and the Philippines*. Proceedings of the World Bank's Thirteenth Agriculture Symposium. Washington, D.C. 1993.

11.6 Cruz, Maria Concepcion J. *Population Growth and Land Use Changes in the Philippines*. New York: The Rene Dubos Forum on Population, Environment, and Development. 1993.

11.7 Davis, Shelton H., James F. Hicks, Herman E. Daly, and Maria de Lourdes de Freitas. *Ecuador's Amazon Region: Development Issues and Options*. World Bank Discussion Paper no. 75. Washington, D.C. 1990.

11.8 Elmendorf, Mary, and Patricia K. Buckles. *Sociocultural Aspects of Water Supply and Excreta Disposal*. Transportation, Water and Communications Department. World Bank. Washington, D.C. 1980.

11.9 World Bank. *Environmental Assessment Sourcebook*. Vols. I-III. World Bank Technical Paper no. 140. Washington, D.C. 1991.

Land and Land Tenure

12.1 Bromley, Daniel, and Michael M. Cernea. *The Management of Common Property Natural Resources. Some Conceptual and Operational Fallacies*. World Bank Discussion Paper no. 57. Washington, D.C. 1989.

12.2 Cernea, Michael M. *Land Tenure Systems and Social Implications of Forestry Development Programs*. World Bank Staff Working Paper no. 452. Washington, D.C. 1981.

12.3 Feder, Gershon, and Raymond Noronha. "Land Rights Systems and Agricultural Development in Sub-Saharan Africa." *World Bank Research Observer* 2(2):143-69. 1987.

12.4 Hecht, Robert M. "Immigration, Land Transfer, and Tenure Changes in Divo, Ivory Coast, 1940-1980." *Africa* 55(3):319-36. 1985.

12.5 Migot-Adholla, Shem E., and others. "Indigenous Land Rights Systems in Sub-Saharan Africa: A Constraint on Productivity?" *The World Bank Economic Review* 5(1):155-75. 1991.

12.6 Noronha, Raymond. "Common Property Resource Management in Traditional Societies." In P. Dasgupta and K.G. Maler, eds. *Environment and Emerging Development Issues.* Oxford: Oxford University Press. 1993.

Water and the Sociology of Irrigation

13.1 Bagadion, Benjamin U., and Francis F. Korten. "Developing Irrigators' Organizations: A Learning Process Approach." In M.M. Cernea, ed. *Putting People First: Sociological Variables in Rural Development.* 2nd ed. New York, London: Oxford University Press. 1991.

13.2 Byrnes, Kerry J. *Water Users' Associations in World Bank-Assisted Irrigation Projects in Pakistan.* World Bank Technical Paper no. 173. Washington, D.C. 1992.

13.3 Cernea, Michael M., and Ruth Meinzen-Dick. "Design for Water User Associations: Organizational Characteristics." In Guy Le Moigne, Shawki Barghouti, and Lisa Garbus, eds. *Developing and Improving Irrigation and Drainage Systems.* Selected Papers from World Bank Seminars. World Bank Technical Paper no. 178. Washington, D.C. 1992.

13.4 Coward, E. Walter, Jr. "Planning Social and Technical Change in Irrigated Areas." in M.M. Cernea, ed. *Putting People First: Sociological Variables in Rural Development.* 2nd ed. New York, London: Oxford University Press. 1991.

13.5 Freeman, David M., and Max K. Lowdermilk. "Middle-Level Farmer Organizations as Links between Farms and Central Irrigation Systems." In M.M. Cernea, ed. *Putting People First: Sociological Variables in Rural Development.* 2nd ed. New York, London: Oxford University Press. 1991.

13.6 Migot-Adholla, Shem E. "Irrigated Agriculture in Africa: Past Accomplishments and Future Directions." In Derick Thron, ed. *Proceedings of the Forum on the Performance of Irrigated Agriculture in Africa.* WMS Report no. 86. Logan Utah: Utah State University. 1988.

13.7 Schuh, G.E., Guy Le Moigne, Michael M. Cernea, and Robert J.A. Goodland. "Social and Environmental Impacts of Dams: The World Bank Experience." In *Transactions of the Sixteenth Congress on Large Dams, San Francisco, June 13-17, 1988* vol. I. Paris: International Commission on Large Dams. 1988.

Forests and Social Forestry

14.1 Barnes, Douglas, and Julia Allen. "The Causes of Deforestation in Developing Nations." *Annals of the Association of American Geographers* 75(2):163-84. 1985.

14.2 Cernea, Michael M. "The Social Actors of Participatory Afforestation Strategies." In M.M. Cernea, ed. *Putting People First: Sociological Variables in Rural Development*. 2nd ed. New York, London: Oxford University Press. 1991.

14.3 Cernea, Michael M. "A Sociological Framework: Policy, Environment, and the Social Actors for Tree Planting." In N.P. Sharma, ed. *Managing the World's Forests*. Iowa: Kendall/Hunt Publishing Co. 1992.

14.4 Cernea, Michael M. "Alternative Units of Social Organization Sustaining Afforestation Strategies." In M.M. Cernea, ed. *Putting People First: Sociological Variables in Rural Development*. New York: Oxford University Press. 1985.

14.5 Cook, Cynthia C., and Mikael Grut. *Agroforestry in Africa: A Farmer's Perspective*. World Bank Technical Paper no. 112. Washington, D.C. 1989.

14.6 Davis, Gloria, and Richard Ackermann, eds. *Indonesia: Sustainable Development of Forests, Land, and Water*. A World Bank Country Study. Washington, D.C. 1990.

14.7 Dyson, Mary. "West and Central African Rain Forest Conservation Conference." *World Bank Environmental Bulletin* 3(1):5. Washington, D.C. 1991.

14.8 Dyson, Mary, Robert Goodland, and others. "Tropical Moist Forest Management: The Urgency of Transition to Sustainability." *Environmental Conservation* 17(4):303-18. 1990.

14.9 Guggenheim, Scott E., and John Spears. "Sociological and Environmental Dimensions of Social Forestry Projects." In M.M. Cernea, ed. *Putting People First: Sociological Variables in Rural Development*. 2nd ed. New York, London: Oxford University Press. 1991.

14.10 Molnar, Augusta, and Janice Alcorn. "Deforestation and Forest-Human Relationships in India." In Les Ponsel, ed. *Tropical Forest Ecology: The Changing Human Niche and Deforestation*. Forthcoming.

14.11 Noronha, Raymond J. "Why Is It So Difficult to Grow Fuelwood?" *Unasylva* 33:3-12. 1981.

14.12 World Bank. *The Forest Sector*. A World Bank Policy Paper. Washington, D.C. 1991.

Rangelands and Pastoralism

15.1 Bonfiglioli, Angelo Maliki. *Agro-Pastoralism in Chad as a Strategy for Survival: An Essay on the Relationship between Anthropology and Statistics*. World Bank Technical Paper no. 214. Washington D.C. 1993.

15.2 Cernea, Michael M. "Pastoralists' Organizations for Resource Management: An African Case." In P. Daniels, and others, eds. *Proceedings of the International Conference on Livestock Services for Smallholders*. Yogyakarta, Indonesia. November 1993.

15.3 Dyson-Hudson, Neville. "Pastoral Production Systems and Livestock Development Projects: An East African Perspective." In M.M. Cernea, ed. *Putting People First: Sociological Variables in Rural Development*. 2nd ed. New York, London: Oxford University Press. 1991.

15.4 Jowkar, Forouz. *Nomadism, Nomadic Support, and Settlement in the Islamic Republic of Iran: The Rangelands and Livestock Development Project*. Working Paper. Institute for Development Anthropology. Binghamton, NY. 1993.

Parks and Biosphere Reserves

16.1 Brandon, Katrina. "Basic Steps toward Encouraging Local Participation in Nature Tourism Projects." In K. Lindberg and D. Hawkins, eds. *Ecotourism: A Guide for Planners and Managers*. North Bennington, Vt. The Ecotourism Society. 1993.

16.2 Brandon, Katrina, and Michael Wells. *People and Parks: Linking Protected Area Management with Local Communities*. World Bank. Washington, D.C. 1992.

16.3   Brandon, Katrina, and Michael Wells. "Planning for People and Parks: Design Dilemmas." *World Development* 20(4):557-70. 1992.

16.4   Brandon, Katrina, and Alvaro Umaña. "Costa Rica's Real Riches." *Americas Magazine*. August 1991.

16.5   Wells, Michael, and Katrina Brandon. "The Principles and Practice of Buffer Zones and Local Participation in Biodiversity Conservation." *Ambio* 22(2-3):157-62. 1993.

Part Five: Social Policy in Sectoral Analysis

Housing and Urban Development

17.1   Bamberger, Michael, and Alberto Harth. "Can Shelter Projects Meet Low-Income Needs? The Experience of El Salvador." In Geoffrey Payne, ed. *Low Income Housing in the Developing World*. Chichester: John Wiley and Sons, Ltd. 1984.

17.2   Bamberger, Michael. "The Role of Self-Help Housing in Low-Cost Shelter Programs for the Third World." *Built Environment* 8(2):95-107. 1982.

17.3   Campbell, Tim. "Environmental Dilemmas and the Urban Poor." In H. Jeffrey Leonard, ed. *Environment and the Poor: Development Strategies for a Common Agenda*. New Brunswick, N.J. and Oxford: Transaction Books. 1989.

17.4   Cernea, Michael M. "Urban Development and Compulsory Population Displacement." *Practicing Anthropology* 12(3):10-19. 1990.

17.5   Keare, Douglas H., and Scott Parris. *Evaluation of Shelter Programs for the Urban Poor: Principal Findings*. World Bank Staff Working Paper no. 547. Washington, D.C. 1982.

17.6   Moser, O. Caroline. "Housing." In L. Ostergaard, ed. *Gender and Development: A Practical Guide*. London: Routledge. 1991.

17.7 Moser, O. Caroline. "The Urban Context: Human Settlements and the Environment." In S. Sontheimer, ed. *A Reader on Women and Environment*. Rome: Italian Association for Women and Development. 1991.

17.8 World Bank. *Urban Policy and Economic Development: An Agenda for the 1990s*. A World Bank Policy Paper. Washington, D.C. 1991

Rural Development

18.1 Barnes, Douglas. *Electric Power for Rural Growth: How Electricity Affects Rural Life in Developing Nations*. Boulder, Col.: Westview Press. Rural Studies Series. 1988.

18.2 Barnes, Douglas. "The Impact of Rural Electrification and Infrastructure on Agricultural Changes in India, 1966-1980." *Economic and Political Weekly* 21(1):26-34. 1986.

18.3 de Wilde, John C., Thayer Scudder, and others. *Experiences with Agricultural Development in Tropical Africa* vol. I. Baltimore: The Johns Hopkins University Press. 1967.

18.4 Hall, Anthony, and others. *Brazil: An Interim Assessment of Rural Development Programs for the Northeast*. A World Bank Country Study. Washington, D.C. 1983.

18.5 Mehta, Shiv R. *Social Development in Mauritius: A Study on Rural Modernization in an Island Community*. New Delhi: Wiley Eastern Limited. 1981.

Additional publications relevant to the topics can be found in Sections 2, 3, 12, 13, 14, and 19.

Agricultural Extension

19.1 Adisak Sreensunpagit. "Monitoring and Evaluation of Extension: Experience in Thailand." In M.M. Cernea, J.K. Coulter, and J.F.A. Russell, eds. *Agricultural Extension by Training and Visit: The Asian Experience*. World Bank. Washington, D.C. 1983.

19.2   Cernea, Michael M., John K. Coulter, and John F.A. Russell, eds. *Research-Extension-Farmer: A Two-Way Continuum for Agricultural Development.* World Bank. Washington, D.C. 1985.

19.3   Cernea, Michael M., John K. Coulter, and John F.A. Russell. "Building the Research-Extension-Farmer Continuum: Some Current Issues." In M.M. Cernea, J.K. Coulter, and J.F.A. Russell, eds. *Research-Extension-Farmer: A Two-Way Continuum for Agricultural Development.* World Bank. Washington, D.C. 1985.

19.4   Cernea, Michael M., John K. Coulter, and John F.A. Russell, eds. *Agricultural Extension by Training and Visit: The Asian Experience.* World Bank. Washington, D.C. 1983.

19.5   Cernea, Michael M., John K. Coulter, and John F.A. Russell. "Strengthening Extension for Development: Current Issues and Prospects." In M.M. Cernea, J.K. Coulter, and J.F.A. Russell, eds. *Agricultural Extension by Training and Visit: The Asian Experience.* World Bank. Washington, D.C. 1983.

19.6   Cernea, Michael M. "Evaluation of Farmers' Reactions to Extension Advice: A Comment." In M. M. Cernea, J. K. Coulter, and J. F. A. Russell, eds. *Agricultural Extension by Training and Visit: The Asian Experience.* World Bank. Washington, D.C. 1983.

19.7   Cernea, Michael M. "Sociological Dimensions of Extension Organization: The Introduction of the T&V System in India." In B. Crouch and S. Chamala, eds. *Extension Education and Rural Development* vol. 2. Chichester: John Wiley and Sons, Ltd. 1981.

19.8   Epstein, T. Scarlett. "The Training and Visit System and Its Socio-Cultural Setting." *Culture and Agriculture.* Issue 20. 1983.

Education

20.1   Colletta, Nat J. *Achieving and Sustaining Universal Primary Education: A Review of the International Experience with Relevance to India.* World Bank Policy Planning and Research Working Paper no. 166. Washington, D.C. 1989.

20.2   Colletta, Nat J. "Worker Education: Revolution and Reform." In John N. Hawkins, ed. *Education and Social Change in the People's Republic of China.* New York: Praeger. 1983.

20.3   Colletta, Nat J., and T. Todd. "The Limits to Nonformal Education and Village Development: Lessons from the Sarvodaya Shramadana Movement." In George Papagianis and John Bock, eds. *Nonformal Education and National Development.* New York: Praeger. 1983.

20.4   Colletta, Nat J. *Worker-Peasant Education in the People's Republic of China: Study of Adult Education in Post-Revolutionary China.* World Bank Staff Working Paper no. 527. Washington, D.C. 1982.

20.5   Colletta, Nat J. "Assessing the Impact of Nonformal Education Programs on National Objectives." In D. Windham and L. Anderson, eds. *Education and Development: Issues in the Analysis and Planning of Post-Colonial Societies.* Boston: Dr. Heath and Co. 1982.

20.6   Colletta, Nat J., and Ross Kidd, eds. *Tradition for Development: Indigenous Structures and Folk Media in Non-Formal Education.* Bonn: The German Foundation for International Development. 1982.

20.7   Colletta, Nat J. *American Schools for the Natives of Ponape: Study of Education and Culture change in Micronesia.* Honolulu: The University Press of Hawaii, East-West Center. 1980.

20.8   Colletta, Nat J., and David Radcliffe. "Nonformal Education: An Educological Approach." *Canadian and International Education* 9(2). 1980.

20.9   Fuller, Bruce, and Aklilu Habte, eds. *Adjusting Educational Policies: Conserving Resources While Raising School Quality.* World Bank Discussion Paper no. 132. Washington, D.C. 1992.

20.10   Fuller, Bruce. *Raising School Quality in Developing Countries: What Investments Boost Learning?* World Bank Discussion Paper no. 2. Washington, D.C. 1986.

20.11   Heyneman, Stephen. "Protection of the Textbook Industry in Developing Countries: In the Public Interest?" *Book Research Quarterly.* Winter 1990. 3-11.

20.12 Heyneman, Stephen. "Economic Crisis and the Quality of Education." *International Journal of Educational Development* 10(2/3):115-29. 1990.

20.13 Heyneman, Stephen. "The World Economic Crisis and the Quality of Education." *Journal of Education Finance* 15:456-69. 1990.

20.14 Heyneman, Stephen, and Bernadette Etienne. "Higher Education in Developing Countries: What, How and When?" *Institute of Development Studies (IDS) Bulletin* 20(1):41-8. 1989.

20.15 Heyneman, Stephen, and Bruce Fuller. "Third World School Quality: Current Collapse, Future Potential." *Educational Researcher* 18(2):12-9. 1989.

20.16 Heyneman, Stephen. "Multilevel Methods for Analyzing School Effects in Developing Countries." *Comparative Education Review*. November 1989. 498-504.

20.17 Heyneman, Stephen, and Ingemar Fagerlind, eds. *University Examinations and Standardized Testing—Principles, Experience, and Policy Options*. World Bank Technical Paper no. 78. Washington, D.C. 1988.

20.18 Heyneman, Stephen, and Joseph P. Farrell. "Textbooks in Developing Countries: Economic and Pedagogical Choices." In Philip G. Altbach and Gail P. Kelly, eds. *Textbooks in the Third World: Policy, Content and Context*. New York: Garland Publishing, Inc. 1988.

20.19 Heyneman, Stephen. "Curricular Economics in Secondary Education: An Emerging Crisis in Developing Countries." *Prospects* 8(1):63-74. 1987.

20.20 Heyneman, Stephen. "Uses of Examinations in Developing Countries: Selection, Research, and Education Sector Management." *International Journal of Educational Development* 7(4):251-63. 1987.

20.21 Heyneman, Stephen, and Daphne White. *The Quality of Education and Economic Development*. A World Bank Symposium. Washington, D.C. 1986.

20.22 Heyneman, Stephen. "The Nature of a Practical Curriculum." *Education with Production* 4(2):91-104. 1986.

20.23 Heyneman, Stephen. "Diversifying Secondary School Curricula in Developing Countries: An Implementation History and Some Policy Options." *International Journal of Educational Development* 5(4):283-88. 1985.

20.24 Heyneman, Stephen, and others. "Textbooks in the Philippines. Evaluation of the Pedagogical Impact of a Nationwide Investment." *Educational Evaluation and Policy Analysis* 6(2):139-50. 1984.

20.25 Heyneman, Stephen. "Research on Education in the Developing Countries." *International Journal of Educational Development* 4(4):293-304. 1984.

20.26 Heyneman, Stephen. "Educational Investment and Economic Productivity: Evidence from Malawi." *International Journal of Educational Development* 4(1):9-15. 1984.

20.27 Heyneman, Stephen, and William Loxley. "The Distribution of Primary School Quality within High- and Low-Income Countries." *Comparative Education Review* 27(1):108-18. 1983.

20.28 Heyneman, Stephen, and William Loxley. "The Effect of Primary School Quality on Academic Achievement Across Twenty-nine High- and Low-Income Countries." *The American Journal of Sociology* 88(6):1162-94. 1983.

20.29 Heyneman, Stephen, guest ed. Special Issue: "Education and the World Bank." *Canadian and International Education* 12(1). 1983.

20.30 Heyneman, Stephen. "Improving the Quality of Education in Developing Countries." *Finance & Development*. March 1983. 18-21.

20.31 Heyneman, Stephen. "Education during a Period of Austerity: Uganda, 1971-1981." *Comparative Education Review* 27(3):403-13. 1983.

20.32 Heyneman, Stephen, and William Loxley. "Influences on Academic Achievement Across High- and Low-Income Countries: A Re-Analysis of IEA Data." *Sociology of Education* 55(1):13-21. 1982.

20.33 Heyneman, Stephen, and others. "Improving Elementary Mathematics Education in Nicaragua. An Experimental Study of the Impact of Textbooks and Radio on Achievement." *Journal of Educational Psychology* 73(4):556-67. 1981.

20.34 Heyneman, Stephen. "Instruction in the Mother Tongue: The Question of Logistics." *Canadian and International Education* 9(2):88-94. 1980.

20.35 Heyneman, Stephen. "Differences between Developed and Developing Countries: Comment on Simmon and Alexander's Determinants of School Achievement." *Economic Development and Cultural Change* 28(2):403-6. 1980.

20.36 Heyneman, Stephen. *The Evaluation of Human Capital in Malawi*. World Bank Staff Working Paper no. 420. Washington, D.C. 1980.

20.37 Heyneman, Stephen. "The Career Education Debate: Where the Differences Lie." *Teachers College Record* 80(4):660-88. 1979.

20.38 Heyneman, Stephen. "Why Impoverished Children Do Well in Ugandan Schools." *Comparative Education* 15(2):175-85. 1979.

20.39 Heyneman, Stephen. *Investment in Indian Education: Uneconomic?* World Bank Staff Working Paper no. 327. Washington, D.C. 1979.

20.40 Heyneman, Stephen, and others. *Textbooks and Achievement: What We Know*. World Bank Staff Working Paper no. 298. Washington, D.C. 1978.

20.41 Jamison, Dean T., Marlaine E. Lockheed, and others. "Education, Extension, and Farmer Productivity." In M. Akin, ed. *Encyclopedia of Educational Research*. New York: MacMillan. 1992.

20.42 Jamison, Dean T. and Marlaine E. Lockheed. "Participation in Schooling: Determinants and Learning Outcomes in Nepal." *Economic Development and Social Change* 35(2):279-306. 1987.

20.43 Jimenez, Emmanuel, and Marlaine E. Lockheed, eds. "Private versus Public Education: An International Perspective." Special Issue of *International Journal of Educational Research*. 15(5). 1991.

20.44 Jimenez, Emmanuel, Marlaine E. Lockheed, and others. "School Effects and Costs for Private and Public Schools in the Dominican Republic." *International Journal of Education Research* 15(5):393-410 1991.

20.45 Jimenez, Emmanuel, Marlaine E. Lockheed, and others. "The Relative Efficiency of Public and Private Schools in Developing Countries." *The World Bank Research Observer* 6(2):205-18. 1991.

20.46 Jimenez, Emmanuel, and Marlaine E. Lockheed. "Enhancing Girls' Learning through Single-Sex Education: Evidence and a Policy Conundrum." *Educational Evaluation and Policy Analysis* 11(2):117-42. 1989.

20.47 Jimenez, Emmanuel, Marlaine E. Lockheed, and others. "The Relative Efficiency of Private and Public Schools: The case of Thailand." *The World Bank Economic Review* 2(2):139-64. 1988.

20.48 Lee, Valerie E., and Marlaine E. Lockheed. "Single-Sex and Coeducational Education in Developing Countries." *International Encyclopedia of Education: Supplementary Volume Two*. Oxford: Pergamon Press 1991.

20.49 Lee, Valerie E., and Marlaine E. Lockheed. "The Effects of Single-Sex Schooling on Student Achievement and Attitudes in Nigeria." *Comparative Education Review* 34(2):209-231. 1990

20.50 Levin, Henry M., and Marlaine E. Lockheed, eds. *Effective Schools in Developing Countries*. Falmer Press. 1993.

20.51 Lockheed, Marlaine E. "Enrollment, Facilities and Finances: International Differences." In M. Akin, ed. *Encyclopedia of Educational Research*. New York: MacMillan. 1992.

20.52 Lockheed, Marlaine E., and Qinghua Zhao. "The Empty Opportunity: Local Control and Secondary School Achievement in the Philippines. *International Journal of Educational Development* 13(1). 1992.

20.53 Lockheed, Marlaine E., and Alastair G. Rodd. *World Bank Lending for Education Research, 1982-89*. World Bank Working Paper Series 583. Washington, D.C. 1991.

20.54 Lockheed, Marlaine E., and Nicholas T. Longford. "School Effects on Mathematics Achievement Gain in Thailand." In S.W. Raudenbush and J.D. Willms, eds. *Schools, Classrooms, and Pupils: International Studies of Schooling from a Multi-Level Perspective*. New York and London: Academic Press. 1991.

20.55 Lockheed, Marlaine E., and Adriaan M. Verspoor, and others. *Improving Primary Education in Developing Countries*. New York: Oxford University Press. 1991.

20.56 Lockheed, Marlaine, E., and Eric Hanushek. "Concepts of Educational Efficiency and Effectiveness. *International Encyclopedia of Education: Supplementary Volume Two*. Oxford: Pergamon Press. 1991.

20.57 Lockheed, Marlaine E., and Andre Komenan. "Teaching Quality and Student Achievement in Africa: The Case of Nigeria and Swaziland." *Teaching and Teacher Education* 5(2):93-111. 1989.

20.58 Lockheed, Marlaine E., Bruce Fuller, and others. "Family Effects on Students' Achievement in Thailand and Malawi." *Sociology of Education* 62:239-56. 1989.

20.59 Lockheed, Marlaine E., and Eric Hanushek. "Improving Educational Efficiency in Developing Countries: What Do We Know?" *Compare* 18(1):21-38. 1988.

20.60 Lockheed, Marlaine E., and Kathleen S. Gorman. "Sociocultural Factors Affecting Science Learning and Attitude." In Audrey B. Champagne and Leslie E. Hornig, eds. *This Year in School Science 1987: Students and Science Learning*. Washington, D.C: American Association for the Advancement of Science. 1987.

20.61 Lockheed, Marlaine E., Stephen Vail, and Bruce Fuller. "How Textbooks Affect Achievement in Developing Countries: Evidence from Thailand." *Education Evaluation and Policy Analysis* 8(4):379-92. 1987.

20.62 Lockheed, Marlaine E. "Farmers' Education and Economic Performance." In G. Psacharopoulos, ed. *Economics of Education: Research and Studies*. Oxford: Pergamon Press. 1987.

20.63 Lockheed, Marlaine E., and Jane Hannaway, eds. *The Contribution of the Social Sciences to Educational Policy and Practice, 1965-1985*. Berkeley, Cal.: McCutchan Publishing Company. 1986.

20.64 Maas, Jacob van Lutsenburg, and Geert Criel. *Distribution of Primary School Enrollment in Eastern Africa*. World Bank Staff Working Paper no. 511. Washington, D.C. 1982.

20.65 Ross, Kenneth, Marlaine E. Lockheed, and others. "Improving Data Collection, Preparation, and Analysis Procedures: A Review of Technical Issues." In K. Ross and L. Mahlck, eds. *Planning the Quality of Education*. Oxford: Pergamon Press. 1990.

20.66 Serageldin, Ismail, M.R. Khater, M.E. Mawgood, I. Werdelin, S. Ibrahim, and others. *The Kingdom of Saudi Arabia: Accelerated Literacy Program*.

Fifteen volumes designed for the experimental program (in Arabic). World Bank. 1978/79.

20.67 Serageldin, Ismail, E. Mawgood, I. Werdelin, and M. Youssef. *Remaining Literate in Egypt: Study Findings and Recommendations for Action*. Final Report of the Study on Literacy and Numeracy Retention. RPO 671-55. World Bank. 1984.

20.68 World Bank. *Primary Education*. A World Bank Policy Paper. Washington, D.C. 1990.

Health

21.1 Hecht, Robert M. *Zimbabwe: Financing Health Services*. World Bank Country Study. Washington, D.C. 1992.

21.2 Moser, Caroline, and P. Sollis. "Did the Project Fail? A Community Perspective on a Participatory Health Care Project in Ecuador." *Development in Practice* 1(1):19-33. 1991.

Roads

22.1 Cook, Peter D., and Cynthia C. Cook. "Methodological Review of Analyses of Rural Transportation Impacts in Developing Countries." *Transportation and Economic Development 1990*. Transportation Research Record no. 1274, pp. 167-78. Washington, D.C.: Transportation Research Board, National Research Council.

22.2 Cook, Cynthia C. "Social Analysis in Rural Road Projects." In M.M. Cernea, ed. *Putting People First: Sociological Variables in Rural Development*. 2nd ed. New York and London: Oxford University Press. 1991.

22.3 Cook, Cynthia C. "Evaluating Alternative Maintenance Strategies for Low-Volume Roads in Sub-Saharan Africa." *Fourth International Conference on Low-Volume Roads, Transportation Research Record no. 1106*. Washington, D.C.: Transportation Research Board, National Research Council. 1988.

22.4 Cook, Cynthia C., and others. *Institutional Considerations in Rural Roads Projects*. World Bank Staff Working Paper no. 748. Washington, D.C. 1985.

Energy Use

23.1 Barnes, Douglas, and others. "The Design and Diffusion of Improved Cooking Stoves." *The World Bank Research Observer* 8(2):119-41. 1993.

23.2 Barnes, Douglas, and Liu Qian. "Urban Interfuel Substitution, Energy Use, and Equity in Developing Countries." In James Dorian and Fereidun Fesharaki, eds. *International Issues in Energy Policy, Development, and Economics*. Boulder, Col.: Westview Press. 1992.

23.3 Barnes, Douglas, and others. "Interfuel Substitution and Changes in the Way Households Use Energy: Estimating Changes in Cooking and Lighting Behavior in Urban Java." *Pacific and Asian Journal of Energy* 1(1):21-49. 1992.

23.4 Barnes, Douglas. "Population Growth, Wood Fuels, and Resource Problems in Sub-Saharan Africa." In G.T.F. Acsadi, G. Johnson-Acsadi, and R.A. Bulatao, eds. *Population Growth and Reproduction in Sub-Saharan Africa*. A World Bank Symposium. Washington, D.C. 1990.

23.5 Campbell, Tim. "Social Feasibility of Densified Fuel for Rural Households of Pakistan." In C. Carpenter and M. Dove, eds. *Sociology of Natural Resources in Pakistan and Adjoining Countries*. Honolulu: East West Center. 1993.

Part Six: Social Research and Methodologies

Social Research Methods

24.1 Bamberger, Michael. "Methodological Issues in the Evaluation of Community Participation." *Sociological Evaluation Practice* 8:208-25. 1990.

24.2 Cernea, Michael M. "Re-Tooling in Applied Social Investigation for Development Planning: Some Methodological Issues." In N.S. Scrimshaw and Gary Gleason, eds. *Rapid Assessment Methodologies for Planning and Evaluation of Health Related Programs*. Boston, Mass.: INFDC. 1992.

24.3	Cernea, Michael M. "The 'Production' of a Social Methodology." In E.M. Eddy and W.L. Partridge, eds. *Applied Anthropology in America*. 2nd ed. New York: Columbia University Press. 1987.

24.4	Cernea, Michael M., and Scott E. Guggenheim. "Is Anthropology Superfluous in Farming Systems Research?" In *Farming Systems Research*. Kansas State University Research Series 4(9):504-17. 1985.

24.5	Cernea, Michael M. *A Social Methodology for Community Participation in Local Investments: The Experience of Mexico's PIDER Program*. World Bank Staff Working Paper no. 598. Washington, D.C. 1983.

24.6	Chambers, Robert. "Shortcut and Participatory Methods for Gaining Social Information for Projects." In M.M. Cernea, ed. *Putting People First: Sociological Variables in Rural Development*. 2nd ed. New York, London: Oxford University Press. 1991.

24.7	Cook, Cynthia C. "Demography of the Project Population." In K. Finsterbusch, J. Ingersoll, and L. Llewellyn, eds. *Methods for Social Analysis in Developing Countries*. Boulder, Col.: Westview Press. 1990.

24.8	Moser, Caroline, and P. Sollis. "A Methodological Framework for Analyzing the Social Costs of Adjustment at the Micro Level: The Case of Quayaquil, Ecuador." *Institute of Development Studies Bulletin* 22(1):23-30. 1991.

24.9	Murphy, Josette, and others. *Farmers' Estimations as a Source of Production Data: Methodological Guidelines for Cereals in Africa*. World Bank Technical Paper no. 132. Washington, D.C. 1991.

24.10	Murphy, Josette. "Farmers' Systems and Technological Change in Agriculture." In M.S. Chaiken and A. Fleuret, eds. *Social Change and Applied Anthropology: Essays in Honor of David Brokensha*. Boulder, Col.: Westview Press. 1990.

Additional publications relevant to the topics in this Section of the Bibliography can be found in Sections 2, 3, and 25.

Social Impact Assessment

25.1 de Kadt, Emanuel. *Tourism: Passport to Development? Perspectives on the Social and Cultural Effects of Tourism in Developing Countries*. A Joint World Bank-UNESCO study. New York, London: Oxford University Press. 1979.

25.2 de Regt, Jacomina P., and Augustin Reynoso y Valle. "Growing Pains: Planned Tourism Development in Ixtapa-Zihuatenejo." In Emanuel de Kadt, ed. *Tourism: Passport to Development? Perspectives on the Social and Cultural Effects of Tourism in Developing Countries*. A Joint World Bank-UNESCO study. New York, London: Oxford University Press. 1979.

25.3 Hecht, Robert M. "The Ivory Coast Economic Miracle: What Benefits for Peasant Farmers?" *Journal of Modern African Studies* 21(1):25-53. 1983.

25.4 Nettekoven, Lothar. "Mechanisms of Intercultural Interaction." In Emanuel de Kadt, ed. *Tourism: Passport to Development? Perspectives on the Social and Cultural Effects of Tourism in Developing Countries*. A Joint World Bank-UNESCO Study. New York, London: Oxford University Press. 1979.

25.5 Noronha, Raymond. "Paradise Reviewed: Tourism in Bali." In Emanuel de Kadt, ed. *Tourism: Passport to Development? Perspectives on the Social and Cultural Effects of Tourism in Developing Countries*. A Joint World Bank-UNESCO Study. New York, London: Oxford University Press. 1979.

25.6 Noronha, Raymond. *Social and Cultural Dimensions of Tourism*. World Bank Staff Working Paper no. 326. Washington, D.C.: 1979.

Additional publications relevant to this topic can be found in Sections 2, 3, 6, 10, and 24.

General Publications in Anthropology and Sociology

26.1 Cernea, Michael M. "Sociology in Rumania: The View of an American Historian." In John W. Cole, ed. *Society and Culture in Modern Rumania*. Amherst Research Report no. 20. Amherst, Mass.: University of Massachusetts Press. 1984.

26.2 Cernea, Michael M. "Rural Community Studies in Rumania." In J.L. Druand-Drouhin and L.M. Szwengrub, eds. *Rural Community Studies in Europe*. Oxford: Pergamon Press. 1981.

26.3 Clark, Maria Donoso. "Anthropology at the World Bank." In A.T. Koons, B.N. Hackett, and J.P. Mason, eds. *Stalking Employment in the Nation's Capital: A Guide for Anthropologists*. Washington, D.C: The Washington Association of Professional Anthropologists. 1989.

26.4 Colletta, Nat J., and T. Todd. *Social and Cultural Influences on Human Resource Development Policies and Programs: Selected and Annotated Bibliography*. Essex, Conn.: Redgrave Press. 1981.

26.5 Eddy, Elizabeth M., and William L. Partridge, eds. *Applied Anthropology in America*. Rev. 2nd ed. New York: Columbia University Press. 1987.

26.6 Gross, Daniel R. *Discovering Anthropology*. Mountain View, Cal.: Mayfield Publishing Company. 1992.

26.7 Gross, Daniel R. *Instructor's Manual for Discovering Anthropology*. Mountain View, Cal.: Mayfield Publishing Company. 1992.

26.8 Partridge, William L., and Elizabeth M. Eddy. "Development of Applied Anthropology in America." In E.M. Eddy and W.L. Partridge, eds. *Applied Anthropology in America*. Revised 2nd ed. New York: Columbia University Press. 1987.

26.9 Partridge, William L. "Towards a Theory of Practice." In E.M. Eddy and W.L. Partridge, eds. *Applied Anthropology in America*. Rev. 2nd ed. New York: Columbia University Press. 1987.

Appendix 3
Index of Authors

All authors and co-authors of bibliographic entries included in this volume are listed below. The vast majority of those listed are sociologists and anthropologists. For multidisciplinary studies, clearly not all co-authors are anthropologists or sociologists, but are nevertheless included in the index. Editors of volumes are listed only with the entry for their own individual chapter(s), not each time their names appear in reference to the volume they edited.

Abadzi, Helen	27.29
Acharya, Meena	8.5
Ackermann, Richard	14.6
Adisak Sreensunpagit	19.1
Ahmed, Viqar	3.4
Allen, Julia	14.1
Ayeni, Julius	10.1
Ardouin, Claude	7.1
Aziz, Abdul	2.1
Bagadion, Benjamin	13.1
Bamberger, Michael	2.1; 3.1; 3.2; 3.3; 3.4; 3.5; 3.6; 3.7; 3.8; 4.1; 5.1; 5.2; 8.1; 17.1; 17.2; 24.1; 27.1
Barnes, Douglas	14.1; 18.1; 18.2; 23.1; 23.2; 23.3; 23.4; 27.2; 27.3; 27.4

Barth, Fredrik	27.5; 27.6
Bartolomé, Leopoldo J.	10.2
Bennett, Lynn	2.2; 8.2; 8.3; 8.4; 8.5
Berger, Thomas R.	10.30
Bhatnagar, Bhuvan	5.3; 5.4
Bonfiglioli, Angelo Maliki	15.1
Bouman, F.J.A.	4.2
Brandon, Carter	11.1
Brandon, Katrina	9.1; 11.1; 11.2; 16.1; 16.2; 16.2; 16.4; 16.5
Brody, Hugh	10.30
Bromley, Daniel	12.1
Bruns, Barbara	27.31
Bryant, Coralie	7.2
Buckles, Patricia	11.8
Butcher, David	1.1
Byrnes, Kerry J.	13.2
Campbell, Tim	17.3; 23.5; 27.8; 27.9; 27.10; 27.11; 27.12; 27.13; 27.14

Index of Authors

Cernea, Michael M.	1.2; 1.3; 1.4; 1.5; 1.6; 1.7; 1.8; 1.9; 1.10; 2.3; 2.4; 2.5; 3.9; 3.10; 4.3; 4.4; 4.5; 4.6; 5.5; 6.1; 7.3; 8.6; 8.7; 8.8; 8.9; 9.2; 10.3; 10.4; 10.5; 10.6; 10.7; 10.8; 10.9; 10.10; 10.11; 10.12; 10.13; 10.14; 10.15; 11.3; 11.4; 12.1; 12.2; 13.3; 13.7; 14.2; 14.3; 14.4; 15.2; 17.4; 19.2; 19.3; 19.4; 19.5; 19.6; 19.7; 24.2; 24.3; 24.4; 24.5; 26.1; 26.2; 27.15
Chambers, Robert	24.6
Cheema, Shabbir	3.2
Clark, Maria Donoso	26.3; 27.16
Clay, Jason W.	27.17
Cole, Donald P.	9.12
Colletta, Nat J.	7.4; 7.5; 7.6; 20.1; 20.2; 20.3; 20.4; 20.5; 20.6; 20.7; 20.8; 26.4
Cook, Cynthia C.	10.16; 10.17; 10.18; 14.5; 22.1; 22.2; 22.3; 22.4; 24.7
Cook, Peter D.	22.1
Coulter, John K.	19.2; 19.3; 19.4; 19.5
Coward, E. Walter	13.4
Criel, Geert	24.64
Cruz, Maria Concepcion J.	11.5; 11.6
Daly, Herman E.	11.7
Davis, Gloria	10.19; 10.20; 14.6
Davis, Shelton H.	7.7; 9.3; 9.4; 9.5; 9.6; 9.7; 9.8; 9.9; 11.7; 27.18

de Freitas, Maria de Lourdes	11.7
de Kadt, Emanuel	25.1
de Maret, Pierre	7.8
de Regt, Jacomina	25.2
de Wilde, John C.	18.3
Dia, Mamadou	27.19
Dichter, Thomas	5.6
Dyson, Mary	8.10; 9.10; 14.7; 14.8
Dyson-Hudson, Neville	15.3
Eddy, Elyzabeth M.	26.5; 26.8
Elder, John	27.20
Elmendorf, Mary	5.7; 11.8
Epstein, T. Scarlett	19.8
Esman, Milton J.	6.2
Etienne, Bernadette	20.14
Etounga-Manguellé, Daniel	7.9
Fagerlind, Ingemar	20.17
Falloux, François	5.7
Farrell, Joseph P.	20.18
Feder, Gershon	12.3
Fong, Vincy	27.24

Freeman, David M.	13.5
Fuller, Bruce	20.9; 20.10; 20.15; 20.58; 20.61; 27.21
Gamble, Donald	10.30
Garrison, Helen	10.18
Goldberg, Mike	2.2
Goodland, Robert	7.10; 9.11; 13.7; 14.8
Gorman, Kathleen	20.60
Grootaert, Christian	6.3; 6.4
Gross, Daniel R.	26.6; 26.7
Grut, Mikael	14.5
Guggenheim, Scott E.	10.3; 10.21; 10.22; 14.9; 24.4; 27.22
Guichaoua, André	27.23
Habte, Aklilu	20.9
Hall, Anthony	18.4
Hannaway, Jane	20.63
Hanushek, Eric	20.56; 20.59
Harth, Alberto	17.1
Hecht, Robert M.	2.6; 2.7; 4.7; 12.4; 21.1; 25.3
Hewitt, Eleanor	3.5; 3.6

Heyneman, Stephen	20.11; 20.12; 20.13; 20.14; 20.15; 20.16; 20.17; 20.18; 20.19; 20.20; 20.21; 20.22; 20.23; 20.24; 20.25; 20.26; 20.27; 20.28; 20.29; 20.30; 20.31; 20.32; 20.33; 20.34; 20.35; 20.36; 20.37; 20.38; 20.39; 20.40
Hicks, James F.	11.7
Hopkins, Nicholas	4.9
Horowitz, Michael	2.8
Hussi, Pekka	4.8
Ibrahim, Saad E.	4.9; 9.12
Jamison, Dean T.	20.41; 20.42
Jimenez, Emmanuel	20.43; 20.44; 20.45; 20.46; 20.47
Jowkar, Forouz	15.4
Kardam, Nüket	1.11
Keare, Douglas	17.5
Khayam, Umar	7.4
Kidd, Ross	20.6
Klitgaard, Robert	7.11
Koch-Weser, Maritta	27.22
Komenan, André	20.57
Korten, Francis F.	13.1
Kottak, Conrad P.	1.12
Kudat, Ayse	8.11; 27.24; 27.25; 27.26; 27.27; 27.28; 27.29

Landell-Mills, Pierre	1.17
Lee, Valerie	20.48; 20.49
Le Moigne, Guy	10.10; 10.23; 13.7
Lethem, Francis J.	2.11
Levin, Henry M.	20.50
Lipset, Seymour Martin	1.14
Lockheed, Marlaine E.	20.41; 20.42; 20.43; 20.44; 20.45; 20.46; 20.47; 20.48; 20.49; 20.50; 20.51; 20.52; 20.53; 20.54; 20.55; 20.56; 20.57; 20.58; 20.59; 20.60; 20.61; 20.62; 20.63; 20.65; 27.21; 27.30; 27.31; 27.32; 27.33
Longford, Nicholas	20.54
Lowdermilk, Max K.	13.5
Loxley, William	20.27; 20.28; 20.32
Maas, Jacob van Lutsenburg	20.64
Magadza, Christopher H.D.	10.24
Marc, Alexandre O.	7.13
Marchant, Timothy	3.12; 6.3; 6.4
Mathur, Hari Mohan	10.25
Mbindyo, Joseph	1.15
Mburugu, Edward K.	10.26
McIntosh, Susan Keech	7.14
McLeod, Scott	2.5

McMillan, Della E.	10.27; 10.28; 10.29
Mehta, Shiv R.	18.5
Meinzen-Dick, Ruth	13.3
Middleton, John	27.30
Migot-Adholla, Shem E.	12.5; 13.6
Molnar, Augusta	2.9; 2.10; 8.12; 14.10; 27.34
Montgomery, John D.	6.2
Morgan, Mara	27.8
Morse, Bradford	10.30
Moser, Caroline O.	8.13; 8.14; 8.15; 17.6; 17.7; 21.2; 24.8
Mukendi, Aleki	10.16
Murphy, Josette	3.11; 3.12; 3.13; 4.8; 8.16; 24.9; 24.10; 27.35
Narayan, Deepa	3.14; 3.15; 5.8; 5.9
Nettekoven, Lothar	25.4
Nettleton, Greta S.	27.30
Noël, Michel	1.19
Noronha, Raymond	2.11; 2.12; 12.3; 12.6; 14.11; 25.5; 25.6; 27.36
Nyang, Sulayman S.	7.15
Painter, Thomas	10.26; 10.28
Parris, Scott	17.5; 27.1; 27.37

Partridge, William L.	4.10; 4.12; 9.13; 10.31; 10.32; 10.33; 10.34; 26.5; 26.8; 26.9
Paul, Samuel	5.10
Perrett, Heli	1.13; 3.16
Pollnac, Richard B.	4.11
Price, David	9.14
Putnam, Robert D.	7.16
Qian, Liu	23.2
Racelis, Mary	5.11
Radcliffe, David	20.8
Ravenhill, Philip	7.17
Reynoso y Valle, Augustin	25.2
Rodd, Alastair G.	20.53
Rogers, Everett M.	1.15
Ross, Kenneth	20.65
Rudquist, Anders	5.12; 27.39
Russell, John F. A.	19.2; 19.3; 19.4; 19.5
Safilios-Rothschild, Constantina	6.5; 8.17
Salmen, Lawrence	2.13; 3.17; 3.18; 6.6; 6.7
Schreiber, Gotz	27.34
Schuh, G.E.	13.7
Schumann, D.	4.12

Scudder, Thayer	10.26; 10.28; 10.35; 18.3
Serageldin, Ismail	1.16; 1.17; 1.18; 1.19; 7.18; 7.19; 7.20; 7.21; 7.22; 7.23; 7.24; 7.25; 20.66; 20.67
Serra, Maria Teresa Fernandez	10.36
Shams, Khalid	5.1
Shihata, Ibrahim	10.37
Shipton, Parker	27.38
Sollis, P.	21.2; 24.8
Sorbo, Gunnar M.	10.38
Spears, John	2.12; 14.9
Stahl, Ann B.	7.26
Taboroff, June	7.18; 7.27
Talbott, Lee	5.7
Tamakloe, Martha A.	10.39
Tepping, Benjamin	3.10
Tobisson, Eva	27.39
Todd, T.	20.3; 26.4
Tshabalala, Mavuso	10.40
Umaña, Alvaro	11.2; 16.4
Uphoff, Norman	1.20; 5.13; 5.14
Uquillas, Jorge	9.4
Vail, Stephen	20.61

Verspoor, Adriaan	20.55
Wali, Alaka	27.18
Warren, D. Michael	9.15
Webb, Maryla	7.10
Wells, Michael	16.2; 16.3; 16.5
White, Daphne	20.21
Wildavsky, Aaron	7.28
Williams, Aubrey	5.3
Williams, Thomas Rhys	27.5; 27.6
Yepes, Guillermo	27.14
Zhao, Qinghua	20.52

Appendix 4
Index of Geographic Locations and Populations

Regions

Africa	1.18; 1.19; 2.1; 4.7; 4.8; 4.12; 5.7; 7.1; 7.2; 7.8; 7.9; 7.13; 7.14; 7.15; 7.17; 7.18; 7.19; 7.20; 7.26; 7.27; 8.6; 8.17; 10.6; 10.16; 10.17; 10.18; 10.23; 12.3; 12.4; 12.5; 13.6; 14.5; 15.2; 16.2; 18.3; 20.9; 20.13; 20.28; 20.34; 20.35; 20.57; 22.3; 23.4; 24.9; 27.17; 27.19; 27.28; 27.35; 27.36; 27.39; 27.40; 27.41
Amazon	11.7; 9.5
Asia	3.2; 3.3; 4.12; 5.1; 8.1; 10.23; 16.2; 19.4; 19.5; 19.6; 19.7; 20.13; 20.29; 27.7
Caribbean	27.8
Central America	11.2
Central Africa	7.8; 9.10; 14.7
East Africa	14.5; 15.3; 20.64
East Asia	2.2; 19.7
Eastern Europe	8.1
Latin America	2.1; 3.17; 4.10; 4.12; 9.4; 9.6; 10.23; 11.8; 16.2; 20.28; 27.8; 27.9; 27.10; 27.11; 27.12; 27.13; 27.14; 27.18
Middle East	7.24; 20.28
North Africa	7.24

North America	20.15; 20.28; 20.36
Sahel	15.1; 23.4
South Asia	2.1; 2.2; 3.4
West Africa	7.1; 8.6; 9.10; 10.27; 10.28; 10.29; 14.5; 14.7

Countries and Provinces

Algeria	27.15
Assam	19.7
Australia	20.20
Azad Kashmir	12.2; 14.2
Bali	10.19; 25.5
Baluchistan	2.6
Bangladesh	3.2; 8.1; 19.2; 19.7
Benin	7.18
Bihar	19.7
Botswana	12.1; 27.39
Brazil	1.2; 3.18; 6.1; 6.8; 9.5; 9.6; 9.14; 10.36; 18.4; 20.50; 27.18; 27.31
Bolivia	3.18; 6.8; 10.32; 27.18; 27.30
Burkina Faso	10.6; 10.28; 10.29; 19.4
Burundi	20.50; 27.23
Cameroon	4.2; 9.10; 10.16
Canada	9.7; 27.30
Central African Republic	9.10

Index of Geographic Locations and Populations

Chad	15.1
Chile	27.13
China	8.1; 10.5; 11.3; 20.2; 20.4; 20.17;27.5; 27.6
Colombia	1.2; 9.6; 10.22; 18.1; 20.45; 20.50; 27.1; 27.18
Congo, The	9.10
Costa Rica	6.8; 10.31; 11.2; 11.5; 16.4
Côte d'Ivoire	4.7; 10.6; 12.4; 14.7; 14.8; 25.3
Divo	12.4
Dominican Republic	20.44
Ecuador	3.17; 3.18; 8.14; 9.3; 9.4; 11.7; 21.2; 24.8; 27.16; 27.18
Egypt, Arab Republic of	6.8; 7.21; 20.67
El Salvador	3.8; 9.9; 17.1; 17.5
Ethiopia	10.4; 10.5
Finland	10.4
Gambia, The	27.38
Ghana	5.14; 7.26; 10.4; 10.6; 10.38; 12.5; 14.8; 20.9; 5.7
Guatemala	6.8; 9.8; 9.9
Guinea	2.7; 5.7
Gujarat	10.30
Honduras	6.8; 27.30
India	1.2; 2.1; 3.10; 6.1; 6.8; 8.1; 8.3; 8.4; 10.25; 10.30; 14.10; 18.1; 18.2; 19.2; 19.4; 19.7; 20.1; 20.39

Indonesia	1.6; 2.12; 6.1; 6.8; 7.4; 10.5; 10.13; 10.19; 10.20; 11.3; 14.6; 18.1; 19.2; 19.4; 19.7; 23.3; 26.5; 27.30
Iran, Islamic Republic of	15.4
Irian Jaya	10.19
Italy	7.16
Java	10.19; 14.6; 23.3
Kalimantan	10.19
Karnataka	6.1; 2.1
Kassala	10.38
Kenya	4.1; 6.1; 9.3; 10.6; 10.26; 12.5; 15.3; 19.4
Korea, Republic of	14.11
Ksar Chellala	27.15
Lesotho	27.30
Liberia	4.2
Libya	7.24
Lombok	10.19
Madagascar	5.7
Madhya Pradesh	10.30; 19.7
Maharashtra	10.30
Mali	10.4
Malawi	6.8; 20.9; 20.26; 20.36; 20.58
Malaysia	6.8; 19.7
Mauritania	27.20

Mauritius	18.5
Mexico	1.2; 3.9; 5.5; 5.14; 6.8; 10.21; 24.3; 24.5; 25.2; 27.11; 27.21
Micronesia, Federated States of	7.6; 20.7
Morocco	12.1
Mozambique	10.5; 10.16
Nepal	5.14; 6.1; 8.5; 19.4; 20.42
Nicaragua	9.1; 20.33
Nigeria	10.1; 14.8; 20.49; 20.57
Norway	27.30
Orissa	10.4; 19.7
Pakistan	2.6; 12.2; 13.2; 14.2; 19.2; 23.5
Panama	9.7; 27.18
Papua New Guinea	14.8; 27.30
Paraguay	9.6; 11.3
Peru	9.7; 27.18
Philippines	9.3; 11.5; 11.6; 13.1; 17.5; 19.4; 20.24; 20.45; 20.52; 27.30; 27.32
Rajasthan	19.7
Romania	8.7; 8.8; 8.9; 10.5; 26.1; 26.2
Rwanda	12.5; 5.7
Saudi Arabia	9.12; 20.66
Senegal	10.6; 11.4; 12.1; 15.2; 17.5; 20.9

Sichuan	27.5; 27.6
Somalia	12.1
South Africa	10.4; 10.40
Sri Lanka	7.5; 19.2; 19.4; 19.7; 20.50
Sudan	7.18; 10.6; 10.38; 11.3; 20.64
Sukumaland	2.4; 2.5
Sulawesi	10.19
Sumatra	10.19
Swaziland	20.57
Tanzania	2.4; 2.5; 10.5; 10.6; 20.45
Thailand	3.18; 12.1; 19.1; 19.2; 19.4; 19.6; 19.7; 20.45; 20.46; 20.47; 20.50; 20.54; 20.58; 20.61; 27.30; 27.33
Togo	10.6
Turkey	19.4; 26.1
Uganda	10.5; 10.16; 20.31; 20.38; 5.7
United States	3.1; 9.7; 20.33; 20.50; 26.5; 26.9; 26.10; 27.30
Venezuela	6.8; 27.18
Viet Nam	8.1
West Bengal	19.7
Zambia	3.7; 10.6; 10.24; 17.5
Zimbabwe	2.8; 10.24; 21.1

Ethnic Groups

Ache	9.6
Arab	4.9; 7.25; 27.29
Bedouin	9.12
Bhil	10.30
Bhilala	10.30
Fulani	10.1
Guahibo	9.6
Hopi	10.4
Karelian	10.4
Maasai	9.3
Maya	9.8
Miskito	9.1
Nambiquara	9.14
Navajo	10.4
Nubian	10.38
Pygmy	9.10
Quichua	9.3
Samburu	9.3
Sukuma	2.4; 2.5
Yanomami	9.6

Appendix 5
Bio-Data

April Adams is an editorial consultant. She has a Bachelor of Arts degree in Political Science from the University of Vermont, and a Master of Arts degree in International Affairs and Economics. In Egypt, Ms. Adams worked in grassroots development with Catholic relief services and several U.S. Agency for International Development contractors.

Michael M. Cernea is the World Bank's Senior Adviser for Sociology and Social Policy and works in the Environment Department. Since he joined the Bank in 1974 as its first in-house sociologist/anthropologist, he has carried out social research, policy work, as well as operational development project work in numerous countries, including Algeria, China, India, Mauritius, Mexico, Pakistan, and Tanzania. Mr. Cernea has taught and lectured in universities in Europe and the United States and is the recipient of the Solon T. Kimball Award for Public Policy and Applied Anthropology, conferred by the American Anthropological Association. He has written and edited numerous books and studies on development, social change, population resettlement, social forestry, grassroots organizations, and diffusion of innovations, including *Putting People First. Sociological Variables in Development* (Oxford University Press, 1985 and 1991); and *Anthropological Approaches to Resettlement: Policy, Practice, Theory* (ed. with Scott E. Guggenheim, Westview Press, 1993).

Ismail Serageldin is Vice President for Environmentally Sustainable Development (ESD) and Chairman of the Consultative Group on International Agricultural Research (CGIAR) at the World Bank. Since joining the Bank in 1972, he has designed and managed a broad array of poverty-focused projects in developing countries. Educated at Cairo University and Harvard University, where he earned a Ph.D., Mr. Serageldin is an internationally published author on economic development, human resource issues, the environment, architecture, urbanism, the Arab world, Islam, and culture. His most recent books include *Nurturing Development* (World Bank, Forthcoming), *Making Development Sustainable: From Concepts to Action* (ed. with Andrew Steer, World Bank, 1994); *Culture and Development in Africa: Proceedings of an International Conference* (ed. with June Taboroff, World Bank, 1994); and *Development Partners: Aid and Cooperation in the 1990s* (Swedish International Development Authority, 1993).

Distributors of World Bank Publications

ARGENTINA
Carlos Hirsch, SRL
Galeria Guemes
Florida 165, 4th Floor-Ofc. 453/465
1333 Buenos Aires

Oficina del Libro Internacional
Alberti 40
1082 Buenos Aires

AUSTRALIA, PAPUA NEW GUINEA, FIJI, SOLOMON ISLANDS, VANUATU, AND WESTERN SAMOA
D.A. Information Services
648 Whitehorse Road
Mitcham 3132
Victoria

AUSTRIA
Gerold and Co.
Graben 31
A-1011 Wien

BANGLADESH
Micro Industries Development
  Assistance Society (MIDAS)
House 5, Road 16
Dhanmondi R/Area
Dhaka 1209

BELGIUM
Jean De Lannoy
Av. du Roi 202
1060 Brussels

BRAZIL
Publicacoes Tecnicas Internacionais Ltda.
Rua Peixoto Gomide, 209
01409 Sao Paulo, SP

CANADA
Le Diffuseur
151A Boul. de Mortagne
Boucherville, Québec
J4B 5E6

Renouf Publishing Co.
1294 Algoma Road
Ottawa, Ontario
K1B 3W8

CHINA
China Financial & Economic
  Publishing House
8, Da Fo Si Dong Jie
Beijing

COLOMBIA
Infoenlace Ltda.
Apartado Aereo 34270
Bogota D.E.

COTE D'IVOIRE
Centre d'Edition et de Diffusion
  Africaines (CEDA)
04 B.P. 541
Abidjan 04 Plateau

CYPRUS
Center of Applied Research
Cyprus College
6, Diogenes Street, Engomi
P.O. Box 2006
Nicosia

DENMARK
SamfundsLitteratur
Rosenoerns Allé 11
DK-1970 Frederiksberg C

DOMINICAN REPUBLIC
Editora Taller, C. por A.
Restauración e Isabel la Católica 309
Apartado de Correos 2190 Z-1
Santo Domingo

EGYPT, ARAB REPUBLIC OF
Al Ahram
Al Galaa Street
Cairo

The Middle East Observer
41, Sherif Street
Cairo

FINLAND
Akateeminen Kirjakauppa
P.O. Box 128
SF-00101 Helsinki 10

FRANCE
World Bank Publications
66, avenue d'Iéna
75116 Paris

GERMANY
UNO-Verlag
Poppelsdorfer Allee 55
53115 Bonn

GREECE
Papasotiriou S.A.
35, Stournara Str.
106 82 Athens

HONG KONG, MACAO
Asia 2000 Ltd.
46-48 Wyndham Street
Winning Centre
7th Floor
Central Hong Kong

HUNGARY
Foundation for Market Economy
Dombovari Ut 17-19
H-1117 Budapest

INDIA
Allied Publishers Private Ltd.
751 Mount Road
Madras - 600 002

INDONESIA
Pt. Indira Limited
Jalan Borobudur 20
P.O. Box 181
Jakarta 10320

IRAN
Kowkab Publishers
P.O. Box 19575-511
Tehran

IRELAND
Government Supplies Agency
4-5 Harcourt Road
Dublin 2

ISRAEL
Yozmot Literature Ltd.
P.O. Box 56055
Tel Aviv 61560

ITALY
Licosa Commissionaria Sansoni SPA
Via Duca Di Calabria, 1/1
Casella Postale 552
50125 Firenze

JAMAICA
Ian Randle Publishers Ltd.
206 Old Hope Road
Kingston 6

JAPAN
Eastern Book Service
Hongo 3-Chome, Bunkyo-ku 113
Tokyo

KENYA
Africa Book Service (E.A.) Ltd.
Quaran House, Mfangano Street
P.O. Box 45245
Nairobi

KOREA, REPUBLIC OF
Pan Korea Book Corporation
P.O. Box 101, Kwangwhamun
Seoul

Korean Stock Book Centre
P.O. Box 34
Yeoeido
Seoul

MALAYSIA
University of Malaya Cooperative
  Bookshop, Limited
P.O. Box 1127, Jalan Pantai Baru
59700 Kuala Lumpur

MEXICO
INFOTEC
Apartado Postal 22-860
14060 Tlalpan, Mexico D.F.

NETHERLANDS
De Lindeboom/InOr-Publikaties
P.O. Box 202
7480 AE Haaksbergen

NEW ZEALAND
EBSCO NZ Ltd.
Private Mail Bag 99914
New Market
Auckland

NIGERIA
University Press Limited
Three Crowns Building Jericho
Private Mail Bag 5095
Ibadan

NORWAY
Narvesen Information Center
Book Department
P.O. Box 6125 Etterstad
N-0602 Oslo 6

PAKISTAN
Mirza Book Agency
65, Shahrah-e-Quaid-e-Azam
P.O. Box No. 729
Lahore 54000

PERU
Editorial Desarrollo SA
Apartado 3824
Lima 1

PHILIPPINES
International Book Center
Suite 1703, Cityland 10
Condominium Tower 1
Ayala Avenue, H.V. dela
  Costa Extension
Makati, Metro Manila

POLAND
International Publishing Service
Ul. Piekna 31/37
00-677 Warszawa

For subscription orders:
IPS Journals
Ul. Okrezna 3
02-916 Warszawa

PORTUGAL
Livraria Portugal
Rua Do Carmo 70-74
1200 Lisbon

SAUDI ARABIA, QATAR
Jarir Book Store
P.O. Box 3196
Riyadh 11471

SINGAPORE, TAIWAN, MYANMAR, BRUNEI
Gower Asia Pacific Pte Ltd.
Golden Wheel Building
41, Kallang Pudding, #04-03
Singapore 1334

SOUTH AFRICA, BOTSWANA
For single titles:
Oxford University Press
  Southern Africa
P.O. Box 1141
Cape Town 8000

For subscription orders:
International Subscription Service
P.O. Box 41095
Craighall
Johannesburg 2024

SPAIN
Mundi-Prensa Libros, S.A.
Castello 37
28001 Madrid

Librería Internacional AEDOS
Consell de Cent, 391
08009 Barcelona

SRI LANKA AND THE MALDIVES
Lake House Bookshop
P.O. Box 244
100, Sir Chittampalam A.
  Gardiner Mawatha
Colombo 2

SWEDEN
For single titles:
Fritzes Fackboksforetaget
Regeringsgatan 12, Box 16356
S-103 27 Stockholm

For subscription orders:
Wennergren-Williams AB
P. O. Box 1305
S-171 25 Solna

SWITZERLAND
For single titles:
Librairie Payot
Case postale 3212
CH 1002 Lausanne

For subscription orders:
Librairie Payot
Service des Abonnements
Case postale 3312
CH 1002 Lausanne

THAILAND
Central Department Store
306 Silom Road
Bangkok

TRINIDAD & TOBAGO
Systematics Studies Unit
#9 Watts Street
Curepe
Trinidad, West Indies

UNITED KINGDOM
Microinfo Ltd.
P.O. Box 3
Alton, Hampshire GU34 2PG
England

ZIMBABWE
Longman Zimbabwe (Pvt.) Ltd.
Tourle Road, Ardbennie
P.O. Box ST 125
Southerton
Harare